W9-DFT-072

Twayne's English Authors Series

EDITOR OF THIS VOLUME

Bertram H. Davis

Florida State University

Sir Richard Blackmore

TEAS 289

SIR RICHARD BLACKMORE

By HARRY M. SOLOMON

Auburn University

TWAYNE PUBLISHERS

A DIVISION OF G. K. HALL & CO., BOSTON

Published in 1980 by Twayne Publishers,
A Division of G. K. Hall & Co.

Printed on permanent/durable acid-free paper and bound
in the United States of America

First Printing

Library of Congress Cataloging in Publication Data

Solomon, Harry M
Sir Richard Blackmore.

(Twayne's English authors series ; TEAS 289)
Bibliography: p. 208-10
Includes index.
1. Blackmore, Richard, Sir, d. 1729.
2. Authors, English—18th century—Biography.
PR3318.B5S6 821'.4 79-23322
ISBN 0-8057-6782-7

Contents

About the Author

Harry M. Solomon received his Ph.D. in Restoration and eighteenth-century English literature from Duke University and is presently associate professor and director of freshman English at Auburn University. He has published articles in various periodicals including *Studies in English and American Literature, Tennessee Studies in Literature, Keats-Shelley Journal,* and *Studies in English Literature.* Currently business manager of *Southern Humanities Review,* he is working on a book on *An Essay on Man.*

Preface

> This way of writing mightily offends in this Age;
> and 'tis a wonder how it came to please in any.
>
> Richard Blackmore, *Prince Arthur* (1695)

In disparaging Spenser's tendency to wander lost "in a Wood of Allegories," Richard Blackmore prophetically characterized his own immortal memory. Although Blackmore is mentioned frequently by scholars of the English Augustan Age, it is almost always as the butt of someone else's joke. Because of his antagonistic relationships to Dryden, Swift, and Pope, he has achieved what Saintsbury calls "an uncomfortable immortality" as the Father of the Augustan Bathous, the Homer of bad eighteenth-century verse. As R. D. Havens notes, Sir Richard has the doubtful distinction of being attacked by more illustrious pens than any minor poet in English literary history. He was one of those men, Samuel Johnson observed, "whose lot it has been to be much oftener mentioned by enemies than by friends."

In the two hundred years since Samuel Johnson included a brief sketch of Blackmore's works in his *Lives of the English Poets,* there has been no critical study of Blackmore's literary output or career. The only modern book on Blackmore is the excellent biography by Albert Rosenberg. Unfortunately, Rosenberg's meticulous research often concerns Sir Richard's medical practice or minor law suits in which he was involved, matters usually not essential to a student of his writings and consequently excluded from the present study. As a biographer, Rosenberg does not survey or criticize the works themselves.

This book attempts three things: (1) to familiarize the reader with Sir Richard Blackmore's literary career; (2) to describe and explain his involvement in the major literary controversies of the time; and (3) to survey and appraise his works. To achieve all three aims the book is organized chronologically. Because even most eighteenth-century scholars know nothing of Blackmore's life, the first chapter provides a biographical overview, emphasizing his education at Oxford and the University of Padua and his flourishing medical practice in London.

Chapters 2–6 give a detailed view of Blackmore's literary career. Chapter 2 deals with his protest against the immorality and profaneness of the Restoration stage and his resultant enmity with John Dryden. The major emphasis of the chapter, however, is on Blackmore's heroic poems *Prince Arthur* (1695) and *King Arthur* (1697) and their role in his arguments with John Dennis over the nature of epic and the sublime in poetry. Chapter 3 describes Blackmore's opposition to Samuel Garth in the dispensary controversy and the ensuing war with the "Covent Garden circle" over the nature of wit and the legitimate function of satire. Tom Brown's opposition to Blackmore's *Satyr against Wit* (1700) and Daniel Defoe's support are central to this chapter.

Chapter 4 shows Blackmore as panegyrist of Queen Anne (*Eliza,* 1705) and the Duke of Marlborough (*Advice to the Poets,* 1706), as the enemy of the famous physician John Radcliffe, and an intimate of Joseph Addison's Whig circle (*The Kit-Cats,* 1708). Chapter 5 demonstrates the central role of Blackmore's most extravagantly praised work, *Creation* (1712), in the rise of physicotheological poetry. Blackmore's theological, scientific, and literary interests are also studied in *The Lay-Monk* (1713–14), his continuation of Addison's *Spectator.* The sixth chapter surveys the tying up of literary loose ends during his last years in London prior to his retirement to Boxted in Essex. Entangled in controversies with young Alexander Pope and Addison by the publication of his *Essays upon Several Subjects* (1716–17), Blackmore also battles the Arians with his poem *Redemption* (1722).

The final chapter describes the development of Sir Richard's reputation as Father of the Bathous. It argues that the judgment of posterity, determined almost entirely by Pope's ridicule in *Peri Bathous* and *The Dunciad,* should be amended to recognize (1) the literary merit of several of Blackmore's compositions and (2) the pervasive effect his works had on epic, religious, and scientific poetry both in England and America.

For the most part, I have allowed the age to voice its own judgments, whether in praising the "British Elijah" or in damning the Homer of the Bathous to outer darkness. For Sir Richard's writings were extremely popular and a study of Blackmore is properly, in part, a study of the tides of English taste in the Early Eighteenth Century. A study of his career leads to a fuller understanding of the literary world within which he quarrelled forcefully with writers greater than himself. I do not argue, as Johnson did, that Blackmore belongs among the "first favorites of the English muse." I cannot feel comfortable calling Blackmore the English Lucretius as John Dennis did. Even less do I agree with John Blair Linn ("The Poet," 1795) that Blackmore is, along with Otway, Dryden, Pope, Thomson, and "youthful Chatterton," an essential influence to the poetic sensibility. Nonetheless, since there was scarcely a single political, scientific, philosophic, theological, or literary controversy during the period in which he was not engaged, I do suggest that few literary figures so adequately mirror the concerns of their own age.

HARRY M. SOLOMON

Auburn University

Acknowledgments

I would like to thank Auburn Unviersity for the grant which allowed me to Xerox or microfilm the many rare works essential to a study of this kind. In addition to the staff of the Ralph Brown Draughon Library at Auburn, I wish especially to thank the staff of the libraries of the British Museum, the Victoria and Albert Museum, Duke, Harvard, Yale, the University of North Carolina at Chapel Hill, the University of Michigan, Princeton, and the Humanities Research Center at the University of Texas at Austin. For valuable criticism of the manuscript, I am indebted to my friends Bert Hitchcock, Dennis Rygiel, and Martha McLaughlin Solomon, to the last of whom this work is affectionately dedicated.

Chronology

1654 Richard Blackmore born on January 22 (O.S.) into the family of a prosperous attorney in the Wiltshire town of Corsham.

1669 In March he matriculates as a commoner at St. Edmund Hall, Oxford.

1674 Receives Bachelor of Arts degree, April 4.

1676 Master of Arts, June 3. Blackmore continues at St. Edmund Hall as a tutor.

1682 Begins European tour.

1684 After study at the University of Padua, Blackmore is examined and pronounced Doctor in Pure Medicine, March 28.

1685 Marries Mary Adams at St. Paul's Church, Covent Garden, February 9.

1687 Admitted as a Fellow of the Royal College of Physicians, April 12.

1695 *Prince Arthur,* advertised in the *London Gazette* for February 28–March 4.

1696 John Dennis's *Remarks on a Book Entituled, Prince Arthur, An Heroick Poem.*

1697 Appointed one of King William's Physicians in Ordinary and knighted for service to the crown. *King Arthur,* advertised in the *London Gazette* for March 18–March 22.

1699 In response to Samuel Garth's *Dispensary,* Blackmore publishes *A Satyr against Wit,* advertised in the *Post Man* for November 21–November 23. Daniel Defoe's *The Pacificator* published February 1700.

1700 *A Paraphrase on the Book of Job,* advertised in the *London Gazette* for February 26–February 29. The same week a group of wits, including Tom Brown, publishes *Commendatory Verses,* a collection of anti-Blackmore lampoons. In early April a collection of *Discommendatory Verses* attacking the wits is issued in his defense. Dryden's last composition, the prologue to *The Pilgrim*, contains an attack on Blackmore.

1702 Blackmore attends William during his final illness and helps draw up *The Report of the Physicians and Surgeons, Commanded to assist at the Dissecting the Body of His Late Majesty at Kensington.*

1703 Emulated Milton in *A Hymn to the Light of the World*, reported in *The History of the Works of the Learned* for December 1702.

1705 Attacks his enemy Dr. John Radcliffe in an epic tribute to Queen Anne, *Eliza*, advertised in the *London Gazette* for July 16–July 19.

1706 Praises and attacks contemporary poets in *Advice to the Poets. A Poem. Occasion'd by the wonderful Success of her Majesty's Arms, under the Conduct of the Duke of Marlborough, in Flanders.* A sequel, *Instructions to Vander Bank*, published and pirated in 1709.

1711 *The Nature of Man*, advertised in the *Spectator* for April 6.

1712 Publication of Blackmore's greatest success and most influential work, *Creation. A Philosophical Poem*, advertised in the *London Gazette* for February 26–February 28. Blackmore variously styled the British Elijah and the English Lucretius.

1713–1714 After the *Guardian* ceases publication, Blackmore, with the aid of John Hughes and the encouragement of Addison, begins a new periodical, *The Lay-Monk*, first issue November 16, 1713. The following year the essays are collected as *The Lay-Monastery*. As one of her Physicians in Ordinary, Blackmore attends Anne during her final illness.

1716 *Essays upon Several Subjects*, advertised in the *Evening Post* for March 6–March 8. The following March a second volume of the *Essays* is published. In the preface to the "Essay upon Epick Poetry" Blackmore praises Pope's translation of the *Iliad*. In the 1717 volume, however, he censures Pope for having burlesqued the First Psalm.

1718 *A Collection of Poems on Various Subjects*, containing most of his shorter poems which had been previously published as well as some new poems.

1721 Blackmore enters the Arian controversy. Publication of *A New Version of the Psalms of David.*

1722 Resigns his position as an Elect of the Royal College of Physicians, October 22. Retires to the Essex village of Boxted to write his medical treatises. Publication of *Redemption.*

1723 *Alfred,* advertised in the *Daily Courant* for September 19.

1728 Blackmore's wife dies on the first day of the new year. Pope's *Peri Bathous* published in March.

1729 Blackmore dies on October 9.

CHAPTER 1

Biography: Arts and Sciences

ON January 22, 1654, Richard Blackmore was born to Robert and Anne Blackmore of Corsham, Wiltshire, the third of four children who would survive infancy. Anne Pilsworth (née Harris) was widowed young and remarried Robert, a practicing attorney of good family who had probably come from Dorsetshire to make his fortune among the wealthy farmers of Wiltshire. Corsham was one of that "very great number of villages" which Defoe observed in Wiltshire flourishing with the wool trade, shearing, spinning, and shipping the superflux downriver to London. For, despite the populousness of the country, Defoe found the land so "exceeding rich and fertile" that it could support its inhabitants in prosperity and still provision the capital. Besides broadcloth every day were shipped to London "very great quantities" of barley made into malt; cheeses, including the delicious green cheese similar to cream cheese but thicker and richer; and innumerable slabs of prime bacon from hogs fed with the "vast quantity" of whey and skim milk which would otherwise be thrown away.[1]

Where there was so much commerce there was opportunity for an industrious young attorney—contracts, titles to land and property, inheritances requiring supervision—and Robert Blackmore made the best of his prospects. The frequency with which his name appears in some professional capacity on mid-century documents provides assurance that his services were in demand, and his continuous acquisitions of land and property recorded in the Court Baron of the Manor and Liberty of Corsham suggest the prosperity which he shared with his fellow townsmen.[2]

I *The Scholar: 1654–1684*

Bustling and bucolic, the village of Corsham, barely eight miles from Bath and an easy day's ride on horseback from

Stonehenge, was Richard's earliest education. The area was rich with historical associations, including an impressive Elizabethan manor still to be seen in Corsham itself. At the same time, it very much looked to London as the hub toward which all things necessarily inclined, the town being only a collecting point for the movement of goods to the great city. As a child Richard must have imbibed the dual sense of tradition and progress which Corsham exemplified, while he derived his love of nature from the woods and meadows surrounding the village.

According to Giles Jacob, Richard's earliest formal education, outside his father's library, was at a "Country School,"from which at the age of thirteen he proceeded to Westminster.[3] Whatever rough edges remained from his Corsham years must have been polished quickly, for he soon left Westminster School and on March 19, 1669, matriculated as a commoner at St. Edmund Hall, Oxford. Blackmore was the "most eager and diligent" student that William Turner, a fellow undergraduate, had ever known: he often studied by candlelight until two or three in the morning, when he fell asleep in his chair, only to be awakened the next morning in time for prayers. In his effort to compensate for what he imagined to be the deficiencies of his background, Blackmore's health failed; but after a short recovery in the country he was back at his books.[4] Another friend during his early years at Oxford testifies that young Blackmore was as earnest in his concern for religion and the reformation of manners as in his dedication to scholarship.[5]

After his initial trepidation, Blackmore came to love the excitement and the quiet of university life. On April 4, 1674, he received his Bachelor of Arts and on June 3, 1676, his Master of Arts; but to avoid leaving Oxford he secured a tutorship. He must have served with distinction in this capacity because Thomas Hearne notes that even years after his departure from Oxford Blackmore was still regarded as "a great Tutor, and much respected."[6] Altogether Blackmore spent thirteen years at St. Edmund Hall as student and tutor, and might have remained at Oxford as scholar and teacher had his earlier application to be appointed to a Demyship at Magdalen College not failed to receive the necessary patronage. In 1672 his father formally petitioned Charles II to nominate his son, who was "of good repute both for his virtuous Disposition and proficiency in his Studies." The petition was accompanied by a testimonial by the principal of St. Edmund Hall to the effect that young Blackmore was sober and hard-working. Thomas Pierce, an elector of Magdalen College, personally examined Richard for the Demyship, finding him to be "hopeful and ingenuous" and in every way prepared for the scholarship, despite minor reservations concerning young Blackmore's weaknesses in music and Greek.[7] Unfortunately, when the final list was posted, Richard was not among those chosen.

Despite this setback he went on to distinguish himself in St. Edmund Hall and might have continued there had not circumstances disrupted the university in the spring of 1681. Unable to arrange a satisfactory compromise with the Whig exclusionists led by Shaftesbury, Charles moved Parliament to Oxford, hoping it would provide a more royalist atmosphere in which to negotiate. Ultimately even this failed and Charles dissolved Parliament. In the interval, however, while the students were being forced to leave Oxford by the sudden influx of influential courtiers and politicians, Blackmore probably had his first mature taste of London society. These were days in which the fate of England and the form of its government were being decided, and even a black-gowned academic like Richard Blackmore could scarcely fail to respond to the excitement.

Robert Blackmore, who had drawn up many a will for other men, died intestate on the eighteenth of August in 1681; and it was probably part of the proceeds of his father's estate that allowed Richard to embark the following spring on that finishing touch to a fine gentleman's education, a continental tour. In his *Treatise of Consumptions* Blackmore says that an Oxford student accompanied him in his foreign travels.[8] Although the facts are somewhat confusing, the student was probably the George Smith who matriculated at St. Edmund Hall in December 1681. It is certain that Blackmore was still at Oxford in February 1682 because of a payment he received at that time. When one considers further that during his tour Blackmore drew bills of exchange on James Smith, an uncle of George Smith, from Nimes, Montpellier, Geneva, Venice, Strasbourg, Rotterdam, and Rome, it seems at least possible that he was engaged or encouraged by the Smith family to accompany the ailing young George to climes more congenial to his consumption. This may also account for the fact that another traveler who met Blackmore in Geneva, John Shower, remembered that he was traveling with a George Smith of Nibly, a graduate of Queen's College, Oxford, who had subsequently received his doctorate of medicine at the University of Padua in 1658.[9] Probably the older George Smith, a physician and relative of the young student with consumption, accompanied Blackmore and the boy through France to Geneva, by which time, as Blackmore says, the signs of consumption had entirely disappeared. Probably the older Smith wished to revisit the university where as a young man he had taken his degree in medicine. This would explain Blackmore's subsequent connection with the University of Padua. With his relative's consumption healed, the physician returned to England and young George Smith continued his tour with his tutor, as Blackmore's *Treatise* reports and as the young man's journal, now lost, suggested.[10]

The France through which Blackmore and his friend passed in 1682 was tightening its restrictions on Huguenots in anticipation of the Revocation of the Edict of Nantes. From the beginning of his reign Louis had been urged by his ministers to move toward revocation of the toleration edict. Children were encouraged to convert and leave their parents' home. Huguenots were forbidden to maintain academies for the education of their young. In 1682, while Richard Blackmore was in France, Louis issued and ordered all Protestant clergymen to read their congregations a proclamation which threatened Huguenots with evils "incomparably more terrible and deadly than before."[11] The atrocities when they did come three years later were more horrible than even the king foresaw.

It must have been with a certain relief, therefore, that Blackmore arrived in Geneva. The province of Gex on the Swiss border had been one of the first in which Louis had formally outlawed Protestant worship; and, as a result, by the time Blackmore arrived there Geneva was already reputed for the heroism of its inhabitants in encouraging and aiding those Huguenots who wished to flee France. Fresh from his experiences of the aftermath of the bogus Popish Plot at home, Blackmore was profoundly affected by this new juxtaposition of the powerful terror and tyranny of Catholic France and the bravery of a city of barely sixteen thousand Protestants. Louis was already fated to become the villain of his later epics; and Blackmore was further confirmed in his commitment to a sincere but tolerant Protestantism.

Despite the tension, however, Geneva was an attractive headquarters for a traveler at this time. The city, as John Evelyn reports in his *Diary*, was strongly fortified, being partially built on rising ground. On open fields surrounding the town the curious might watch citizens, and especially the young, practicing with long bows, cross-bows, and muskets. For the academically inclined the University housed a good library and there was an "aboundance of Bookesellers." The Rhone flowing clear as crystal through the city provided "the most celebrated Troute, for largenesse and goodnesse of any in all Europ." Moreover, such fish of three feet and more were, like all provisions in the markets of Geneva, both "good and cheape." Lining the river just outside the city were cherry gardens and lovely villas where the foreign traveler was welcome. On the other side of the city lay Lake Leman, over which "never had Travelers a sweeter passage." Here Blackmore enjoyed the sublimity of "one of the most delightfull prospects in the World, the *Alps*, cover'd with Snow, though at greate distance, yet shewing their aspiring tops."[12]

When Blackmore decided to take a degree in medicine is uncertain, but it seems likely that he did much of his reading during his residence in Geneva. Circumstances conspired to pique his interest in physic. The younger of his companions was seriously ill when they left England and the older was already a physician. In the progress of their journey Blackmore inevitably became interested in consumption and its treatment, an enduring interest which produced a treatise on the subject in his last years. Furthermore, while they were in Geneva another Oxford man, Thomas Bent, died; and his Latin epitaph, attached to the wall of the church of St. Gervais, was written by Richard Blackmore.[13] Bent's death, intensified by the communal intimacy of fellow Oxford men together in a foreign country, may have confirmed Blackmore in his decision to ask George Smith to recommend him as a student to the University of Padua.

As early as the fifteenth century the University of Padua had become one of the great intellectual centers of Europe, boasting an Aristotelianism which made observation rather than theology its guide.[14] The Faculty of Medicine was renowned then and, if anything, its reputation had increased in the intervening years. It was Harvey's great teacher at Padua, Girolamo Fabrizio d'Acquapendente, who had discovered the valves in the veins and done the research on the effect of ligatures which led to his pupil's demonstration of the circulation of the blood. So respected and popular was its school of medicine that in the seventeenth century a council was appointed to oversee the English students working at Padua, one of whom was Dr. George Rogers, a friend of Evelyn's who had taken his degree there. In fact, Evelyn was so impressed with the "flourishing and antient" university that he matriculated to study medicine and anatomy under a faculty which boasted the best professors in Europe. It was during his study that Evelyn commissioned the anatomical charts, unknown at home, which medical men in England so frequently visited him to admire. Doubtless Blackmore attended anatomy lectures similar to those Evelyn witnessed a few years earlier. They were held in the celebrated "Theater for Anatomies" which Evelyn found "excellently contriv'd both for the discector and spectators." Using the most modern—to Evelyn "extraordinary"—instruments, the teachers took a full month to dissect three bodies, those of a man, woman, and child, demonstrating as they did so "all the manual operations of the Chirurgion upon the humane body." Instruction was empirical with frequent hospital visitation. Observation of female patients was so open that Evelyn feared for the virtue of the younger students, for some of the women were "not very modest, and when they began to be well, plainely lew'd."[15]

The city of Padua also provided an atmosphere almost uniquely congenial to a serious student of the classics like Blackmore. It was the birthplace of the historian Livy, whose house near the university was open for inspection. A city of brick arches, the streets shady in summer and sheltered from rain, Padua teemed with the treasures of the Renaissance. Its reddish marble piazza and great hall Evelyn, among others, judged the most magnificent in Europe. Roman buildings made an invigorating contrast for the reputation of a city so recently associated with Galileo's new cosmology. The university provided a microcosm of this contrast: the venerable old buildings of the colleges so inappropriate to the medical innovations proceeding within their walls. As in Geneva, an Englishman found the market plentiful and cheap. A student wintering in Padua might buy grapes inexpensively by the bushelful and press his own excellent wine. Herbariums, so necessary to the medical school, invited interesting and aromatic afternoon walks, as did the groves of olive, orange, and fig trees which skirted the city.

On March 27, 1684, his preparations completed, the faculty assigned Blackmore two subjects on digestion from Avicenna's *Canon of Medicine.* The following afternoon he discoursed before the doctors and a large audience of the curious, as was customary. The archives of the university record that Blackmore "conducted himself with merit both in considering anew and solving the most involved propositions submitted to him, and also in his treatment of a case submitted to him with no previous knowledge of it on his part, and this gave abundant proof to all of his learning."[16] The faculty was unanimous in pronouncing him Doctor of Pure Medicine.

II *The Physician: 1685–1727*

Returning up the Rhine and through Rotterdam, Richard Blackmore set up practice in a London which very much needed the services of a competent physician. To a community ravished by the miseries of plague, smallpox, tuberculosis, gout (among the upper classes, including Queen Anne), venereal disease (all classes), and "fever," a generic term which included malaria, typhoid, typhus, and other assorted ills, health became, as one historian notes, the *summum bonum* which all sought "through prayers, stars, kings, toads, and science."[17] According to estimates Charles II touched one hundred thousand of his subjects who were afflicted with scrofula. William, who rightly regarded the practice as ridiculous, antagonized the people by his good sense; and Anne returned to the laying on of hands. Astrology was respected by many in all classes, and even among those who passed themselves off as scientific practitioners it was the golden age of quackery. Furthermore, a medical degree from Oxford or Cambridge was in itself no guarantee that the physician was qualified, for the training was too often theoretical or incompetent.[18] Robert Boyle correctly affirmed that the people feared their doctor almost as much as their disease; they were probably wise to do so.

Blackmore entered the practice of medicine at the top. Physicians were the only ones allowed to treat patients internally. Surgeons could not prescribe medicines. Other than their work as barbers, the surgeons' practice typically involved treating fractures, bruises, and contusions; bleeding by opening veins, applying leeches, or using cupping glasses; extracting teeth; operating to remove bladder stones; and amputating. Because the patient had to be conscious during the operation without aid of anesthetics, speed was essential to a surgeon who desired to establish a thriving practice. The celebrated William Cheselden was able to amputate an arm in two minutes. Less brutal was the craft of the apothecary or pharmacist. Strictly forbidden to prescribe, he was only to provide ingredients and prepare them according to the physician's directions. Of course, the apothecaries frequently abused their office by diagnosing and prescribing; and physicians who were less than absolutely scrupulous might make a good living by being available at one or another of the coffeehouses in order that puzzled apothecaries might describe their patients' symptoms.

The coffeehouse was also frequently the unofficial office for physicians practicing legitimately. Richard Blackmore, for example, might be found at Garraway's, a coffeehouse in Exchange Alley near the Royal Exchange which Defoe says was frequented by the "more considerable and wealthy citizens." Dressed in the obligatory black garments and large powdered wig, he would sit in state to receive and prescribe during lulls in conversation. For more prosperous patients or those who were indisposed, he would put on his three-cornered hat, also black, take up the insignia of his profession, a gold or silver-knobbed cane containing disinfectant (protection equally against contagion and the stench of London streets), and mount his gilt carriage. The more ostentatious physicians, including Blackmore's enemy John Radcliffe, insisted on six horses and two running footmen to accompany their carriage.[19] These august trappings were, of course, reflected in the physician's fee.

Partially as a legacy of the "English Hippocrates," Thomas Sydenham, the physician was often able to make an accurate diagnosis by observing respiration, pulse, the condition of the patient's tongue, temperature, and the nature and location of discomfort. The appearance and odor of urine were also believed to provide useful clues as was the blood, which physicians were convinced changed shade according to the disease. The emphasis on observation of the patient's symptoms was characteristic of Sydenham's method, a subordination of theory to experience. Physicians who followed his lead were less likely than most to kill their patients, for he emphasized the ability of the body to overcome illness with a minimum of medication. In truth, even if the physician had made a correct diagnosis, as he frequently had, there were no effective drugs except Peruvian or Jesuit's bark (the source of quinine) for malaria and mercury to combat syphilis. While the herbal remedies often prescribed were usually harmless, they were also useless; and most metallic medications were positively dangerous.[20]

Sydenham was working as a general practitioner in London when Blackmore returned from the Continent in 1684; and the young physician sought him out. When he asked Sydenham what books he should read to prepare him for practice, the older physician recommended *Don Quixote.*[21] In warning Blackmore against what John Locke described as "the romance way of physic," Sydenham was urging that he not view medicine through the spectacles of books, those repositories of other men's preconceived ideas.[22] Blackmore took his advice to heart and was soon "so far faln out with all Hypotheses in *Philosophy*, and all Doctrines of Physic which are built upon them" that he believed nothing hampered an intelligent physician more than the abstractions he had been taught to operate in terms of.[23] This radical empiricism ultimately carried over into his literary practice as well.

Within a year of his return from Padua, Blackmore married Mary Adams and through her became related to the Verneys of Claydon House, Buckingham, an important Whig family who probably helped Richard extend his practice among the rich and fashionable. They chose to live in Sadler's Hall, Cheapside, near St. Paul's in a section of London rebuilt since the great fire of 1666. Although John Hughes and Isaac Watts, two of his closest friends, were Dissenters, Blackmore was always a devout communicant of the Church of England, and he and Mary regularly attended services at St. Vedast in Foster Lane.[24]

Three days before the Blackmores were married on February 9, 1685, Charles died and was succeeded by his brother James, Duke of York, a Catholic. In spite of the anxiety this must have caused a traveler, like Blackmore, recently returned from a firsthand view of the Huguenot persecution in France, the accession proved beneficial in one respect. James enlarged the Royal College of Physicians from forty to a maximum of eighty and, for the first time, allowed physicians who had not taken their degrees at Oxford or Cambridge to be admitted Fellows of the College. Consequently, on the twelfth of April, only a week after James had proclaimed a Declaration of Indulgence suspending all laws against Roman Catholics and Dissenters, Richard Blackmore was admitted to the elite group that made up the Royal College. He was active in the college and by the turn of the century was respected sufficiently to be a major opponent of the Dispensarians, a group of physicians within the college who, partly out of pique at the apothecaries' insolence in prescribing and partly out of charity, wished to establish dispensaries where poor Londoners could obtain medical advice and drugs.[25]

Physicians have always been noted in England for their love of learning and the liberal arts, and Blackmore was no exception. In 1693, when William Cole, a fellow physician and friend, published his new hypothesis concerning intermittent fevers, Blackmore contributed complimentary verses in Latin. Thereafter he worked seriously on a poem allegorically celebrating William's entry into England and his expulsion of James. The result was published as *Prince Arthur. An Heroick Poem. In Ten Books* in late February of 1695. Though the immense popularity of *Prince Arthur* (a second edition was printed the same year and a third in 1696) irritated some critics, as did his attack on the misuse of the stage in the preface to the poem, Blackmore was generally recognized as a powerful writer and an effective apologist for the court. Thus, when Sir George Barclay's plot to assassinate William was discovered, and the court thought it advisable to have an official account, Blackmore was selected to write it.[26]

Prince Arthur had been published at a fortunate time. When Queen Mary died two months earlier William was automatically isolated as an object of Jacobite intrigue.[27] The timely publication of *Prince Arthur* probably helped arouse popular support for the king and his policies. As a reward the king presented Blackmore with a gold chain and medal valued at £150. He was also appointed one of William's Physicians in Ordinary with a salary of two hundred pounds a year.[28] Most importantly, however, on March 18 of 1697 Blackmore was summoned to the new royal palace of Kensington which William had purchased because Mary so liked the gardens and because he hoped the location would be more congenial to his asthma than Whitehall or St. James's. There he knelt to be made Sir Richard Blackmore. On the same day the *London Gazette* contained an advertisement for a new epic, *King Arthur,* written by "Sir Richard Blackmore, Kt. M.D. Fellow of the College of Physicians in London, and One of his Majesty's Physicians in Ordinary."

Even Kensington was too near the coal smoke and dust of the city to be much of a relief to William, and consequently his favorite residence was Hampton Court. As Physician in Ordinary Blackmore was provided rooms for himself and his servant at the Thames retreat. His access to the court must certainly have helped his practice among the wealthy; but too many expressions of his ability as a medical man survive, John Locke's among them, to attribute his popularity as a physician solely to the king's patronage.[29] In the final few years of his own life, William seems to have relied increasingly on Sir Richard; and when the king died from lacerations of the lung which he received when he fell from his horse and broke his collarbone, Blackmore was in attendance and afterward helped prepare the official report of the autopsy.[30]

Queen Anne was a moral and pious but sympathetic Protestant sovereign destined to be especially appealing to a man who was already serving as governor of two London hospitals and as vice-president of the new society for the propagation of the Gospel in America.[31] Perceiving a significant parallel between Anne's position in opposition to Louis and that of Elizabeth in her defense of Protestantism earlier, Blackmore published another epic, *Eliza,* in the summer of 1705. The character of Lopez, the Portuguese physician executed for involvement in a plot to poison Elizabeth, was immediately recognized as an attack on Blackmore's arch medical antagonist, the supercilious, suspected Jacobite Dr. John Radcliffe. Radcliffe's contemporary biographer, William Pittis, attributes the animosity between the two to a misdiagnosis by Blackmore which caused the death of the young Duke of Gloucester in 1699. When, at the urging of Sarah Churchill, Anne (then Princess of Denmark) called him in for consultation, Radcliffe is reputed to have contemptuously warned that Blackmore should stick to schoolteaching and be "whipp'd with one of his own Rods" rather than meddle in a profession about which he knew nothing.[32] Blackmore's part in this story is probably apocryphal;[33] but Radcliffe's callousness in dealing with the child goes far toward explaining Anne's later dislike. In *Eliza* Blackmore pointedly alludes to Radcliffe's failure to secure an appointment as Physician to the Queen, an honor bestowed upon Sir Richard in 1708. After Radcliffe's death, however, Blackmore's antagonism ceased, and he later refers to Radcliffe as highly esteemed and relied on during his lifetime.[34]

Blackmore's experience with William must have helped him treat Anne's husband, Prince George of Denmark, who also suffered with asthma. However, when an increasingly serious dropsy sent George into a coma in October 1708, there was little besides bleeding that Blackmore or any of his physicians could do. When he died, Anne was present with the doctors. Blackmore's aid was also ineffective in saving his friend Arthur Maynwaring in 1712, despite compassionate efforts.[35] Apparently Anne was favorably impressed by the treatment her husband received, for she rewarded Blackmore with a gift of £100 on that occasion and desired his attendance together with Arbuthnot and others during her own final illness in the summer of 1714. Cupping and a vomit proving ineffectual, the queen died early on Sunday, August 1.

After signing an account of Anne's last illness, Sir Richard ended his career as a court physician. When George of Hanover arrived in England he brought physicians with him whose language he could understand. Still, Blackmore, a staunch Whig, must have welcomed the Protestant succession. When in 1723, already retired from practice, he celebrated the new monarch in yet another epic, *Alfred,* he did not do so out of ambition. In any case, by the time of George's accession his eminence in the medical profession was secure. He rose in the Royal College to Censor and finally to the position of Elect; and his practice included such notable men as the Marquess of Wharton and the Earl of Halifax.[36]

When Blackmore resigned as an Elect of the Royal College on October 22, 1722, he left the home in Earl's Court, Kensington, to which he had moved five years earlier, to retire to Boxted in Essex. Perhaps for a man of sixty-eight the inconveniences of city life and the demands of his profession had become too much. The last surviving personal reference to Sir Richard as physician occurs in a letter written two years prior to his retirement. A distraught husband whose ailing wife later recovered records that he "sent for Sir R.B. at 12 at night, but he would not come out of his bed."[37]

Following Sydenham, Blackmore had made observation and experience his chief guides in practicing medicine; and now, after a lifetime of both, he settled in the quiet of the country to write his reflections on what he had seen. In a commendatory poem prefixed to Blackmore's *Treatise of Consumptions,* a colleague, George Sewell, celebrated Blackmore's opposition to "VAIN HYPOTHESIS" and his championing of an empirical method:

> The Field, judicious SYDENHAM left untill'd,
> Thy Hand has planted, and thy Bounty fill'd.

Blackmore wrote in English, convinced that medical knowledge should be accessible to as many people as possible. Physicians who think it beneath the dignity of medicine to write in the vernacular, he identifies with those who opposed the translation of the Bible.[38] He also states his determination to adapt his English to the nonspecialist, using only "the most familiar, significative and unscholastick Terms."[39]

The treatises themselves are now only of historical interest. When an outbreak of the plague in France seemed to threaten England, memories of the great plague during his boyhood stimulated Blackmore to share his knowledge with his countrymen. As in his *Treatise upon the Small-Pox* published the following year, Blackmore frankly admits he knows no medicine which is effective in treating plague or any of the other fevers with which the volume deals.[40] Instead, the physician is limited to removing the cause and helping the body's natural mechanisms fight the disease. Inoculation, introduced only six years before his treatise on smallpox, Blackmore cautiously opposes pending a more adequate study of its effects. Various kinds of melancholia or depression which the Augustans designated "spleen" especially fascinated Blackmore, perhaps because he had seen so much of the fashionable malady during his career. He is sensitive to the seriousness of psychosomatic disorders and wishes that his fellow physicians were more aware of them. He finds the amusement of visiting Bedlam to ridicule and laugh at the inmates disgusting.[41] In another work he praises William III and George for their enlightened rejection of touching for scrofula.[42] His final medical work treats five diseases, from dropsy to diabetes; and his collected medical writings touch on almost every major disease afflicting early eighteenth-century England. Again and again he inveighs against a reliance on authority, no matter how venerable. Nothing commands absolute respect but what the physician actually observes in practice, some of which may defy the doctor's best attempts to analyze and categorize. In some cases there seem, to Blackmore, to be such "secret and occult Operations of Nature" at work that the wise physician does well to reflect on the limitations of human intellect in dealing with the intricacy of creation.[43]

III *The Man of Letters: 1695–1729*

The reaction to Blackmore's *Prince Arthur* in 1695 was not all patronage and praise. Some of the more excessive encomiums irritated a critic who was later recognized as notably irascible, John Dennis. His *Remarks on Prince Arthur*, published the following year, contrasted Blackmore with Virgil, admitting the young author's strengths but vehemently criticizing his lapses. In the preface to *King Arthur* (1697), Sir Richard admitted in turn that some of the barbs he had received were justified; and he was apparently not resentful of Dennis since they subsequently became friends and correspondents. Some coffeehouse critics, however, Blackmore had no desire to pacify. The preface to *King Arthur* continued his attack on the lewd and irreligious misuse of the stage. Dryden, Blackmore felt, was chief among the offenders; and insults were exchanged.

The argument over whether the Royal College was usurping the prerogative of the apothecaries by establishing a dispensary for the service of the poor found Dr. Samuel Garth and Sir Richard in opposite camps, although here too the later relationship was amicable. In response to Garth's *Dispensary*, Blackmore published *A Satyr against Wit* (1699). Both poems attacked other physicians and poets. The factions confronted one another in two volumes: (1) forty lampoons ridiculing Blackmore in *Commendatory Verses, on the Author of the Two Arthurs, and the Satyr against Wit* followed quickly by (2) a parodic counterblast in his support, *Discommendatory Verses.* Blackmore's *A Paraphrase on the Book of Job* was published at the same time and drew its shaft of darts, especially from Grub Street writer Tom Brown.

This war of wits raged on into the early years of the new century. In some circles "Blackmore" was becoming synonymous with "poetaster." In others he was revered as a champion of religion and a practitioner of the sublime. Works were dedicated to him; others were written against him. In the course of celebrating the Duke of Marlborough's victories against Louis on the Continent in *Advice to the Poets* (1706), Blackmore stirred up his political and literary enemies, especially the friends of John Philips. When a sequel appeared under the title *Instructions to Vander Bank* (1709), even Steele, a friend of Sir Richard, indulged in a little good-natured gibing in the *Tatler*.[44] As early as 1695 Blackmore was apparently engaged with Addison, among others, in preparation of an edition of Herodotus for the publisher Jacob Tonson.[45] Although nothing came of the project, Blackmore's poem *The Kit-Cats* (1708) suggests that his association with the Whig literary men was close and continuous.

Admirers had suggested to Blackmore that he was, as a physician and scientist, uniquely qualified to write "a natural history of the great and admirable phaenomena of the universe."[46] *The Nature of Man* (1711) suggested, in its study of the effect of climate on character, Blackmore's increasing interest in philosophical poetry; and the following year his masterpiece appeared, *Creation. A Philosophical Poem. In Seven Books.* An immediate success, the poem enjoyed edition after edition and received almost universal praise. Blackmore further pursued his interest in scientific and philosophical subjects when, the *Guardian* having ceased publication, he and John Hughes published forty issues of a periodical entitled *The Lay-Monk* (1713–14).

Pope had paid his respects to Sir Richard after the publication of *Creation*, and in the first volume of his *Essays upon Several Subjects* (1716) Blackmore praised Pope's translation of the *Iliad*. However, he characterized Swift, as author of *A Tale of a Tub*, as an "impious Buffoon." This characterization, and his condemnation of Pope's burlesque of a Psalm in the second volume of the *Essays* published the next year, earned Blackmore the Twickenham wasp's undying enmity. Blackmore's detestation of anything that tended to detract from the dignity of religion is wholly characteristic, and his crusade on behalf of divine poetry continued in the preface to his collected shorter *Poems* (1718). In 1721 he published two books against the "fashionable heresy" of Arianism,[47] both preparatory to his definitive defense of Christ in the poem *Redemption* (1722). During his involvement in this theological controversy, Blackmore also found time to compose *A New Version of the Psalms of David* (1721), which he hoped would be adopted for services in the Established Church. Feeling that his work and the efforts of others to strengthen religion had failed, Blackmore tried one final time in *Natural Theology* (1728) to demonstrate that the moral imperatives of Christianity were inherent in the nature of the universe.

While in retirement at Boxted writing his theological and medical treatises, Blackmore was being regularly abused by the wits in London. Pope's ingenious *Peri Bathous* pilloried Sir Richard as the prime exemplar of dull composition just two months after Blackmore's wife died on New Year's Day, 1728. When Blackmore died on October 9 of the following year, the wits had so worn down his reputation that Abel Boyer notes his death as the passing of "an eminent Physician but a very indifferent Poet."[48] He was buried near his wife in the parish church of Boxted. According to the specific instructions of his will, the ceremony was held between eleven and midnight with no pallbearers. His coffin, as instructed, was completely unadorned, without escutcheons.[49]

CHAPTER 2

Prince Arthur: *"An Almost Virgin Muse"*

Heroic poems without number,
Long, lifeless, leaden, lulling lumber.
Robert Lloyd on Blackmore's epics (1782)

I *The Epic*

DURING the Restoration and early Eighteenth Century in England the epic was the preeminent type of poetry. In the hierarchical genre criticism of John Sheffield's *An Essay upon Poetry* (1682), epic poets occupy the "airy top" of Parnassus, for

Heroic poems have a just pretense
To be the chief effort of human sense.[1]

Marshaling the authority of Aristotle, Longinus, and Horace, John Dryden argues that the epic or heroic poem "has ever been esteemed, and ever will be, the greatest work of human nature" (1677).[2] In stating his own preferences in "A Discourse Concerning . . . Satire," he dissents from Aristotle by finding the perfections of tragedy "mechanical" in contrast to the true nobility of epic (1692).[3] In a dedication to Sheffield, Dryden only voiced the consensus of the age in agreeing with the Earl that "a heroic poem, truly such, is undoubtedly the greatest work which the soul of man is capable to perform" (1697).[4]

Only by "painful steps," by inspired wit and careful judgment, invention and decorum, could an author attain this greatest of neoclassical literary goals. For the epic was not merely a narrative poem of heroic action; it was an encyclopedic distillation of all religious, philosophical, political, and scientific knowledge.[5] On such an ambitious journey, Sheffield wonders,

> who has strength to go?
> Who can all sciences exactly know?
> Whose fancy flies beyond weak reason's sight,
> And yet has judgment to direct it right?

Only Homer and Virgil, he finds, have succeeded in the genre. Even Spenser and Milton have failed.[6] Against such odds, for such glory, the best of poets felt the epic fire. Jonson, Dryden, and Pope proposed epics which they never wrote. Lesser poets wrote epics which are no longer read.[7] Ironically, the age which most revered the epic and which, in Dryden's *Aeneid* and Pope's *Iliad,* produced the greatest English translations of the genre gave the world no great original heroic poem. Despite its date of publication, *Paradise Lost* is rightly regarded as the masterpiece of an earlier sensibility.

Perhaps the temper of the times was simply uncongenial to epic, despite the profusion of contemporary opinions to the contrary. Perhaps, as one critic suggests, the Augustans moved away from epic to excellence in mock-heroic and other varieties of satire "without fully realizing what they were doing—almost against their will."[8] Certainly Jonathan Swift's shift from Pindaric panegyric to prose satire even in the face of Sir William Temple's distaste for malicious wit suggests that something more irresistible than aesthetic theory was in the air. And despite the adulation accorded epic, it was one of the first casualties in the Augustan war of wits.

Almost as soon as Sir William Davenant's preface to *Gondibert* and Hobbes's answer initiated much of the theory of the epic that reigned in England for the next 150 years,[9] John Denham led a group of wits in publishing satires on *Gondibert.* Cowley's *Davideis* drew similiar criticism as did the efforts of a lesser precursor of Blackmore, Edward Howard. His presumption in ranking Spenser and Davenant with the greatest of the writers of epic combined with his own poor practice in *The British Princes* (1669) caused Charles Sackville, among others, to ridicule Howard's "strange alacrity in sinking"[10] in phrases which clearly anticipate Pope's abuse of Sir Richard in *Peri Bathous* sixty years later. Perhaps nothing so clearly illustrates the ambivalent attitude toward epic as the authorship of the prefatory poem to Howard's *British Princes.* It is by the same John Denham who found *Gondibert* so absurd.[11]

II Prince Arthur: *The Preface*

Perhaps prompted by Dryden's inspirational words in "A Discourse Concerning Satire" in 1692, Blackmore apparently decided that the rewards of writing an epic outweighed the risk of ridicule; and for the next two years in the "Vacancies and Intervals" of his practice as a physician he worked on the poem that was issued as *Prince Arthur* in late February 1695.[12] The publication of Blackmore's poem had been in some measure prepared for by a short article in the *Athenian Mercury* on January 26. The answerer to the query "What is the Nature of a true Epic Poem? who have best observed it amongst the Poets, and what are the rules for it?" drew heavily on Le Bossu's *Traité du poème épique* (1675), which Sheffield had enthusiastically recommended as disclosing the "sacred Mysteries" of heroic poetry. Possibly Blackmore wrote the answer in the*Athenian Mercury* himself. Several of John Dunton's friends, Samuel Wesley, for example, were also friends of Blackmore, and Blackmore's discussion of the epic in the preface to *Prince Arthur* is clearly indebted to Le Bossu.

Although he acknowledges the authority of Aristotle, Horace, Rapin, and André Dacier, Blackmore clearly visualizes the epic according to the categories provided by Le Bossu, "the best of modern critics," according to Dryden. So influential was the *Traité du poème épique* that its reflection in Blackmore's preface to *Prince Arthur* may serve as a touchstone for what most men thought about the heroic poem during this period. To Blackmore an epic poem is "a feign'd or devis'd Story of an *Illustrious Action,* related in Verse, in an *Allegorical, Probable, Delightful* and *Admirable* manner, to cultivate the Mind with Instructions of Virtue." The hero must have courage and be involved in "important" actions. Although an epic requires variety, it must, insists the physician Blackmore, have an organic unity similar to the body's—"no Episode being out of its place, of a *disproportion'd* size to the Rest, or that could be spar'd from its place, without *maiming,* or at least *deforming* the Whole." Of the epic poets only Virgil has utilized allegory successfully by making his hero Aeneas represent the emperor Augustus. Homer has only a literal sense while both Ariosto and Spenser err to the opposite extreme by proposing allegories "so *wild, unnatural,* and *extravagant*" that they "mightily offend."

Nothing, Blackmore observes, is more essential than that probability be observed; but since admiration is the passion preeminently aroused by the epic poet, he must delight by "*astonishing* and *amazing* the Reader." To stimulate admiration within the bounds of probability the poet must present "sublime Thoughts, clear and noble Expression, Purity of Language, a just and due Proportion, Relation, and Dependance between the Parts, and a beautiful and regular Structure and Connection discernable in the Whole." Verisimilitude and admiration are most likely to conflict when "machines" (i.e., gods) are introduced into the poem. Yet Blackmore disagrees with Boileau's injunction against the use of the Christian religion in the epic.[13] Indeed, Blackmore insists, one of his motives in writing *Prince Arthur* was to demonstrate that Christian theology might "enter into an Epick Poem, and *raise* the Subject without being it self *debas'd.*"

His other motive for writing *Prince Arthur* is the degeneration he sees in contemporary poetry. Overflowing from what Dryden termed "the steaming ordures of the stage," irreligion and lewdness were infecting other kinds of writing. Moreover, Blackmore says, "The sweetness of the Wit, makes the *Poison* go down with Pleasure, and the Contagion spreads without Opposition." Ingenious playwrights contend that the degeneracy of the age obliges them to write as they do or to starve. Blackmore argues that true poets scorn to satisfy the appetites of a "vain and wanton" audience. Yet the comedies of the age are calculated to do nothing else. The hero is usually "a *Derider* of Religion, a great *Admirer* of *Lucretius,* not so much for his *Learning,* as his *Irreligion,* a Person wholly *Idle,* dissolv'd in Luxury, abandon'd to his Pleasures, a great Debaucher of Women, profuse and extravagant in his Expences, and in short, this *Finish'd Gentleman* will appear a *Finish'd Libertine.*"[14] The heroine is, if anything, worse. Clergymen are inevitably presented as pimps, fools, or hypocrites while the "*Diligent, Thriving* Citizen is made the most Wretched, Contemptible Thing in the World."

If Blackmore's remarks on the abuses of the stage seem

obvious, it is because other men manned the wall from which he had fired the first shot. As Samuel Johnson correctly observes, the preface to *Prince Arthur* anticipates "almost all that was alleged afterwards" by Jeremy Collier in *A Short View of the Immorality and Profaneness of the English Stage* (1698). Moreover, Blackmore's criticism was uniquely well timed, for the Licensing Act expired in 1695, and with the relative freedom of the press which that insured, increased abuses could be expected. In *The Stage Condemn'd,* published in the same year as Collier's tract, George Ridpath cites Blackmore repeatedly, observing that Sir Richard urges reasonable reform rather than abolition of the stage. The anonymous author of *The Stage Acquited* (also 1698) proposed to write a separate volume answering Blackmore's objections.[15] Blackmore's attack on immodest and irreligious wit in the preface to *Prince Arthur* registers and defines a major shift in the sensibility of the English people.[16] His presentation of Arthur as the heroic ideal in contrast to the "Finish'd Libertine" anticipates his friend Steele's conception of the fine gentleman or man of honor, and Steele's attack on Etherege's *Man of Mode* in *Spectator* No. 65 repeats several of Blackmore's general observations.

One other interesting aspect of Blackmore's preface is his praise of "our own *excellent Critick Mr. Rymer.*" Doubtless Blackmore admired the common-sense insistence on probability and decorum which Rymer inherited from the French neo-classicists and advocated in the preface to *Monsieur Rapin's Reflections on Aristotle's Treatise of Poesie* (1674). The translation and preface had been reissued only a year before *Prince Arthur* and it must be that work and not the more notorious 1693 *Short View of Tragedy* (in which Rymer discourses of Shakespeare much as a pig might grunt at his pearl) which Blackmore admired.[17] In his preface to Rapin, Rymer considers the epics of Spenser, Davenant, and Cowley, praising and criticizing each. His contention that the Spenserian stanza and the quatrain of Davenant are not as appropriate to epic as Cowley's heroic couplets may have confirmed Blackmore in his choice of verse form. Similarly, Blackmore was put on guard by Rymer's objection to Davenant's choice of an unfamiliar hero and action and by his warning, in discussing Cowley's *Davideis,* of the difficulty of utilizing Christianity and still remaining within the bounds of probability.[18]

III Prince Arthur. An Heroick Poem

Book I of *Prince Arthur* opens with the hero, who had fled Britain when the Saxons overcame King Uter, on his way back to recover his crown. Ambitious Lucifer, however, moving among the Miltonic "silent, lonesome Walks of ancient Night," resolves to frustrate Arthur's plans and further his subject Octa's domination of Britain. In a passage which is the first incorporation of Nordic mythology in English epic, Lucifer has Thor release the winds, causing a storm designed to sink all Arthur's ships. Lucifer's comrade in the war against heaven, Thor recalls the great defeat:

> Thou led'st in Heav'n our bright Battalions on,
> And bravely did'st attempt th' Almighty's Throne;
> I saw thy mighty Deeds, and kept my Post
> Close by thee, till that Glorious Day was lost.
> Thy faded Splendor, and illustrious Scars,
> From Ghastly Wounds, receiv'd in those just Wars,
> I view with Reverence, 'tis true subdu'd
> Headlong we fell from Heav'n's high Tow'r's, pursu'd
> With whirlwinds, and loud Thunder, down to Hell,
> And Storms of Fire beat on us as we fell.
> Yet after that. . . . (p.8)

The storm Thor raises terrifies Arthur and his men:

> The raging Seas in high ridg'd Mountains rise,
> And cast their angry Foam against the Skies.
> Then gape so deep, that Day Light Hell invades,
> And shoots grey Dawning thro' th' affrighted Shades.
> Low bellying Clouds soon intercept the Light,
> And o'er the *Britions* spread a Noon Day Night.
> Exploded Thunder tears th' Embowel'd Sky,
> And Sulphurous Flames a dismal Day supply. (p.9)

In response to Arthur's prayers Uriel descends to calm the waters. The survivors abandon their wrecked ship and scramble onto the Armorican shore. Arthur assures his men that their misfortune does not indicate God's disapproval of their actions, for the ways of divine providence are too profound for the easily perplexed mind of man. After feasting, his men hear Arthur draw an analogy between the tempest they have just survived and "this transient mortal State." They have deserted their sandlocked ship just as the soul, "Long beaten off from the bright Coasts of Bliss," departs the body.

Having calmed his men, "the Pious British Prince" retires to a shaded cave and confides his uncertainties in prayer. Raphael appears, reassuring Arthur that he has been shipwrecked in the land of King Hoel for a purpose and that he should proceed to Hoel's court. Just as Raphael returns "up the steep Crystal Mountains of the Skies," Lucifer calls a council in hell to meditate further mischief. The most monstrous of the assembled furies is Persecution:

> Her squallid, bloated Belly did arise,
> Swoln with black Gore, to a prodigious Size.
> Distended vastly, by a mighty Flood
> Of slaughter'd Saints, and constant Martyrs Blood.
> Part stood out prominent, but part fell down.
> And in a swagging heap, lay wallowing on the ground. (p. 18)

She reminds the council that "sacred Zeal" often inflames even Christian monarchs to extreme cruelties. Catholic Rome, she brags, owes its glory to her methods. Commissioned by hell, Persecution assumes the shape of Almon, high priest of Odin in Hoel's court, and convinces the king that he will be serving heaven's cause in killing the unsuspecting Arthur. However, Hoel is intercepted in his zealous march to Arthur's camp by the "soft, still" voice of "the Christians God" and instructed to aid Arthur and receive religious instruction from him. The book concludes with the joyous meeting of Hoel and Arthur, which both now realize has been providential.

The following fifth of the epic is devoted to Arthur's instruction of Hoel. In Book II Arthur describes creation and the heavenly celebration which follows. He tells of Adam's dominion in Eden:

> The twining Branches weave him shady Bowers,
> And Hony-Dews fall in delicious Showers.
> Birds with their Songs their Soveraign salute,
> From Boughs that bend beneath their Golden Fruit. (p. 45)

After Adam's disobedience, Arthur describes God's summoning of his angels for judgment. Mercy pleads for Adam's sentence of death to be amended; and the book concludes with the life of Christ. At Hoel's insistence, Arthur describes the end of the world, Christ's judgment, and the New Jerusalem in Book III. Arthur contrasts the horrors of hell with the glories of eternal life in heaven.

In Book IV, Arthur and Hoel journey to the imperial city. At a great feast in Arthur's honor, the bard Mopas sings "in lofty Verse" of "the secret Maze of Nature." Among the wonders of creation Mopas ingeniously describes how God

> . . . spread the Airy Ocean without Shores,
> Where *Birds* are wafted with their feather'd Oars. (p.96)

Hoel remains with the Britons after Arthur retires to ask about the history of their country and Arthur's story in particular. Lucius relates how the Saxons, coming as friends, remained as masters. Determined to wage one last battle for liberty, King Uter opposed the Saxon forces of Octa. Although Arthur distinguished himself in the battle, Carvil, trusted by Uter, betrayed the Britons for Saxon gold. Uter and many Britons were killed in a night attack. Gabriel appeared to Arthur, telling him that after ten years he would conquer but that now he should flee to Odar's court, where the Britons would be graciously received by Odar and invited to remain until the right time for a return home. Lucius describes a "noble" speech made by Arthur on contentment in adversity and narrates Arthur's fight against the Goths to save Odar's peaceful kingdom. After the ten years, Lucius continues, Tylon was dispatched by the British lords who still hold the west country to persuade Arthur to return. It was in the process of sailing for Britain that they were tossed on the Armorican shore.

As Book V begins, Hoel assures Arthur of his aid. But as the rebuilding of the fleet progresses, Lucifer blocks the Britons exit with unfavorable winds. Meanwhile, in the shape of Odin, he inspires Octa to engage Arthur in a sea battle, in which his ship is burned by Arthur's fireship and he is forced to seek refuge in Horsa's vessel while Lucifer covers the Saxon retreat. Sailing the coast of Britain, Arthur finally takes harbor at Malgo's castle, where the dead King Uter appears to him in a dream, telling him of his glorious future and counseling him in good government. Then Uter shows Arthur all the English kings down to the warrior-saint William, his arch-foe Louis, and his recently dead spouse, Mary. After Uter's tribute to Queen Mary, Arthur awakens to contemplate his vision.

Book VI relates the British preparations for war and catalogues those troops who joined Arthur's forces. As the Britons move to Gallena, Octa calls a council of his lords, which after much debate resolves to sue for a peaceful division of the land. Emissaries from Octa arrive during games celebrating Arthur's birth and offer marriage to Octa's daughter Ethelina as a symbol of the union. Arthur retires for two days' deliberation before accepting. Infuriated by the peace and resolved to frustrate even if he cannot ultimately defeat Arthur, Lucifer again holds court in hell. There the subtle seducer Asmodai, "who Men inspires/With wanton Passions, and unclean Desires," is chosen to tempt the Britons to offend heaven. A vicious army of debauched Britons defiles the land while Magaera, goddess of disease, infects the camps, "Deforming every Tent with Heaps of Dead." In response to Arthur's prayers, Raphael is sent with a "crystal Vial" of balms to cure the troops. As he reproves Arthur for failing to keep a strict reign on his subordinates, the book ends.

Convinced that the Britons are greatly weakened, Lucifer commands the fierce Bellona to assume the shape of Octa's mother in order to convince Octa to break his truce. Inspired by their king, the Saxons prepare anew for war as the Muse catalogues their troops. Meanwhile, with Arthur emphasizing the justice of God's wrath, the British camp prays for forgiveness. Hearing of the Saxon preparations, Arthur fears the weakened condition of his army until Raphael reassures him. In the Saxon camp, although he has seen many ill omens, Octa hides his fears and encourages his men. In desperation Octa hires Merlin to curse Arthur; but after a night of demonic preparation, Merlin's curse is changed into a benediction as he prophesies British victory. As battle nears, Michael guards the field from Lucifer's intrusion. Arthur appears dressed for battle. Book VII closes with the history of Arthur's sword and a description of the Christian battle scenes emblazoned on his shield.

In the battle which Book VIII narrates, Arthur fights furiously:

> As when Tempestuous Storms o'erspread the Skies,
> In whose dark Bowels in born Thunder lies.

The watry Vapours numberless conspire,
To smolder, and oppress th' imprison'd Fire.
Which thus collected gathers greater Force,
Breaks out in Flames, and with impetuous Course
From the Cloud's gaping Womb in Light'nings flies,
Flashing in ruddy Streaks, along the Skies.
So *Arthur's* flaming Sword cuts thro' the Cloud,
Around him spread, and rends th' opposing Crowd.
With daz'ling Arms, he flies upon the Foe,
Flashes amidst the throngs, and terribly Thunders thro'. (p. 235)

In a pathetic scene Elda successfully pleads with Arthur for the life of her vanquished husband, Lothar, with whom in her declining years

Th' inhospitable Desart will appear,
A flowry Paradise, when he is there.
O'er Snows with him and Hills of Ice I'll stray,
I know not how, but Love will find the way. (p. 242)

Disguised as a seraph Lucifer sneaks past the angelic guards and intimidates the Britons with a vision of Arthur's severed head. As the Britons flee, Arthur appears to inspire them. Night coming on quickly obscures the Saxon retreat.

A ten-day truce allows the honorable preparation of Macor's body for burial as Book IX opens. The slain on both sides are buried or burned and victory games celebrated with huge bonfires and horseraces. In the Saxon camp orators from Tollo inform Octa that, if offered Ethelina's hand, he is ready to aid the Saxons. The promise made, Tollo assumes command from the wounded Octa and, reinforced by Mordred and his Picts, leads the united armies against the Britons. In the final book, as the advantage inclines to the Britons, Lucifer causes a storm. The troops return to their respective camps. In Saxon council the wise Pascentius urges that Arthur and Tollo fight for Ethelina. Arthur kills Tollo in single combat as *Prince Arthur* ends.

IV *Blackmore's Eclecticism*

As Blackmore mentions later in the preface to *King Arthur*, the historical authority for Arthur's exploits is Geoffrey of Monmouth's *Historia* with which *Prince Arthur* loosely agrees in its narration of Arthur's battles against the Saxons, his march to London, and his victories over Ireland and Scotland. In *Poly-Olbion* (1613) Michael Drayton urged the use of Arthurian material for an epic:

> For some abundant brain, oh, there had been a story,
> Beyond the blind man's might to have enhanced our glory.

But although Jonson, Milton, and Dryden planned Arthurian heroic poems, only Blackmore actually completed his.[19]

It is to Virgil, however, rather than to British sources that Blackmore is chiefly indebted in *Prince Arthur.* "I do not make any *Apology* for my *Imitation* of *Virgil* in so many places of this Poem," he insists in the preface, arguing that Virgil was as deeply indebted to Homer. A comparison of the opening of *Prince Arthur* with Dryden's translation of the *Aeneid* published two years later suggests the pervasive resemblance of Blackmore's poem to Virgil's:

> I sing the *Briton,* and his Righteous Arms,
> Who bred to Suff'rings, and the rude Alarms
> Of bloody War, forsook his Native Soil. . . .
> *Prince Arthur* (1695)

> ARMS, and the Man I sing, who, forc'd by Fate,
> And haughty *Juno's* unrelenting Hate;
> Expell'd and exil'd, left the *Trojan* shoar. . . .
> *Virgil's Aeneis* (1697)

In Blackmore, Lucifer replaces Juno as enemy of the hero, and just as Juno has Aeolus raise a storm so Lucifer has Thor do the same. In the *Aeneid* Neptune calms the waters; in *Prince Arthur,* Uriel. The parallels, often quite ingenious, continue throughout the epic.

Although the *Aeneid* provides the formal model for *Prince Arthur,* Blackmore has obviously studied the other authors of epic carefully. The councils in hell and the pious hero assisted by heaven and assaulted by the forces of hell derive from his reading of Tasso's *Gerusalemme Liberata* as well as from Milton. Similarly, Arthur's instruction of Hoel recalls Adam's instruction of Seth in Du Bartas's *La Semaine* and *La Seconde Semaine* (translated into heroic couplets by Joshua Sylvester as *Du Bartas*

His Divine Weekes and Workes in 1592–99) more perhaps than it recalls Raphael's instruction of Adam in *Paradise Lost.* Of course, Milton's manner fully as much as his matter is an important influence. One recent critic feels that Blackmore's Lucifer has something of the "fine spirit" of Milton's Satan;[20] and another critic believes that, as in his use of Virgilian material, his adaptions from Milton "often have much originality and force."[21] As his preface indicates, Blackmore feels that both Ariosto and Spenser, having failed to observe the "judicious Conduct of *Virgil,*" are too often lost in a wild wood of allegories. Nonetheless, the influence of Spenser is strong in *Prince Arthur.* The descriptions of the fiends Persecution and Asmodai, for example, recall the villains and the themes ("Holinesse" and "Temperaunce") of the first two books of *The Faerie Queene.* Spenser's use of Prince Arthur must have impressed a classicist like Blackmore as hopelessly episodic. Yet despite his repeated insistence on unity of action—"The regular Succession of one *Part* or *Episode* to another"—there was simply too much richness in Spenser for Blackmore to reject his influence entirely, as the Alexandrine belly of Persecution suggests.

Blackmore's "Allegory" in *Prince Arthur* is something entirely new in the epic. Virgil and Spenser, among others, had drawn vague parallels between the characters and actions in their poems and those in contemporary public and political life; but Blackmore made exact and clearly recognizable identifications of persons and events. Two unpublished epic allegories of the reign of Charles I survive in manuscript, both written as continuations of the unfinished adventures of Arthur in *The Faerie Queene*;[22] and doubtless the popularity of French prose romances, which invited very specific identifications, and the more explicit *roman à clef,* influenced Blackmore. In addition, Restoration poems and plays often depended for heightened interest on the portrayal of contemporaries as historical or fabulous personages, as in Dryden's *Albion and Albanius* or *Absalom and Achitophel.*

In his later "Essay upon Epick Poetry" (1716) Blackmore suggests that this "very agreeable" kind of allegory should "be drawn so thin, that the real Characters in the View and Intention of the Poet may appear underneath, and be seen with ease through the transparent Veil."[23] No reader need ponder long to discover that the British Arthur represents King William, champion of Protestantism. Blackmore altered Geoffrey's account in the *Historia* to have his hero exiled to the court of Odar (Holland), where he successfully defended the country against the Goths (the French). The petition from the oppressed British lords, the unpropitious storm which scattered the fleet and delayed passage to England, the landing and the march to London all accurately reflect incidents in the autumn of 1688. But Blackmore did not limit himself to the facts. The sea battle with Octa (James II) is fictitious and the marriage to Ethelina (Mary), which is still not consummated when the epic ends, had, in real life, occurred much earlier. Despite these dramatic liberties, however, contemporaries would have recognized Thomas Osborne, the Earl of Danby, as the wise Pascentius advising his king to negotiate a peaceful settlement. In Magaera's coming from hell, they saw the rain and disease which debilitated the Duke of Schomberg's Irish expedition, and in Raphael's reproof of Arthur they saw Parliament's censure of the conduct of the campaign in Ireland, after which William resolved to go himself and direct affairs. The great battle of Book VII is the Battle of the Boyne, and Arthur's defeat of Tollo in single combat is a symbolic rendering of the defeat and death of John Graham of Claverhouse, Viscount Dundee, and the consequent end of Scots support of James. The religious allegory appropriately pits Christian Arthur (Protestant William) against pagan Octa (Catholic James) quite as transparently as the political allegory.

V *John Dennis*

Whether attracted by the patriotic appeal of a British epic or the intriguing allusiveness of the poem's allegory, many readers ventured over the frosty cobblestones to the sign of the black swan in Pater-Noster-Row, where the folio *Prince Arthur* was for sale in the bookseller's shop af Awnsham and John Churchil. A second edition was quickly needed, and then a third. This popularity must have relieved Blackmore of some anxieties about publishing so ambitious a work as his poetic debut. As Johnson noted, Blackmore is the only English author whose first public poem was an epic.[24] He had chosen to forgo the usual apprenticeship in lesser genres, beginning with the lyric or the pastoral. He was, therefore, that much more open to criticism.

To write an epic at all demands considerable courage because the undertaking is on such a colossal scale that failure invites ridicule which may reverberate for centuries. One need only think, Northrop Frye relevantly suggests, "What the name 'Blackmore' still suggests to students of English literature, many of whom have not read a line of Blackmore's epics."[25] If Pope is being candid when he says that *Prince Arthur* was unpopular, the reverberations raised by the wits of Covent Garden against it must have subverted the truth.[26] For even those who for political, religious, or aesthetic reasons disliked the work seem to have read it, including the aspiring Jonathan Swift.[27] "That *Prince Arthur* found many readers," Johnson observes succinctly, "is certain."[28]

Before the end of the year Blackmore's reputation as one of England's leading men of letters was established. When friends called John Phillips's attention to the fact that the preface to *Prince Arthur* had already voiced many of the objections he made in *A Reflection on our Modern Poesy*, Phillips replied that he was "very glad to see so *Eminent* an *Author* of the same opinion."[29] More significantly, shortly after the publication of *Prince Arthur* one "W. J.," praising Blackmore's poem enthusiastically, dedicated his own translation of Le Bossu's *Traité du poème épique* to the new epic poet. W. J.'s praise is not indiscriminate panegyric. He suggests that some of Blackmore's digressions and descriptions are tedious and would benefit from shortening. On the other hand, more episodes would add a welcome variety. Nonetheless, he judges Blackmore to be the finest of English epic poets:

> All the *Characters* are nobly drawn, and look like the Curious Strokes of a great Master. . . . His *Machines* are very Natural, and adapted to the *Genius* and Notions of our times, as *Virgil's* were to those of his Age. His *Expression* is Noble and Majestical; his *Verse* Sonorous, Masculine, and Strong; his *Thoughts* are Sublime; his *Similes* natural. . . . In a word throughout the whole he seems in a great Measure to have confin'd himself to the Rules of *Aristotle* and *Horace*, to have copy'd the best of any Man the Perfections of *Virgil*, and to have shewn a Strength of *Genius*, and Height of *Fancy*, and a correctness of *Judgment*, that comes but little behind that of the two *Ancient* Poets.[30]

Because of minor lapses the "Excellent *Heroick Poem*" of the "Learned and Ingenious Dr. *Blackmore*" must rank "*Next* to, though not an *Equal* with" those of Homer and Virgil. In any case, W. J. hopes that his translation of Le Bossu may be useful to those who wish to judge *Prince Arthur* themselves.[31]

Perhaps provoked by what he considered W. J.'s excessive deference to the ancients, Edward Howard defended *Prince Arthur* as superior to either the *Iliad* or the *Aeneid*. "The two Elaborate Poems of *Blackmore* and *Milton*, the which, for the dignity of them, may very well be looked upon as the two grand Exemplers of Poetry," Howard writes in *An Essay upon Pastoral*, "do either of them exceed, and are more to be valued, than all the Poems both of the *Romans* and the *Greeks* put together."[32] An anonymous admirer praised Blackmore as the savior of poetry in an epistle "To the Learned *Rich Blackmore* M. D. on his Ingenious Poem Prince Arthur." Borrowing strains from *Cooper's Hill*, he paid tribute to Blackmore's epic:

> Such is thy *Arthur*, such thy matchless song,
> Sweet, yet Majestic; beautiful, yet strong.[33]

Probably urged on by his coffeehouse elders, young John Oldmixon initiated his literary career with several attacks on Blackmore in his Anacreonic *Poems on Several Occasions*. He specifically attacks Howard's *Essay upon Pastoral*, observing sarcastically that "if this Honorable Critick has been so severe with the Ancients, he is wondrous kind to the Moderns." Although Oldmixon admits that *Prince Arthur* "stands fair in the opinion of some honest, well-meaning Gentlemen," he objects to Howard's equating Blackmore with Milton. Oldmixon's imitation of Boileau's second satire invites comparison with the anonymous imitation of the same satire which praised Blackmore so lavishly. His literary fortunes, he laments, are

> So low, that B[lackmore] can my Envy raise,
> Oh! happy B[lackmore] thy Prodigious Muse,
> Huge Books of Verse can in a year produce.
> True—Rude and Dull, to some she gives offence,
> And seems Created in despite of sense;
> Yet she will find, whatever we have said,
> Both Sots to Print her Works, and Fools to read.[34]

Such assured impudence from a twenty-three-year-old novice suggests a strong undercurrent of coffeehouse dissatisfaction with the laurels heaped on *Prince Arthur*. Dryden felt understandable irritation over the appearance of a successful epic when his own epic translation was imminent. In his preface, W. J. had called attention to Dryden's projected *Aeneid*. Add to that Blackmore's praise of Rymer, who had assumed Dryden's old post of historiographer royal only three years earlier, and some enmity seems inevitable. Most importantly, however, in Book VI of *Prince Arthur*, Blackmore had directly attacked the Catholic Dryden as the sycophantic, pagan bard Laurus.

Oldmixon, morever, was probably already a friend of John Dennis;[35] and it is difficult to believe that the small shot of his *Poems on Several Occasions* was not intended as prelude to Dennis's heavier artillery. Blackmore's deference to Rymer would also have incensed Dennis, whose recent *Impartial Critick: Or, Some Observations Upon a Late Book, Entituled, A Short View of Tragedy, Written By Mr. Rymer* (1693) treated Rymer's pronouncements on English drama as the mumblings of a baboon. After Dennis had carefully pondered W. J.'s recommendation that *Prince Arthur* might be evaluated according to Le Bossu's analysis of the epic, in mid-June of 1696 and soon after Blackmore's poem appeared in its third edition, the *London Gazette* carried an advertisement for Dennis's *Remarks on a Book Entituled, Prince Arthur.* Despite Johnson's dismissal of Dennis's *Remarks* as "a formal criticism, more tedious and disgusting than the book which he condemns,"[36] it was perhaps the first modern review[37] and is certainly one of the longest and most thorough literary criticisms of the age.

Dennis's slavish reliance on Le Bossu's "rules" inevitably produces *a priori* criticism full of "purely arbitrary preceptist statements"[38] and "various specious arguments."[39] Consequently, the most interesting and original observations occur when Dennis wanders from his subject to discuss the necessity of genius or the nature of the sublime and pathetic. In dealing with Blackmore, Dennis writes consistently as an antagonist, and despite the objections of Edward Niles Hooker[40] Johnson's characterization of his tone as "insolent and contemptuous" is generally accurate. Despising the popular taste for "Rhyming Heroick Fustian," Dennis looks upon his criticism of *Prince Arthur* as an "Antidote" to be taken "before or immediately after the Poem." He admits that *Prince Arthur* "has been very agreeable to a great many Readers" but attributes its popularity to unsophisticated palates.[41]

Dennis agrees with Boileau that "the Terrible Mysteries" of Christianity should not figure in an epic poem.[42] Moreover, he cannot understand why the clergy of the Church of England espouse Blackmore's work. No true patriot should defend Blackmore, Dennis feels, because he frequently shows Arthur afraid, which Dennis denounces as a blasphemy on the acknowledged bravery of King William.[43] Blackmore's "Servile" imitation of Virgil, Dennis contends, destroys the surprise which many of the incidents might otherwise have. The unity of the action is violated by several episodes, most notably by the "tedious" account of creation in Book II, of which Dennis prophetically remarks:

> If this part of the Poem had been publish'd before the rest, it would never have been thought to have been a relation, or indeed a part of any thing else, but it might have pass'd upon the world very well with the Title of a religious Poem upon the Creation of the World and the Redemption of Man.[44]

Employing various sophistries, Dennis finds Arthur "neglectful, impious, and fearfull," wholly unsuited to be the hero of an epic poem.[45] In similar manner, despite Arthur's speeches in the poem concerning the incomprehensible nature of providence, Dennis objects that Blackmore does not observe strict poetic justice. The war councils, both mortal and demonic, Dennis dismisses as congregations of "dull dogmatizing Politicians." Sneering at various verses, Dennis ultimately concludes that *Prince Arthur* lacks the passion which characterizes the best heroic poetry:

> If Mr. *Blackmore's* Narration is not pathetick, it cannot be very delightful. Indeed, a Poet ought always to speak to the Heart. And the greatest Wit in the World, when he ceases to do that, is a Rhimer and not a Poet.[46]

Dennis does not, however, consider Blackmore completely destitute of that genius which animates the true sublime. In an "annotation" explaining why he believes Books II and III, which narrate biblical history from creation to the final judgment, were written separately from the rest of *Prince Arthur*, Dennis admits that even the Verses in these two Books are of a different Character from those of the rest of the Poem. For there are more good Verses in these two than in any four of the rest; and there is more of the Pathetick in them, than there is in all the rest of the Poem. For in some Places of them, there appears to be something terrible, whereas that Passion is but very faintly mov'd, throughout the rest of the Poem.[47]

Repeatedly Dennis says not that *Prince Arthur* is worthless but that it is absurd to claim it to be the equal of the *Aeneid*. It is not a sufficient critical argument, Dennis insists, for Blackmore's panegyrists to declare that "*Prince Arthur* pleases me, and pleases ten thousand more, and therefore it is delightful." The vogue enjoyed by Quarles, a writer inferior to Blackmore, Dennis maintains is ample proof that popularity alone cannot be the grounds for assessing literary merit. Yet, Dennis fairly admits, good critics have commended the poem and "there are several things in it which may stand before the strictest Judges."[48]

If the strait jacket of Le Bossu's theory keeps Dennis from proving himself "a perfect Critick" in his *Remarks* as his friend Charles Gildon claimed,[49] Dennis's criticisms of digressions, unaffecting characterizations, tedious descriptions, bloated similes, didacticism, and frequently turgid verse remain pertinent today. However, Dennis's motive in publishing the *Remarks* seems more likely to have been a desire to please his protégé John Dryden by leading the wits' attack against the Cheapside physician rather than a simple concern for the integrity of English taste. The occasionally respectful tone which alternates in the *Remarks* with passages of pure vitriol and which has led some subsequent critics to comment on Dennis's aesthetic disinterestedness in treating Blackmore's epic was actually essential to disguise the partisan nature of the work.

However, despite some bickering in the years that followed, Dennis and Blackmore were destined to become friends when Dennis disassociated himself from the coffeehouse wits after Dryden's death. Their views on religion, politics, and poetry were too close for the two men to remain perpetual antagonists. By 1704 they must have been on good terms, for Sir Richard is listed as a subscriber to Dennis's *Grounds of Criticism*, many of the ideas of which appear in embryo in his *Remarks on Prince Arthur*. As the preface to *King Arthur* in 1697 proves, Blackmore, finding several of Dennis's criticisms sound, attempted to revise his practice accordingly. By 1723 he was prepared to rate Dennis as a greater critic than Boileau.[50] Dennis, for his part, apparently encouraged Blackmore in the productive directions which led him to become, in Dennis's opinion, a greater poet than Lucretius.[51] As Dennis's letters show, the two men continued an amicable, mutually respectful discussion on the nature of epic poetry at least until Sir Richard's retirement to the country.[52] Ironically, by the time the two men became friends, Dennis's *Remarks* had done much to permanently undermine Blackmore's reputation as an heroic poet. In 1724 Aaron Hill wrote in *The Plain Dealer* that despite "some Genius, and a sufficient Stock of Learning" which Dennis perceived in *Prince Arthur*, Blackmore would not mend his errors according to the prescriptions given in the *Remarks* and that consequently his epics are now "equally secure, as well from Criticism as Imitation."[53] In this case, "as the poet sinks, the man rises"; and Johnson was correct to praise Blackmore for his generous attitude toward John Dennis.[54]

Although one edition exhausted the demand for Dennis's *Remarks*, it had its intended effect on the reading public. Since almost twenty years elapsed before a fourth edition of *Prince Arthur* was issued, the wits at Will's Coffeehouse must have exulted over the damage done to the good doctor's reputation. The war of wits, however, was only beginning. In the same year William Pittis justified an attack on Dryden's darling Congreve by analogy to the criticisms of Blackmore. He does not see why "the friends of *Prince Arthur*" should not take the same liberty "with a Gentlemen of *Will's*, as those Gentlemen took with *Dr. Blackmore*."[55] Nor did Dryden's coterie intimidate all of those who shared Blackmore's opposition to lewd and profane poetry. In the second edition of "A Reflection on our Modern Poesy" (1697), John Phillips inveighed against poets who pandered to a depraved public taste:

> . . . sure Great *Homer* got not thus a Name:
> Nor Greater *Maro* his Eternal Fame;
> *Maro* whose lofty Soul now animates
> Our *Blackmore's* Breast with true Poetic Heats![56]

Before Dennis's devasting *Remarks* was published, Colley Cibber noted in *Love's Last Shift* that the criticism of

Blackmore's epic sometimes had an effect different from that which the critics intended. Witty Narcissa tells Young Worthy that what she has heard of him previous to their meeting "had much the same effects as the coffee critics ridiculing Prince Arthur, for I found a pleasing disappointment in my reading you, and till I see your beauty's equalled I shan't dislike you for a few faults."[57] The same year, in vindication of the judgment of women, Judith Drake quarreled with Narcissa's taste: "I reverence the *Fairy Queen*, am rais'd, and elevated with *Paradise Lost; Prince Arthur* composes and reduces me to a State of Yawning indifference."[58] Not everyone, however, was so affected. In his frequently reprinted *Art of English Poetry*, Edward Bysshe cites *Prince Arthur* time after time for its "Most Natural, Agreeable, and Noble Thoughts."[59] William Coward praised the poem in *Licentia Poetica Discuss'd, or the True Test of Poetry* for showing "the true elegancies of the English tongue."[60] The copy of *Prince Arthur* in the Harvard library contains an indignant marginal comment in a contemporary hand: "Let them say what they please, damn them, this is a great epick poem."[61] Finally, Dr. Carlyle notes in his *Autobiography* that in a lonely inn in rural Scotland, in 1744, he found no books but the Bible and Blackmore's *Prince Arthur*.[62]

VI King Arthur

Prince Arthur established Blackmore as an important defender of the king just at a time when such support was especially useful. With Mary's death public opposition to William grew, and Jacobite intrigues stirred out of their temporary lethargy. In January of 1696, Sir George Barclay, a Scots Catholic who had served as an officer in the army of James, landed secretly in England to organize William's assassination. The plot to ambush the king in a narrow lane as he returned from hunting failed only because one conspirator, struck by conscience or hopeful of reward, confessed all. The invasion of James's fleet which was to follow the assassination was also aborted when, warned of the plan, William ordered Admiral Russell to stage a show of force off Calais. When William informed Parliament of the attempted assassination, it rallied to his defense. Pledges of allegiance were circulated for signature. Whether Blackmore organized it or not, he signed the Royal College of Physicians' pledge to revenge any injury done the king.[63] Despite the spasm of indignant patriotism which followed public disclosure of Barclay's attempt, some persons, perhaps remembering the bogus Popish Plot, were suspicious of the story. Accordingly the court thought it advisable to have an official report published containing the dates, names, and places needed to substantiate the details of the plot. Blackmore, because of his Whig connections and because of the success of *Prince Arthur*, may have already been known to the king; or he may have been recommended to write the report by William's historiographer royal, Thomas Rymer. In whatever manner, Blackmore was selected to write the history of the conspiracy, was given access to Lord Keeper Somers and other government officials, and was provided all documents and depositions relating to the case.

After William's return to the war in Flanders in May, public opinion shifted. Sir John Fenwick, a general under James, was implicated in the plot; but since he had suborned one of the two witnesses against him the Parliament was forced to bring in a Bill of Attainder to execute him, an act sufficiently tyrannical to infuriate many Englishmen. In October William returned to England to oversee the final stages of Fenwick's long trial, which ended with his beheading on 28 January. Sometime in February one poet voiced the sadness that many felt over the whole unsavory affair in a eulogy, "On Sir John Fenwick":

> Here lie the relics of a martyred knight,
> Whose loyalty, unspotted as the light,
> Sealed with his blood his injured
> Sovereign's right.[64]

With such sentiments abroad, William was undoubtedly pleased to hear that a new poem by the popular Dr. Blackmore was ready for the press, a poem which presented William's arguments in the most propitious light. To bestow the mark of royal favor on the endeavor, William summoned Blackmore to Kensington Palace, made him a valuable gift of a gold medal and chain, appointed him His Majesty's Physician in Ordinary, and knighted him for services to the crown. On exactly the same day that Blackmore became Sir Richard, March 18, the *London Gazette* advertised the publication of *King Arthur. An Heroick Poem. In Twelve Books.*

The new epic continued the transparent allegory of the Prince of Orange, now King of England. In writing the sequel Blackmore used his recently acquired knowledge of the Barclay plot as well as his memories of the Huguenot persecution he had witnessed in his travels on the Continent. As the epic opens, Gallic lords (Huguenots) implore Arthur to intervene against the outrages they endure under the government of vicious King Clotar (Louis XIV). Other emissaries from Neustria (Normandy) complain that their court is overrun with "wits":

> By artful Eloquence they strive to show
> Those Pleasures Lawful, which they wish were so.
> Against their Country they their Wit engage,
> Refine our Language, but corrupt the Age. (p. 15)

After a long praise of English love of liberty, Arthur agrees to fight Clotar. The eager Britons enthusiastically prepare for war:

> Some in the Hills with loud repeated Strokes
> Dismember nodding Pines and groaning Oakes.
> The lifted Ax thro' all the Mountain sounds
> To heal the Navy's with the Forest's Wounds. (p.20)

Seeing Arthur advance and fearing the destruction of his Roman Catholic empire, Lucifer sends Discord to Britain to subvert Arthur's own subjects. Disguised as a priest, Discord inflames Botran (Barclay) and others against William's weak "moderation" in religious matters. They, in turn, urge all possible objections against Arthur's "foreign" wars, attempting to spread dissension. Amid the predictable battle scenes, one with "AEsculapian Skill inspir'd," Gibbonius (William Gibbons, a medical colleague of Blackmore's) heals the injured. Summoned by the faithful British lords, Arthur returns home leaving the victorious army in the charge of Solmar (Count Solms). By his tolerance and justice, Arthur discourages resistance; the rebels capitulate and are pardoned.

Book VI is the most intriguing in the poem. This eclectic and ingenious Book clearly draws on Homer, Virgil, the Armida and Rinaldo episode in *Gerusalemme Liberata,* Spenser, Milton, and Job, which Blackmore came to regard as the first and greatest epic. Forsaking classical models, Blackmore's description of

Lucifer's subversion of mankind is unmistakably Miltonic despite its verse form:

> And spite of Heav'n the mighty Deed was done,
> And from th' Allmighty this fair World I won. (p.151)

When Lucifer pleads with God to allow him to tempt Arthur both the situation and the diction are directly from Job:

> Hast thou observ'd my Servant *Arthur's* Ways
> The just and perfect Man. . . . (p.153)

But most significantly, Lucifer's early reference to Arthur as "this proud Wight" suggest the strongly Spenserian cast of the majority of Book VI. After a furious storm and other adventures designed to test Arthur's courage, Lucifer bears him to "a shady wood":

> So black the Shade, so thick the stagnent Air,
> That no reviving Sunbeams enter'd there.
> Nothing but here and there a straggling Ray
> Which lost itself in wandering from the Day:
> Which serv'd not to Refresh, but to affright,
> Not to Dispel, but to Disclose the Night. (p. 165)

In the ruin of an ancient castle surrounded by a moat of blood, Arthur faces the monster Anelpis unafraid. For his final test Lucifer transports Arthur to a gardenlike land modeled on Spenser's Bower of Bliss. There lives the sensuous and seductive Fascinia:

> Her Amber Locks loose on her Shoulders lay,
> Whither lascivious *Zephyrs* came to play.

Like Homer's Circe, Fascinia delights in changing men into beasts or into women, a metamorphosis which Blackmore describes in the manner of Ovid. The book concludes abruptly as Arthur, unable to resist Fascinia's sexuality, is miraculously rescued by the angel Gabriel and conveyed to his anxious troops.

Dispirited by Arthur's absence, the Britons wage a defensive war. After King Clotar kills Solmar they debate whether to return to England in phrases that frequently suggest Dryden's influence. Echoing the description of Shaftesbury in *Absalom and Achitophel,* Coril advises caution:

> Meer Courage is to Madness near ally'd,
> A brutal Rage, which Prudence do's not guide. (p. 201)

As the British council adjourns unresolved, the scene shifts to Clotar's camp where Clovis, now a prisoner, views his impending death as a glorious martyrdom:

> Martyrs *Elijah*-like, to Heav'n aspire
> On ruddy Steeds, and rapid Cars of Fire. (p. 207)

In a long passage full of almost metaphysical wit, as Blackmore's verses frequently are, Clovis reflects on the reluctance of the flesh to die despite the dictates of faith and reason:

> If tender Infants who imprison'd stay
> Within the Womb, prepar'd to break away,
> Were conscious of themselves, and of their State,
> And had but Reason to sustain Debate,
> The painful Passage they would dread, and show
> Reluctance to a World they do not know.
> They in their Prisons still would chuse to ly
> As backward to be born, as we to dy. (p. 209)

Clovis's wife, Merula, visits him in prison with the confession that under torture she renounced Christ and became pagan. Clovis chooses rather to "swim to Heav'n thro' a red tyde of Blood" than convert to the worship of ikons. In a Lockean passage, philosophic Clovis responds to Merula's argument that the faithful can form no notion of God save through the senses:

> Sense do's, 'tis true, it's object first enjoy,
> And that first object do's our Thoughts employ.
> All knowledge previous to the Acts of Sense
> And in-born Notions, are a vain Pretense.
> But then, 'tis true, that when our Minds embrace
> Those Images which thro' our Senses pass,
> They stop not there, but quickly higher go,
> And on themselves reflecting know they know.
> They their own Actions oft review, and thence
> Conceptions form above the Sphear of Sense. . . . (p. 220)

Moved by her husband's dialectic Merula calls for tears sufficient to drown her grief (pp. 230–31) and asks Clovis how the almighty's vengeful hand may be averted. Wild with joy, Clovis welcomes her "pure contrition" as Uriel descends to convey them unharmed to the British camp.

The final third of the epic narrates Arthur's return and conquest. In Book IX Caledon, a "man of God," prophesies Arthur's heroic role in God's awesome providence:

> The Constellations shine at his Command,
> He form'd their radiant Orbs, and with his Hand
> He weigh'd, and put them off with such a Force
> As might preserve an Everlasting Course. (p. 243)[65]

Enraged at the defeat Clotar's forces suffer in the battle of Book X, Lucifer organizes an unsuccessful assassination attempt which resembles closely that against William the previous year. The battle in the last book concludes with Clotar's decapitation and the beginning of an age of peace.

The final siege of Lutetia (Paris) allegorically represents William's victory over Namur. Although the topicality of the poem is obvious throughout, its timeliness is clearly evinced by the signing of the peace at the conclusion, which foreshadows the agreement William was negotiating at his country home at Ryswick in the first months of *King Arthur's* publication. The epic's political interpretation tells only a portion of the story, however. In *King Arthur* Blackmore ambitiously attempts an abstract and brief chronicle of the times and thoughts of his own age. The meticulous description of fortified warfare no less than the summations of Lockean psychology and Newtonian cosmology illustrates Blackmore's determination to distill the essence of the age into his epic.

The heterogeneity implicit in the encyclopedic nature of heroic poetry is further complicated in *King Arthur* by Blackmore's apparent reaction to three of Dennis's criticisms. To obviate the objection that close parallels to Virgil destroyed surprise in his first poem, Blackmore resolved not to imitate. Thus, he no longer had the discipline of a beaten path to rely on for overall structure. With the sole exceptions of "some Images" from Homer and "a few Allusions" to Milton, whom he looks upon "as a very Extraordinary Genius," Blackmore eschews any indebtedness.[66] Reacting to Dennis's emphasis on passion as the distinguishing characteristic of genius, Blackmore seems, in his preface, to have shifted from his admiration of Virgil's regularity to a greater appreciation of Homer's "wild Luxuriance." This is reflected in *King Arthur* partially by an increased subtlety in portraying emotions. Arthur's sexual temptation and the scene between Clovis and Merula are excellent examples of this new trend. Finally, Blackmore met Dennis's objection that *Prince Arthur* lacked variety by making *King Arthur* more episodic. The result of all three changes is increased interest at the expense of coherent organization. Blackmore probably assumed and hoped that the dual historical reference, to Geoffrey's Arthur and to William III, would insure that unity which the poem, in fact, lacks.

In the preface Blackmore admits that "several considerable Defects" did mar his earlier epic but argues, backed by Longinus, that writers of the first rank have such "extraordinary and admirable Thoughts" as are sufficient to atone for any number of faults. This greater emphasis on genius rather than judgment explains Blackmore's praise of Homer and, more important, of Milton, that daring genius who produced what Dennis regarded as a brilliant but "irregular" poem.[67] Perhaps nothing indicates the limited familiarity Milton enjoyed at this time so clearly as the fact that no reviewer of *Prince Arthur* suggested its indebtedness to Milton despite resemblances which would strike a modern reader as unmistakable. Blackmore is one of the earliest writers to have adequately recognized the grandeur of *Paradise Lost.*[68] An orthodox Anglican, Blackmore invariably rejected Milton's theology and ethics where they deviated from the established church and is only subservient in matters of style, where his adaptations "often have much originality and force."[69] Interestingly, Blackmore's adaptations are often in the direction of classical precedent. His demons and angels resemble the deities of the *Iliad* and *Aeneid* almost more than they resemble Milton's good and evil angels. Even Blackmore's linguistic borrowings reveal the same bias. The description of Satan, "Squat like a Toad, close at the ear of *Eve*" (*Paradise Lost*, IV, 800), expands to an Homeric simile in *Prince Arthur*:

> So when a Toad, squat on a Border spies,

The Gardner passing by, his bloodshot Eyes
With Spite, and Rage inflam'd, dart Fire around
The verdant Walks, and on the flowry Ground,
The bloated Vermin loathsome Poison spits,
And swoln and bursting with his Malice sits.
So the faln Angel sate. . . . (p. 177)

Although to claim that Blackmore "contributed largely" to the spread of Milton's fame and influence[70] may be excessive, the popularity of *Prince Arthur*, the preface to *King Arthur*, and Blackmore's subsequent associations with Dennis and Addison, both champions of *Paradise Lost*, suggest that his emulation of the greater poet played some part in enhancing Milton's reputation during the age.

VII *John Dryden*

The most intriguing aspect of Blackmore's early career, his enmity with Dryden, has, paradoxically, never been adequately researched.[71] As a result most critics dismiss Blackmore as a priggish plagiarist, at once defaming Dryden's accomplishments and stealing his ideas. The truth is much more complex. To understand it the reader must refer back to Dryden's "Discourse Concerning the Original and Progress of Satire" which prefaced his *Juvenal* in the fall of 1692, over two years before the appearance of *Prince Arthur*. In the "Discourse" Dryden digressed to pay that glowing tribute to heroic poetry which may have inflamed Blackmore to his first epic ambitions. Dryden's motive, however, was not solely aesthetic. He was also appealing for patronage. The "Discourse" was addressed to Charles Sackville, Earl of Dorset, who had been appointed Lord Chamberlain only three years earlier. A supporter of William of Orange and a patron of worthy authors of both political persuasions, Dorset was himself known as the author of songs and satiric pieces, including the sarcastic "To Mr. Edward Howard on his Incomparable, Incomprehensible Poem, Called *The British Princes*," which had circulated extensively in manuscript.

Like Dorset, Dryden has observed the "Failings of many great Wits amongst the Moderns, who have attempted to write an Epique Poem," Spenser and Milton among them. In answering the objection that Christian machinery is unsuitable to epic,

Dryden proposes that modern poets use guardian angels and, following the example of Satan in Job, evil angels as well. This would give modern heroic poets the strength heretofore lacking in their emulations of Homer and Virgil. Dryden continues:

> Thus, my Lord, I have as briefly as I cou'd, given your Lordship, and by you the World a rude draught of what I have been long labouring in my Imagination, and what I had intended to have put in practice, . . . and to have left the Stage, to which my Genius never much inclin'd me, for a Work which wou'd have taken up my Life in the performance of it. This too, I had intended chiefly for the Honour of my Native Country, to which a Poet is particularly oblig'd: of two Subjects, both relating to it, I was doubtful, whether I shou'd chuse that of King *Arthur*, conquering the *Saxons*; which being farther distant in Time, gives the greater Scope to my Invention: or that of *Edward* the Black Prince. . . .[72]

Had the leisure been afforded him to write an epic, Dryden pointedly tells Dorset, he would "have taken occasion to represent my living Friends and Patrons of the Noblest Families" in his characters. "But being encourag'd only with fair Words, by King *Charles* II, my little Sallary ill paid, and no prospect of a future Subsistance, I was then Discourag'd in the beginning of my Attempt; and now Age has overtaken me; and Want, a more insufferable Evil, through the Change of the Times, has wholly disenabl'd me."[73]

To accuse Blackmore of plagiarism[74] is to overestimate Dryden's originality and to misunderstand at least part of Blackmore's motive in writing *Prince Arthur*. Readers of Milton would have found nothing new in Dryden's recommendation of Christian machinery; and Dorset's own satire on *The British Princes* was a reaction to Howard's poor use of English kingship in an heroic poem. Dryden's deliberately pathetic plea amounts to a declaration that had the world been kinder to him he would have written a great epic poem. Moreover, the suggestion to Dorset that timely patronage might yet enable him to write that poem for England's honor and the glorious memory of certain "Friends and Patrons of the Noblest Families" appeals respectively to Sackville as Lord Chamberlain and as the sixth Earl of Dorset. Admittedly, Dryden had long desired to write an epic and finances doubtless played some part in his failure to do so. Certainly, as he realized, his final years were being spent in the translation of other men's works rather than the creation of his own because, simply stated, he needed the money.

Those not predisposed in Dryden's favor or inclined to share his politics or religion, however, could see this cosmic injustice as divine providence and his present distresses as the punishment for past crimes. Had not Dryden added his own "fat pollutions" to the stage and had he not spent his poetic talents prodigally in partisan political service? And was Dryden not the center of a group of wits at Will's Coffeehouse who had forgotten that the chief aim of poetry is the improvement and not merely the amusement of mankind? What irritated Blackmore most, as he indicates in the preface to *Prince Arthur*, was Dryden's pious insistence in the "Discourse" that although his hands were dirty his heart was pure, that the viciousness of the age rather than his own inclinations had dictated the sort of poetry he must write. To Blackmore it seemed the rankest sophistry to contend that the most renowned poet of the age had no influence upon public taste. He is clearly sneering at Dryden in his denunciation of the logic which argues that "Poets must Starve if they will not in this way humour the *Audience*." Moreover, the best of such poets are the most pernicious, for there is no greater "prostituting" of abilities than employing "excellent Faculties and abundance of Wit, to humour and please Men in their Vices and Follies." As his repeated tributes after Dryden's death attest, Blackmore sincerely admired Dryden's talent, [75] but he abhorred the use he had frequently made of it.

Still, despite Blackmore's audacity in writing in two years the very heroic poem which Dryden envisioned as his lifetime's labor, the attack on Dryden in the preface and the implicit comparison between Dryden's empty ambition and his own epic accomplishment might have escaped general attention. After all, Blackmore had not mentioned any names in his condemnation of the stage and the state of modern poetry. Thus, to insure that no one missed the comparison he intended, Blackmore inserted the satiric portrait of Laurus in Book VI. After praise of the "British Maecenas" Sakil (Sackville, Earl of Dorset), Blackmore sketches a sychophantic Dryden:

> *Laurus* amidst the meagre Crowd appear'd,
> An old, revolted, unbelieving Bard,
> Who throng'd, and shov'd, and prest, and would be heard.
> Distinguish'd by his louder craving Tone,

So well to all the Muses Patrons known,
He did the Voice of modest Poets drown.
Sakil's high Roof, the Muses Palace rung
With endless Cries, and endless Songs he sung.
To Bless good *Sakil Laurus* would be first,
But *Sakil's* Prince, and *Sakil's* God he curst. (p. 167)

The appellation "Laurus" (Bayes) alerted even the most unsophisticated readers to the identification with Dryden. The scene invited remembrance of the fulsome dedication to Sackville in the *Juvenal* preface and made Blackmore's contention in his own preface that *Prince Arthur* was written in the brief intervals of a busy medical practice ring with heightened irony. Far from covertly plagiarizing, Blackmore is deliberately calling attention to and ridiculing the tone of Dryden's "Discourse".

Even had his translation of Virgil not been in progress, this would have sufficiently antagonized the aging Dryden. The sheer audacity of this unknown Cheapside physician in publishing as his first poetic effort an admittedly hastily written heroic poem could only be topped by flinging his gauntlet directly in the teeth of the reigning literary lion. Yet added to this audacious insult was Dryden's genuine feeling of recrimination over a career not entirely well spent. Blackmore must have seemed an unwelcome nemesis. *Prince Arthur* had to be shown to be rubbish and Blackmore exposed as a buffoon. Otherwise, Dryden was faced with the ignominious prospect of an antagonistic upstart amateur cropping his laurels. Considering it beneath his dignity to reply directly but chagrined by the immediate popularity of Blackmore's poem, Dryden may have encouraged Dennis to publish his *Remarks.*[76] No choice could be more logical, for the preface to Dennis's *Miscellanies in Prose and Verse* (1693), which defers repeatedly to Dryden, was likewise dedicated to Charles Sackville, Earl of Dorset.

In the preface to *King Arthur* Blackmore leaves no doubts as to who he thinks is behind many of the attacks on his earlier poem. How could he have hoped for applause from Dryden's protégés, he asks, "having never kiss'd their Governour's hands, nor made the least Court to the Committee that sits in *Covent Garden,*" the location of Will's. Arguing from the success of *Prince Arthur* that lewdness and impiety are not necessary for popularity, Blackmore again insults Dryden:

This is a meer Pretence of ill Poets, whose Imaginations are fill'd only with base and contemptible *Ideas*; Men of a poor and narrow *Genius*, scarce above the level of Writers of Farce, who would not have Images enough left in their Minds to furnish out a Poem, if the prophane and obscene Ones were struck out.

And finally he reemphasizes the "less than two years time" in which *Prince Arthur* was written. Is perfection to be expected, Blackmore asks, from a poem "written in *Coffee-houses*, and in passing up and down the Streets; because I had little leisure elsewhere to apply to it?" Conversely, he intimates, how barren must a poet be not to finish one translation in the same period of time sufficient for another man, prosperously pursuing another career, to write two original epics?

When *King Arthur* was published in March, Dryden's *Aeneis* was in the press. Perhaps stung by the remembrance of his own *King Arthur*, an opera intended to strengthen the power of Charles II but which had to be altered until it was unrecognizable after William assumed the throne, Dryden lashed out at Blackmore in the dedication, finally published in June: "The file of heroic poets," Dryden says, "is very short; all are not such who have assumed that lofty title in ancient or modern ages, or have been so esteemed by their partial and ignorant admirers."[77] Dryden harangues against Blackmore's supporters as "a company of warm young men, who are not yet arrived so far as to discern the difference between fustian, or ostentatious sentences, and the true sublime."[78] Blackmore himself "affects greatness" in all he writes; but it is "a bladdered greatness, like that of the vain man whom Seneca describes; an ill habit of body, full of humours, and swelled with dropsy. . . . How many of those flatulent writers have I known, who have sunk in their reputation, after seven or eight editions of their works!"[79] Perhaps, as Dryden insisted in the Postscript to the *Aeneis*, Blackmore did not have it in his power to defame him;[80] but his attempts provoked Dryden nonetheless.

Less than a month before Dryden's *Aeneis* was ready for sale, in late May 1697, Dennis ridiculed Blackmore's boasting admission that he had written his heroic poems at Garraway's Coffeehouse near the Royal Exchange or while traveling the streets in pursuit of his livelihood. "This Play," the character Joe Haines in *A Plot, and No Plot* announces in the prologue,

in a little space
Of time was writ, and a damn'd scurvy place.
The time Six weeks, the place I have forgot:
Dammee, this Brandy makes a man a sot.
Were but the Author here, perhaps he'd tell you,
'Twas in some Coffee-house in *Exchange-alley.*
A place of late to Epick Muse well known,
Perhaps that 'twas compos'd in's Coach he'd own,
But that alas poor Devil he has none.[81]

The "Petty Merchants of small Conceits," as Dennis was later to dub his own confederates, intensified their attacks on Sir Richard, finally organizing the *Commendatory Verses;* but after his covert attack on Blackmore in the *Aeneis* in June, Dryden drops out of the picture for a time, although he almost certainly continued active behind the scenes.

When in April of the following year Collier's attack on the stage appeared, both Dryden and Dennis were quick to respond to this new, more vehement disciple of Blackmore's gospel. In less than two months Dennis's *The Usefulness of the Stage* led a procession of indignant replies by Vanbrugh, Congreve, Oldmixon, Tom Brown, Peter Motteux, and others who composed the circle at Will's. Almost simultaneously with Dennis's vindication, Dryden contributed an epistle to the first printing of Motteux' *Beauty in Distress* in which he criticizes Collier's excessive zeal in what he admits could be a worthy cause:

Were they content to prune the lavish Vine
Of straggling Branches, and improve the Wine,
Who but a mad Man wou'd his Faults defend?
All wou'd submit; for all but Fools will mend. . . .
What I have loosly, or profanely writ,
Let them to Fires (their due desert) commit.[82]

Although he would have been quick to disassociate himself from the extreme position advocated by Collier, a nonjuring clergyman who had been outlawed in 1696 for absolving on the scaffold two of the plotters to assassinate William, Blackmore may have influenced the king to issue the writ of *nolle prosequi* which protected Collier after publication. In any event, he watched the controversy closely, later using one of the metaphors in Dryden's epistle to attack its author again.

Unsold folio volumes of *King Arthur* groaned heavily on his bookseller's shelves as Blackmore saw the demand for his epic dwindle. No second edition was necessary. Perhaps, as Tom Brown later suggested, had Blackmore stopped after one epic "he had gone off with some applause" if not with a knighthood. More charitable to Sir Richard, William Coward nonetheless reached the same conclusion:

> Tho' some *Refiners* envious Verdicts spend,
> On BL——RE'S *Prince*, the *Poem* I commend.
> Had he stop'd *there*, vain were the *Critics* Scorn,
> None more politely cou'd that *Theme* adorn;
> I know some *scatter'd Faults* lie here and there,
> *Faults* found in every Poem, every where.
> But in the main, the Verses and Design,
> With *more than common English* Beauty shine.
> Only the *King*, with second Effort pen'd,
> *Clog'd* the *brisk Wings*, with which he strove t'ascend.[83]

Blackmore should have found solace in the recognition that *King Arthur* was, as he claimed, written in the infrequent intervals of other business. Besides attending to his flourishing medical practice, Blackmore had worked diligently on his history of the conspiracy against William. In the same demanding and august role of historiographer, he was busied not long after the appearance of *King Arthur* in producing a defense of the Whig Junto's handling of Parliament.[84] Also, if the public reacted indifferently to *King Arthur*, *Prince Arthur* still flourished. His prefaces had earned him the admiration of fledgling poets like John Hughes, who dedicated his *Triumph of Peace* to Blackmore as "One who has vindicated the Reputation of the Muses from the Dishonour reflected on 'em by the loose Lines and Writings of some witty Men."[85]

Sager heads also dissented from the wits' denunciation. William Molyneux of Trinity College, Dublin, wrote his friend John Locke shortly after the publication of *King Arthur* that his esteem for Blackmore was "not at all lessened" by his second epic. After reading *Prince Arthur* Molyneux communicated to Blackmore through Sir Richard's publisher "how excellently I thought he might perform a philosophic poem." In the preface to *King Arthur* Blackmore waved aside suggestions that he should write on philosophic subjects with the disclaimer that "I am so far faln out with all Hypotheses in *Philosophy*, and all Doctrines of Physic which are built upon them that in such matters I am almost reduc'd to a *Sceptical Despair*. The *Almighty's Creation* is like his *Providence*, unsearchable." Evidently Molyneux's suggestion was muddled in transmission, for he intended to urge Blackmore to write "a natural history of the great and admirable phenomena of the universe" such as he found in Mopas's song in *Prince Arthur* or in the description of the order of the heavenly bodies in *King Arthur*. [86] When Locke replies that he knows Sir Richard, equally admires his poetry and his empirical bias, and will tell Blackmore of his friend's ideas for a "sublime" nature poem, Molyneux congratulates Locke on his acquaintance with that "extraordinary person" and requests a complete key to the names used in *King Arthur*. "All our English poets (except Milton)," he enthusiastically proclaims, "have been mere ballad-makers, in comparison to him."[87]

CHAPTER 3

War with the Wits

'Twas in his carriage the sublime
Sir Richard Blackmore used to rhyme,
 and (if the wits don't do him wrong)
'Twixt death and epics passed his time
 Scribbling and killing all day long.

Thomas Moore (1850)

BLACKMORE'S pen was busied by the upcoming Parliamentary elections of 1698, which had been guaranteed by the triennial bill that William, under pressure because of difficulties in his foreign campaigns, had reluctantly signed. Tories seeking election objected most vehemently to the financial repercussions of the Continental war and attempted to frighten voters by resurrecting the goblin of a standing army. The Whig Junto, in response to these successful tactics, engaged Blackmore to write a defense of William's third Parliament, emphasizing accomplishments achieved in the face of a difficult war abroad, Tory defeatism at home, and a currency crying for reform.[1] The new Parliament ushered in "a very darke, rainy gloomy Autumn"[2] for the Junto whose future, despite the prop of such pens as Blackmore's and Daniel Defoe's, was clearly uncertain.

I The Dispensary

His preoccupation with affairs of state made it easier for Blackmore to ignore the sniping of literary small fry like Tom Brown, who urged the busy physician,

As ye hope to succeed, let alone the Nine *Sisters,*
And instead of the *Muse,* invoke *Purges* and *Glysters.*
Then your Bus'ness is done, and your needs must prevail,
For He'll please the *Head* best, who best Tickles the *Tail.*[3]

However, the furor which surrounded the publication of the mock-heroic *Dispensary* in May 1699 inevitably drew Blackmore away from the court and into the fray.

The author of *The Dispensary,* Samuel Garth, had distinguished himself rapidly after his admission to the Royal College in 1692 as a leader of the "Society-Physicians," a group within the college which advocated free treatment of the deserving poor. To what extent the charitable dispensary which this faction wished to establish represents the embryonic stirrings of true philanthropic zeal was much debated at the time. The apothecaries reproached these "Dispensarians" as hypocrites determined to destroy the apothecaries' business and thus extinguish competition. Before Parliament their attorney argued that physicians "would not come to the poor without Fees, nor to the Rich, if at Dinner or in Bed, whilst [the apothecaries] came at all times, and gave their advice and physick to the poor for Nothing."[4] In fact, he argued, nineteen-twentieths of all the medical practice in London was carried on by apothecaries, including virtually all treatment received by the poor. Physicians, as a rule, the apothecaries argued, were negligent, careless, and uncharitable.[5] The apothecaries, consequently, interpreted the plans for a dispensary as an attack motivated by the apothecaries' request to Parliament that they be allowed to practice medicine as well as to prescribe. Those members of the college who tried to obstruct the dispensary, Blackmore foremost among them, were labeled "Apothecaries Physicians" and were contemptuously charged by the "Society-Physicians" with attempting to curry favor with the apothecaries.

Interesting as the controversy is, and though Blackmore's role in the dispensary quarrel was prominent, the specific details are not vital to the war of wits which ensued.[6] For Canto 4 of *The Dispensary,* which reads like a catalogue of those who opposed establishing the dispensary, denigrates Sir Richard in his literary rather than his medical capacity—one fact which helps explain the later congenial professional relationship between Garth and Blackmore. Canto 4 is set in the City, where, in unmistakable reference to Blackmore's recent efforts in support of the government,

> The Politicians of *Parnassus* prate,

And Poets canvass the Affairs of State;
The Cits ne'er talk of Trade and Stock, but tell
How *Virgil* writ, how bravely *Turnus* fell. (*4*, 21-24)

The action, mock-heroic deliberately reminiscent of similar scenes in *Prince Arthur* and *King Arthur,* is a council of antidispensarians met to summon the goddess Disease to their aid. William Gibbons, whom Blackmore had characterized as "one with AEsculapian Skill inspir'd" in *King Arthur,* is the "AEsculapius" who opens the declamations, assuring his fellow physicians that his hand

when Glory calls,
Can Brandish Arms as well as Urinals. (*4*, 49–50)

Blackmore undertakes to raise Disease by citing some of his more horrific verses. This jumble of Blackmore's worst from both epics arouses the goddess who warns him to

dare not, for the future, once rehearse
Th' offensive Discord of such hideous Verse.
But in your Lines let Energy be found,
And learn to rise in Sense, and sink in Sound.
Harsh words, tho' pertinent, uncouth appear,
None please the Fancy, who offend the Ear. (*4*, 204–209)

Garth apparently considers Blackmore's works unpolished rather than devoid of inspiration, for the goddess advises him to moderate his epic ambitions and to study poets who will teach him to

Slide without falling, without straining soar.
Oft tho' your Stroaks surprize, you shou'd not choose,
A Theme so mighty for a Virgin Muse. (*4*, 231-33)

Despite Johnson's judgment that *The Dispensary* was mostly mediocrity,[7] it enjoyed great and immediate popularity, certainly stimulated, as Goldsmith perceived, by partisan interest in the controversies involved. For besides the matter of the dispensary, Garth also defended young Charles Boyle against Richard Bentley in the Ancients-Moderns controversy. Bentley's devastating *Dissertation upon the Epistles of Phalaris* had been published barely two months before *The Dispensary* appeared. And, of course, the juxtaposition of "Men of Wit" and "Men of Sense," of Covent-Garden elite and the city mob, of principled Society-Physicians and unprincipled Apothecaries Physicians pandering to their unenlightened self-interest, carries all the implications of an emerging class struggle—Garth's privileged aristocracy contrasted to Blackmore's bourgeoisie.

Whatever the source of its popularity, *The Dispensary* was in a third edition within five weeks; and by late June an anonymous author had been emboldened to follow Garth in putting specific lines from Blackmore's epics to burlesque use in *A Funeral Oration upon Favorite, My Lady ——'s Lap Dog. Together with an Heroic Elegy, out of the Author of Prince Arthur*. Meanwhile, the *"Forty thousand Arm'd Lampoons"* Defoe mentions in *The Pacificator* circulated in manuscript. The mockery which the wits lavished on Blackmore after the appearance of *King Arthur* intensified in the wake of Garth's popularity. Even in poetry, as the author of *The Present State of Physick* insisted, the summer battle inclined to the Society-Physicians.[8]

II A Satyr against Wit

As if to prove that wars waged in folio admit of turnabouts no less sudden than those fought on bloodier fields, the publication of Blackmore's rebuttal to *The Dispensary* in November found the literary world in the possession of the Apothecaries Physicians once again. Good-humored and consistently clever, *A Satyr against Wit* develops Garth's suggestion in Canto 4 of *The Dispensary* that the typical Cheapside lawyer first "grows a Mad-mad, and then turns a Wit" (*4*, 28). Blackmore inveighs against the contagious "Plague of Wit":

> It takes Men in the Head, and in the Fit
> They lose their Senses, and are gone in Wit. (ll. 34–35)

The metaphor of wit as a disease serves the physician in Blackmore admirably, as when

> Some seiz'd like *Gravar*, with Convulsions strain
> Always to say fine Things, but strive in vain
> Urg'd with a dry Tenesmus of the Brain. (ll. 39–41)

Had Will's Coffeehouse been shut up and the infected moved to Bedlam upon the first appearance of this "Bantring Spirit" many would have been saved. Now, however, the "Mob of Wits" stalks the streets, led by their Captain Tom—probably a reference to young Sir Christopher Codrington who had abused Blackmore in commendatory verses published with *The Dispensary.*[9] Codrington, who among other accomplishments during his brief career in London fought a duel over the etymology of a Greek word, supported Boyle in his antagonism to Bentley. In the *Satyr* Blackmore praises Bentley's scholarship at the same time he censures his arrogance. Blackmore glances at Codrington as "Codron" later in the poem:

> By Hearsay he's a Scholar, and they say
> The Man's a sort of Wit too in his way. (ll. 250-51)

Despite the indication on the title page of a 1700 Dublin edition that *A Satyr against Wit* was "Design'd an Answer to a Poem Stil'd the Dispensary," the first quarter of the poem attacks the Wits' opposition to "right Reason" and "common Sense" without allusion to Garth's poem. Lines 109-56, however, praise the Apothecaries Physicians lampooned in *The Dispensary.* Blackmore objects to Garth's ridicule of Francis Bernard in the character of Horoscope since Bernard had died over a year before *The Dispensary* was published. The surviving physicians are advised to ignore the attack:

> But let Invectives still your Names assail,
> Your Business is to Cure, and theirs to Rail.
> Let 'em proceed and make your Names a Sport
> In leud Lampoons, they've Time and Leisure for't.
> Despise their Spite; the Thousands whom you raise
> From threaten'd Death will bless you all their Days,
> And spend the Breath you sav'd, in just and lasting Praise.
> (ll. 150-56)

Although Blackmore's use of "wit" throughout the poem is usually ironic and metaphorical and may be at various times equated with "malice," "impiety," "lewdness," and "stupidity," he is making a more serious point in defending Bentley (despite his bad manners) and in praising the medical practice of his fellow physicians. For, as he argues in "An Essay upon Wit," "a pleasant Man is always caress'd above a wise one, and Ridicule and Satyr, that Entertain the Laughers, often put solid Reason and useful Science out of Countenance."[10] To admire the grace of Boyle's style while ignoring the sound learning supporting Bentley's argument, or to ridicule those who oppose the dispensary in mock-heroic without giving the slightest attention to the propositions they advance in defense of their position, seemed deliberately perverse to Blackmore. Within its proper province "the Exercise of Wit and a pleasant Genius, excels all other Recreations," for wit not only adds "intellectual Enameling" to something that is otherwise unadorned, it also "animates and warms a cold Sentiment." Properly wit is the "Accomplishment of a warm, sprightly, and fertile Imagination, enrich'd with great variety of proper Ideas."[11]

Wit becomes destructive only when it strays into provinces where its exercise is impertinent, as in "History, Philology, Philosophy, or in the greater Lyrick or Epick Poems." The application of Blackmore's argument to the satiric attacks on Bentley's "pedantry" and to Garth's ridicule of personalities rather than ideas is clear. More relevant to the mockery of quoting passages from his epics out of context, Blackmore cites Archbishop John Tillotson's opinion that "the gravest Book that ever was written, may be made ridiculous, by applying the Sayings of it to a foolish purpose, for a Jest may be obtruded upon any thing."[12] Although it is too harsh to maintain that Blackmore's "values are not literary or aesthetic at all, but utilitarian,"[13] it is important to remember that in his hierarchical scheme of values the accomplishments of wit are subordinate to reason and the Christian virtues, just as satire is a lesser kind of literature than epic. Consequently, delightful as the wit may be in his proper province, he is engaged in affairs less august than those "who are either busied in governing the State, defending their Country, improving the Minds, or relieving the Bodies of other Men."[14]

After defending his fellow physicians, Blackmore suggests the establishment of a "Bank of Wit" along the lines of the fiscal reorganization described in his *Short History of the Last Parliament.* If the Muse's Exchequer would refuse to accept "false wit" any longer, then defective monies might be recoined, salvaging the true metal and discarding the "Allay":

'Tis true, that when the course and worthless Dross
Is purg'd away, there will be mighty Loss.
Ev'n *C[ongrev]e, S[outher]n, Manly W[ycher]ly,*
When thus refin'd will grievous Suff'rers be.
Into the melting Pot when *D[ryde]n* comes,
What horrid Stench will rise, what noisome Fumes?
How will he shrink, when all his leud Allay,
And wicked Mixture shall be purg'd away?
When once his boasted Heaps are melted down,
A Chest full scarce will yield one Sterling Crown.
Those who will *D[e]n[ni]s* melt and think to find
A goodly Mass of Bullion left behind,
Do, as th' *Hibernian* Wit, who as 'tis told,
Burnt his gilt Leather to collect the Gold. (ll. 202-15)[15]

As Frank H. Ellis's annotations suggest, Blackmore's coinage metaphor allowed him the freedom of allusion which he loved. In a poem passed about only in manuscript, Dryden had been praised as a "refiner" of the English language which "like mettle in the Mine, / He purg'd the Dross and Stampt it into Coin."[16] In *An Essay on Translated Verse* Roscommon noted the difficult beauty involved in the "weighty Bullion of One Sterling Line"; and Dryden himself feared that no modern could match the sublimities of Shakespeare: "If Shakespeare were stripped of all the bombast in his passions, and dressed in the most vulgar words, we should find the beauties of his thought remaining; if his embroideries were burnt down, there would still be silver at the bottom of the melting-pot."[17] In *A Satyr against Wit* Blackmore cleverly turns Dryden's own metaphor against him while still admitting the beauty and worth of his best work, a courtesy not accorded Dennis.

After advising ambitious poets to imitate the genuine wit of Prior and censuring "Felonious" Garth for smuggling French wit[18] (a reference to Garth's debt to Boileau's *Le Lutrin*), Blackmore alludes by way of compliment to Dorset's satire "To Mr. Edward Howard on his . . . *British Princes,*" insisting that it is preferable to be lampooned rather than praised by men beneath contempt:

For all their Libels Panegyrick's are,
They're still read backward like a Witch's Pray'r.
(ll. 348-49)[19]

Dorset himself provides the pattern for the beneficial use of satire, a striking contrast to the would-be wits at Will's:

> Therefore let Satyr-Writers be supprest,
> Or be reform'd by cautious *D[or]set's* Test.
> 'Tis only *D[or]set's* judgment can command,
> Wit the worse Weapon in a Madman's Hand.
> The Biting Things by that great Master said,
> Flow from rich Sense, but theirs from want of Bread.
> Whatever is by them in Satyr writ
> Is Malice all, but his excess of Wit.
> To lash our Faults and Follies is his Aim,
> Theirs is good Sense and Merit to defame.
> In *D[or]set* Wit (and therefore still 'twill please)
> Is Constitution, but in them Disease. (ll. 352–63)

Those wits who "make *Parnassus* worse than *Shooter's Hill,*" a notoriously dangerous spot on the Dover road, should be "seiz'd and set to Work." In another insulting glance at Dryden's appeal to Dorset in the *Juvenal* preface, Blackmore advises mercy for

> the Impotent,
> That in your Service have their Vigor spent.
> They should have Pensions from the Muses State,
> Too old to Write, too Feeble to Translate. (ll. 364–67)

He further advises the construction of an hospital upon Parnassus for such "Muses *Invalids*" to be staffed by the undistinguished physicians who are so eager to maintain their own dispensary. In an "impressive"[20] and defiant climax, Blackmore scornfully assures the reader that there are "some such Doctors" whom

> you may persuade
> To labour at th' Apothecary's Trade.
> They'll Med'cines make, and at the Mortar sweat,
> Let 'em pound Drugs, they have no Brains to beat.
> (ll. 387–90)

The appearance of *A Satyr against Wit* on November 23 created a sensation. As Abel Boyer notes, when Blackmore published his satire "what Tumults, what Storms did he raise? All *Will's* was presently in Arms."[21] Tom Brown's indignation may be taken as representative of the furor Blackmore's poem caused:

'Tis the most fantastical Mixture of *Hypocrisie* and *Scandal* you ever saw: The Writer of it sets up for an Advocate of *Religion* which he shews by his Scurrility, and want of good Manners, and pretends that a *Confederacy* is carrying on in *Covent-Garden*, to Banish *that* and *Learning* out of the World. By the terrible Description he makes of some People, one wou'd be apt to think that the *Goths* and *Vandals*, who have been buried under Ground for so many hundred *Ages*, were newly *sprung* up in *Russel-Street*, and going with Fire and Faggot in hand to set all our Libraries in Ashes; and when that was done, to knock all the *Parsons* on the Head, and ravish all the Women between *White-Hall* and *White-Chapel*. But Dr. *Oates's* forty thousand *Pilgrims*, with their *Black Bills*, and so forth, don't smell so rank of the *Legend*. All the Reason I know he has to make this *hideous* Out-cry is, because the *Dispensary* has made bold to expose the *rumbling Fustian* of his two *Arthurs*, and some honest Gentlemen, that now and then use to *drink* a *Dish* of *Tea* at *Will's*, have been guilty of speaking the same truth. A strange thing this! that a Man must be an *Atheist*, only for calling *Dullness* by its proper Name, and a *Rake*, because he has too much *Honesty* to Flatter one of the most execrable *Poems*, that has plagu'd the World since the Days of *Quarles* and *Ogilby*.[22]

Attempting to salve the obvious smart caused by Blackmore's poem, the Wits immediately put a series of shoddy rebuttals such as "Extempore Verses on the Author of the Satyr against Wit" into manuscript circulation.[23] By mid-December the *Post Boy* advertised publication of *A Satyr Upon a late Pamphlet, Entituled, A Satyr against Wit*, a feeble defense of "the Nation's glory":

Wit is a Radiant Spark of Heav'nly Fire,
Full of Delight, and worthy of Desire;
Bright as the Ruler of the Realms of Day,
Sun of the Soul, with in-born Beauties gay.

The satire against Blackmore is furious but ineffectual. The reader may recognize Blackmore by the "rumbling Tone" of his *Arthurs* but to so describe *A Satyr against Wit* is simply silly. After some offensively facile wordplay on Blackmore's name, the anonymous author offers the obligatory jokes on the poet-physician:

'Twixt *Pen* and *Potion* is his Time assign'd;
This mortifies the *Body*, That the *Mind;*

Both to Tormenting make some vile pretence,
One Tortures *Souls*, and t'other *Limbs* and *Sence.*[24]

Such toothless lampoons merely confirmed Blackmore's allegations against the wits.

III The Pacificator

A more moderate reaction appeared in the second week of January. Samuel Cobb's *Poetae Britannici: A Poem, Satyrical and Panegyrical, upon our English Poets* lauds Dryden in verses which are at least not contemptible, while attempting a just evaluation of Blackmore's talent. Cobb dismisses the Laurus portrait in *Prince Arthur*, assuring Dryden,

Thou shalt immortal be, no Censure fear
Tho' angry B[lack] more in Heroicks jeer.

Despite obvious talent, Cobb asserts, Blackmore ceases to please as an heroic poet when he either follows Virgil too closely or deserts his discipline altogether. And, unlike Virgil, Blackmore insufficiently polishes his verses, too frequently rumbling on "like the King of Winds":

His flat Descriptions, void of Manly Strength,
Jade out our Patience with excessive length.
While Readers, yawning o'er his *Arthurs*, see
Whole Pages spun on one poor Simile.
We grant he labours with no want of Brains,
Of Fire, or Spirit; but He spares the Pains,
One happy Thought, or two, may at a Heat
Be struck, but Time and Study must compleat
A Verse, sublimely Good, and justly Great.

Blackmore's Homeric energy and imagination require, Cobb concludes, the smoothing of the file.[25] Such moderation was unrepresentative, of course; and during the same week that Cobb's poem went on sale Tom Brown noted the "Pious Design" being engendered at Will's to "Squib" Blackmore with epigrams.[26]

The call for contributions apparently reached the ears of Daniel Defoe, for he alludes to the project near the conclusion of

The Pacificator published on February 15.[27] Although he does not disparage wit, Defoe is, as was the ministry he served, solidly on the side of the Men of Sense in their struggle against the Men of Wit. *The Pacificator*, capitalizing on the popularity of *The Dispensary*, narrates the mock-heroic battle of Covent Garden and Cheapside. Blackmore (Great Nokor) first offered battle in *Prince Arthur*, but even though he successfully "threw *Dram-matick Wit* upon its Back" his own "hasty Talent threw him on his Knees," leaving him open to Dennis's "Storm of Words" in the *Remarks* as well as to the annoyance of numerous lampoons. Dennis, Commander of "the Forlorn of Wit," receives harsher treatment than most of the other habitués of Will's. Able to "find out all Mens Errors but his own," Dennis is

> Easie to be distinguish'd by his Works,
> With equal Havock, and destructive Hate,
> Leaves all the Land he treads on Desolate. (ll. 164–66)

Undeterred, Blackmore routed the field with the publication of *King Arthur*, for which service William (Apollo) "Knighted him upon the spot." Collier's "thin Squadrons" appeared next but were "over-power'd by multitudes of Wits." The impetuosity of Blackmore's *Satyr against Wit*, however, reclaimed the field for the Men of Sense:

> His Squadrons in Poetick Terror shone,
> And whisper'd Death to Wit as they came on:
> The strong Brigades of his Heroic Horse,
> Dreadful for Sense, for Pointed Satyr worse,
> Wing'd with Revenge, in fiery Raptures flew,
> And dipt in Poison'd Gall the Darts they threw;
> Nothing cou'd *Nokor's* furious Troops withstand,
> Nor cou'd he check them with his own Command.
> The Troops of Wit, Disorder'd, and O'r-run,
> Are Slain, Disperc'd, Disgrac'd, and Overthrown;
> The Shouts of Triumph reach the distant Sky,
> And *Nokor* lies Encamp'd in the Field of Victory.
> (ll. 296–307)

Defoe's estimate of the effectiveness of Blackmore's satire was shared by others less partisan. The anonymous author of *A Satyr against Satyrs* refuses to take sides in the controversy but agrees that

B[lackmo]re the Prince of Satyrists has Writ,
The Noblest Satyr 'gainst the Plagues of Wit.

Like Defoe, he argues against this kind of literary civil war. If Garth failed to settle the dispensary quarrel and if no wits reformed in the wake of Blackmore's powerful assault, clearly nothing can be expected of further satires except continued dissension.[28] Furthermore, as Defoe points out, wit and sense should be mutually dependent, for

Mere Sense is sullen, stiff, and unpolite,
Mere Wit is apoplectick, thin, and light. (ll. 365–66)

The consequence of a decisive victory for either side would be a "Dearth of Sense, or else a Plague of Wit," both undesirable extremes. Yet, Defoe fears, the success of Blackmore's *Satyr* has disturbed the hive in Covent Garden:

For Wit, by these Misfortunes desperate,
Begins to arm at an unusual rate,
Levies new Forces, gives Commissions out,
For several Regiments of Horse and Foot,
Recruits from every side come in amain. . . . (ll. 317–20)

The commonplace book at Will's lay open receiving contributions toward the counterattack.

IV *"The Blood-thirsty Hussars of* Parnassus"

Invigorating as literary quarrels are, the vehemence with which the wits responded is difficult to account for unless one assumes, with Richard C. Boys, that the *mores* that Blackmore stood for threatened the kind of life the wits cherished.[29] In this respect, Swift is right to lump Blackmore with the Moderns in *The Battle of the Books,* for to Dryden especially he must have seemed conspicuously of a different age, a post-Restoration Whig who partook of none of the growing gloom of the Tory satirists. In one sense, Blackmore's divergence from the aristocratic assumptions shared by men like Bolingbroke and Alexander Pope serves to define his "dullness"; and the counterattack against Blackmore launched by the wits deserves study as the origin of a surprising number of the satiric thorns that were used over a generation later in *Peri Bathous* and *The Dunciad*.

On February 27, less than two weeks after the appearance of Defoe's *Pacificator*, the brief peace was broken by the publication of *Commendatory Verses, on the Author of the Two Arthurs and the Satyr against Wit.*[30] Adopting the outworn wit and format of *Certain Verses Written by Several of the Author's Friends* which had ridiculed Sir William Davenant's epic *Gondibert* in 1653 and marshaling the same metaphors raised against Edward Howard's epics in the late sixties, a group of Blackmore's "Particular Friends" indicted the City Bard in this twenty-eight-page folio diatribe. *Commendatory Verses* finds Sir Richard guilty of the multiple audacities of: (1) having taught school; (2) of living in unfashionable Cheapside; (3) of mixing medical malpractice with the composition of wretched poetry; and (4) of having flattered the King into honoring him with a knighthood. The quality of the poems mustered in defense of wit is so feeble that Boys suggests that many of them must have been written while their authors were drunk.[31] Apparently the writers themselves realized the ephemeral nature of their contributions, for they are seldom reprinted in collected works.[32] And if the original intention, as seems likely, had been to have authors who had been attacked in *A Satyr against Wit* reply in *Commendatory Verses,* it was not successful. From attributions in Tom Brown's *Works,* in *Discommendatory Verses,* and by contemporary annotations, it is clear that few of the major authors contributed.

Young Christopher Codrington seems to have been behind the volume. Almost a year earlier, in May 1699, just as *The Dispensary* was published, Codrington succeeded his father as governor general of the Leeward Islands. After *A Satyr against Wit,* he was anxious, therefore, to leave the London scene and take up his new duties with something other than Blackmore's ridicule ringing in his ears. Consequently, he seems to have hired the enterprising Tom Brown to organize and publicize the rebuttal to *A Satyr against Wit.* Always ready to soil his hands for solid cash, Brown went about his commission with relish, producing one-fourth of the poems himself in addition to the preface. Unfortunately it was his savorless wit rather than his indefatigable energy which communicated itself to the poems gathered together as *Commendatory Verses.* Insofar as the poems pretend to be anything more than defamatory lampoons, they defend wit, the stage, the dispensarians, and the authenticity of the Epistles of Phalaris, which Charles Boyle maintained. Next to Blackmore, Bentley draws more sneers than anyone, doubtless a reflection of the instructions Brown received from Boyle's close aristocratic friend Codrington.

Brown's preface, written in the persona of a citizen of London, advises his fellow citizens to patronize Blackmore as poet but to avoid him as physician. For though he "has eas'd many of you of those heavy Burdens, call'd Wives and Children" in his practice of medicine, his poetry is a mainstay of the London economy. "He's a particular Benefactor to the Manufacture of the Nation," the persona of "O.S." elaborates, "and, at this present Minute, to my certain Knowledge, keeps Ten Papermill a going with his *Job* and *Habakkuk*, and his other *Hebrew* Heroes."[33] Nor need pious citizens fear an infusion of wit in Sir Richard's rhymes:

> He is a Poet, pray be not scandalized at the Word, he is a Poet, I say, but of sober solid Principles, and as hearty an Enemy to Wit as the best of you all: he has writ twenty thousand Verses and upwards without one Grain of Wit in them; nay, he has declar'd open War against it, and, despising it in himself, is resolved not to endure it in any one else. When he is in his Coach, instead of pretending to read where he can't see, as some Doctors do; or thinking of his Patient's case, which none of them do, he is still listning to the Chimes, to put his Ear in tune, and stumbles upon a Distick every Kennel he is jolted over.[34]

Codrington's epigram, appearing first, in the position of honor, initiates a toothless assault. The second poem by Sir Charles Sedley is somewhat better. Sedley had opposed Blackmore's arguments in *A Short History of the Last Parliament* the previous year by arguing against a standing army in peacetime, and he seems to have been interrogated during the investigation of the assassination attempt on William III, either of which may account for his antipathy. Sedley's contemptuous conclusion, however, implies that he needs no provocation beyond Blackmore's poetry:

> It is a common Pastime to Write Ill;
> And Doctor, with the rest e'en take thy fill.
> Thy Satyr's harmless: 'Tis thy Prose that kills,
> When thou Prescrib'st thy Potions, and thy Pills. (*CV* 2)

Giving a new turn to the Thames simile in *Cooper's Hill*, Henry Blount, a university friend of Codrington, warns Blackmore to cease burlesquing the king in his laborious epics and instead continue an enemy to wit:

> So Dullness thou may'st write into Esteem,
> Thy great Example, as it is thy Theme. (*CV* 3)

Frequently Blackmore is labeled heir to Flecknoe or Quarles or Ogilby as Prince of Dullness, an honor accorded for his alacrity in sinking, a recurrent metaphor. The Countess of Sandwich, Rochester's witty second daughter, typifies the genteel tone of the collection when she refers to Blackmore as

> Thou only Stain to Mighty WILLIAM's Sword!
> Old *Jemmy* [James] never Knighted such a *T—d.*
> For the most nauseous Mixture GOD can make,
> Is a dull Pedant, and a busy Quack. (*CV* 12).

She commands Blackmore to return to teaching and "pore upon Boys A—es" rather than write "Heroick Farces." More ingenious, if not more entertaining, is Tom Brown's lengthy "Epitome of a Poem, truly call'd *A Satyr against Wit*; done for the Undeceiving of some Readers, who have mistaken the Panegyrick in that Immortal Work for the Satyr, and the Satyr for the Panegyrick" (*CV* 40). This close parody uses line references and italics to indicate Brown's alterations of Blackmore's verses.[35] More lively is his briefer "Upon King ARTHUR, partly written in the Doctor's Coach, and partly in a Coffee-house":

> Let the malicious Criticks Snarl and Rail,
> *Arthur* immortal is, and must prevail.
> In vain they strive to wound him with their Tongue,
> The Lifeless *Foetus* can receive no wrong.
> As rattling Coach once thunder'd through the Mire,
> Out dropt Abortive *Arthur* from his Sire.
> Well may he then both Time and Death defie,
> For what was never born, can never die. (*CV* 20)

The *Post Boy* for April 4–6 announced the publication of *Discommendatory Verses*, evidence that Blackmore's defenders had not slumbered through the onslaught from Will's. The preface ridicules men who would select so contemptible a buffoon as Tom Brown to be their leader and who would pen poems notable for nothing but stale puns and obvious rhymes often repeated. As their poems demonstrate, the authors of *Discommendatory Verses* knew to whom most poems in *Commendatory Verses* belonged and answered each in kind. Thus "Upon seeing a Man light a Pipe of Tobacco in a Coffee-house, with a Leaf of King ARTHUR" (*CV* 21) is correctly attributed to Tom Brown and answered by a poem "Upon seeing a Man wipe his A—se with *T*[*om*] *B*[rown]'s *Satyr* against the *French King*" (*DV* 24), the editor having warned that scurrilous attacks would be "return'd a suitable Roughness."[36]

Apparently the wits at Will's, for their part, knew nothing of the contributors to *Discommendatory Verses* and their identity has somewhat miraculously remained a secret ever since.[37] If, as he implies in a letter, "To a Physician in the Country; giving a true State of the Poetical War between Cheapside and Covent-Garden," Tom Brown knew the identity of the "Mendicant *Rhymer*" whom he accuses Blackmore of engaging to head the "Body of Mercenaries" who wrote *Discommendatory Verses*,[38] Brown did not bequeath the knowledge to posterity. Because of the "suitable Roughness" of *Discommendatory Verses* critics have perhaps been too quick to disassociate Blackmore's friends Isaac Watts and Samuel Wesley from complicity, especially since Wesley, the author of *Maggots*, had the requisite cleverness and had been repeatedly attacked in *Commendatory Verses* as a precursor of Blackmore's heroic bombast. Neither man, however, fits Brown's description of the leader of this "attempt to Poison . . . with *Stinkpots*." Nor does Thomas Rymer, despite his name. Defoe remains a possibility but, lacking sufficient evidence, nothing more.

Because Brown describes the "Mendicant *Rhymer*" as earlier intimate in the circle of the wits, a fact certainly born out by the Rhymer's detailed knowledge concerning the authorship of *Commendatory Verses*, John Dennis may have been the man. He subsequently inveighed against the "Petty Merchants of small Conceits" who populate coffeehouses, venting their spleen in extempore lampoons.[39] Further, Dennis quit frequenting the haunts of the wits at some indeterminate time during this period and was very shortly to become friendly with Blackmore, who subscribed to his *Grounds of Criticism* in 1704. Also, it was in the early months of 1700 that Dennis fell out with Thomas Cheek, one of his closest friends and a contributor to *Commendatory Verses.* Dennis and Cheek quarreled over Abel Boyer's play *Achilles, or Iphigenia in Aulis.* The next year Dennis was abused, as was Blackmore, by Cheek or Boyer or both in Boyer's *Letters of Wit, Politicks, and Morality.* Dennis is specifically excluded from the circle at Will's while Cheek is included.[40] Because none of Dennis's abiding friends, neither Dryden, Garth,[41] Wycherley, nor Congreve, contributed to *Commendatory Verses,* they were unscathed in the rejoinder which consists entirely of mockeries of the lampoons in the earlier volume.[42] If Dennis's revulsion against the wits did take this form at this time, it would explain the cessation of hostilities between Dennis and Blackmore; and to the circle at Will's Dennis's behavior would seem the act of a turncoat, as Tom Brown maintains.

Blackmore's part in the "Stinkpots" is almost as obscure as that of the mysterious Rhymer. Boys feels certain the *Discommendatory Verses* was not solely Blackmore's work, that it "was the fruit of several poets' labors."[43] Both Yoffie and Rosenberg think it improbable that Blackmore had any hand in the "scurrilous" and "indecent" volume, observing that while Blackmore wrote thousands of dull lines he wrote not a one which could be considered scurrilous.[44] Perhaps just as Dryden did not contribute to *Commendatory Verses,* Blackmore elected not to sully his hands in a battle waged mostly by small fry.

Despite occasional flashes both volumes are largely innocent of wit; and the modern reader is likely to concur with one of the authors in *Discommendatory Verses* who finds the lays in *Commendatory Verses* only useful as "Lethargick *Opiats*" (*DV* 18) or with another author who improves the metaphor by recommending that one read the wits' poems as one would

> *Opiats* take,
> And only run 'em o're for *Sleepings* sake. (*DV* 21)

Although *Discommendatory Verses* are more original, the contributors doubtless had a wise eye toward their reputation when they buried their authorship in oblivion. Neither volume offers a single poem of the caliber of Garth's *Dispensary* or Blackmore's *Satyr against Wit.* Nahum Tate, whose "slowness" in composition Blackmore had glanced at good-humoredly in his *Satyr*, perceptively observed that replying to lampoons was "paying Nonsense in its own Coin" and that it was high time for both sides "to return to their Sense; they have so long Ridicul'd One Another, till the Men, that had some Wit, are become Diversion for them that have None."[45] In his preface to Sedley's *Poetical Works*, William Ayloffe made a similar point in noting, "If a Man sets up for a Poet, he is Immediately attacqu'd by a Satyrical Party; Destruction is the Word; and, as for Quarter, they give none: These are the Blood-thirsty Hussars of *Parnassus*, cut out for the Ruin of others, tho' rarely with any great Honor to themselves."[46]

The thirstiest of the Hussars was the ill-fated Tom Brown "of facetious memory." The editor of *Commendatory Verses* was, as always, quick to pick up and pander to the changed temper of the town when it grew tired of petty squabbling:

> Such swarms of Wits on Blackmore; most absurd!
> Two Thousand Flies attack a new-fall'n T—,
> In which great Fray, each unsuccessful Fly
> Loses his Sting, beshits his little Thigh:
> From whence this useful Moral's clearly shown,
> Better the Fly had let the T— alone.[47]

Nonetheless Brown waged the war more doggedly than any of Blackmore's antagonists. He may have been the author who added a poem to the unsold volumes of *Commendatory Verses* in 1700[48] and he certainly had a part in publishing a 1702 edition. Clearly Brown intended to follow the original issue of *Commendatory Verses* with a similar volume ridiculing Blackmore's forthcoming *Paraphrase of Job*, for the last page of *Commendatory Verses* announces that upon the publication of *Job* "new Subscription-books will be open'd at *Will's* Coffee-house in *Covent-garden*, and all Gentlemen, that are willing to Subscribe, are desired to send in their *Quota's*."[49] Perhaps because some were more squeamish than Brown about burlesquing the paraphrase of a religious work no matter how execrable or perhaps because *Commendatory Verses* preempted Brown's plan by ridiculing *Job* repeatedly before it issued from the press, the proposed volume never appeared. The most lamentable news Job ever received, Brown himself says in "on *Job* newly

Travestied by Sir *R[irchard] Bl[ackmore],*" is that

> A *Cheapside* Quack, whose vile unhallow'd Pen
> With equal Licence Murders Rhimes and Men,
> In fumbling Fustian has burlesqu'd thy Page. . . . (*CV* 30)

Such verses, intended by Brown to pique the taste of the town, only palled it.

V "*Sir* Richard*'s Poetical* Powdering-Tub"

A Paraphrase on the Book of Job was advertised for sale[50] only two days after *Commendatory Verses* appeared. Upon sending a female friend a copy, Tom Brown promised that she would see Job "just as he escap'd out of Sir *Richard's* Poetical *Powdering-Tub,* which has prov'd more unfortunate to him than his Dunghill."[51] Brown could not charge Blackmore with failing to serve his apprenticeship in the composition of divine poetry, as so many critics had alleged when *Prince Arthur* appeared. Blackmore's emphasis on the moral and religious responsibilities of poetry in the preface to *Prince Arthur* caused Nahum Tate, the following year, to solicit some of his shorter compositions for a collection of religious verse to be dedicated to Princess Anne, patroness of "the Reformation of Poetry, and Restoring the *Muses* to the Service of the Temple." Tate's dedication echoes Blackmore's preface, even to inveighing against all but "legitimate Off-spring of Wit, which are useful to the World."[52]

Blackmore's contributions to Tate's *Miscellanea Sacra* match the temper and style of the other inclusions which, as might be expected even if Herbert, Cowley, and Jeremy Taylor were not quoted, is often extravagantly metaphorical. In Blackmore's "Solitude" the contemplative soul

> chides the interposing Clay,
> And bars of Flesh that take away
> Her heavenly Prospect, and retard her flight—

a conceit reminiscent of the metaphysicals. Similarly, in "The Enquiry" earthly satisfactions are as

> one poor drop to him that almost bursts
> With fierce desires, and for an Ocean thirsts.

And, as in Herbert's "The Pulley," only God "shall be the Minds last Rest and End." Blackmore's facility ranges from occasional felicitous phrases as when sin "gluts the *grave*" in "Soliloquy" to hapless lapses as when the pious Essenes in "Solitude" dine frugally on the bounty of nature:

> Of the next Silver Stream they drank,
> Got a cheap Meal from some green Bank.

The themes are obligatory, necessarily displaying little originality but encouraging the kind of verbal and visual experimentation characteristic of devotional meditation. If one topic more than another seems to fire Blackmore's imagination, it is Nature's vast "Volumes of Divinity," already a recurrent theme.[53]

Remembering Blackmore's interest in natural theology, his choice of Job for his first major religious poem should not surprise, for as Sir William Temple noted in "Of Poetry," the subject of the Book of Job "is instruction concerning the attributes of God, and the works of nature." The Psalms Blackmore elected to paraphrase as well as most of the other biblical selections included in the *Paraphrase* volume emphasize the sublime aspects of God's creation. Paraphrases of Job, although not nearly as common as paraphrases of the Psalms, were nothing new in 1700. Most respected was George Sandys' *Paraphrase Upon the Divine Poems* (1648), which included Job and most of the other verses in Blackmore's volume. Symon Patrick's less successful *The Book of Job Paraphras'd* was published in 1679; and as recently as 1697 another anonymous paraphrase of Job had appeared.

Blackmore's *Paraphrase on the Book of Job* had, however, as he explains in a most interesting and original preface, a new emphasis to offer. *Job* is intended as a third example of poems which may both entertain and instruct and is offered in opposition to "the Universal Deprevation of our Manners" which has employed poetry to the most "detestable Purposes." Disclaiming any personal hostility in his censures of the wits, Blackmore praises Dryden's recantation in the verses prefixed to Peter Motteux' *Beauty in Distress* two years earlier:

> What I have loosly, or profanely writ,
> Let them to Fires (their due desert) commit.

Blackmore does continue to needle Dryden when later in the preface he argues that "if it should *hereafter* happen, that *Homer* or *Virgil* should be well *Translated* into the English *Language*" Job, if similarly executed, would "outshine" either. The comparison between Blackmore's *Paraphrase* and Dryden's *Aeneis* is clear.

Arguing for less imitation of the ancients, Blackmore wishes for "some *good Genuis*" to "assert the *Liberty* of *Poetry*, and set up for an *Original* in *Writing*" in a way accommodated to the religion, manners, and circumstances of contemporary England. Despite the ingenuity of commentators, he finds little attempt in the classical epics to instruct. They seem rather intended solely for diversion. "Rules" are also the product of commentators rather than of the original authors. And although translating and commenting on classical epics is "an inoffensive Amusement and a pardonable sort of Idleness," it is not likely to yield morals or improve manners in any way useful to a Christian commonwealth. An unfounded admiration for classical scholarship, in fact, elevates narrow pedantry while disparaging truly learned men. In distinguishing those who merely labor to "stop a Period more exactly" or "rectifie a Word" from men of more profound learning, Blackmore is setting the record straight for those who might otherwise misinterpret his support of Bentley's meticulous scholarship.

Blackmore's denial of the authority of the ancients makes him difficult to categorize in terms of contemporary literary argument, representing as it does a radical departure from his deference to "the *Rules* of Writing set down by the great *Masters*" in the preface to *Prince Arthur*. H. T. Swedenberg notes that in his "Essay upon Epick Poetry" (1716) Blackmore presents himself as a liberal in criticism, scoffing at the influence of Aristotle and contending that reason and experience should supersede any "rules."[54] Undoubtedly, Richard F. Jones is partially correct in attributing Blackmore's rebellion against Aristotelian principles in literary criticism to the contemporary attitude of scientific skepticism which insisted on questioning all assumptions.[55] The motto of the Royal Society, after all, was "Upon the Word of No One," an eschewing of all authority. It was Blackmore's empirical bias which so impressed Locke in the preface to *King Arthur*.

An equally important motivation for Blackmore, however,

comes from his determination to establish Job as the archetype of the Christian epic. The influential Boileau objected that Christianity did not lend itself to nor could it benefit from epic treatment,[56] an objection Blackmore answers most fully in the preface to *Alfred* (1723). Others objected that epic fiction should not be mixed with the awful truths of religion. Nonetheless, Vida, Tasso, Du Bartas, and Milton used Christian machinery in the epic before Blackmore;[57] and Edward Howard and Dryden advocated its use, as did Dennis and Isaac Watts later. The novelty of Blackmore's preface is that he argues from the authority of a Christian epic which utilizes Christian machinery and which antedates even Homer's epics. For in Job, "if it be not depress'd by the Paraphrase," the reader may find the "*Sublime Stile, elevated Thoughts, magnificent Expressions* where the *Subject* requires them, and great *richness* and *abundance* throughout the whole, without the *Aids* of the *Pagan System* of *Divinity.*"

Unlike the heroes of Homer and Virgil, Job is "passive"rather than active and not a prince or great commander. One has to examine the history of epic theory to realize just how revolutionary Blackmore's contentions are, for virtually everyone assumed that epic could only deal with the "great and glorious."[58] But what commission, Blackmore argues, had either Homer or Virgil "to *settle* the *limits* and *extent* of *Epick Poetry*, or who can prove that they ever intended to do so?" in "An Essay upon Epick Poetry," Blackmore further dismisses the "servile" assumption that "the chief Hero ought to be engag'd in some eminent Action," citing his "Contrary Position" in the preface to *A Paraphrase of Job.* There, he recalls, he endeavored to prove "that the principal Character of the Poem may be as well unactive and in a State of Suffering and Calamity." It is the failure to recognize this, Blackmore contends, that has led so many critics astray in their search for a hero of *Paradise Lost.* Despite the universal assumption, based on classical epic theory, that the hero must be either Satan or Christ, reason, Blackmore insists, shows Adam is obviously the "hero."[59] Nor, Blackmore asserts in the preface, should the hero be drawn without some defects for "a perfect *Idea* of *Vertue* and *Excellency* may amaze and dazzle us; but when propounded for our *Imitation* it will rather discourage, than excite us." Virtue beyond probability is sterile.

Thus Job, in his misfortune doubting the justice of his God, makes a hero "every way proper" for an epic intended to demonstrate divine providence. Blackmore's providence, however, is no simple "poetic justice" of the kind Dennis found sometimes deficient in *Prince Arthur* and argued with Blackmore in defense of throughout his career.[60] In the same dedication to *Juvenal* which influenced the writing of *Prince Arthur*, Dryden refused to consider *Paradise Lost* an epic because it did not conclude happily.[61] Blackmore astutely realized the *a priori* foolishness implicit in such judgments but, again, was alone in his contention that an unfortunate conclusion might instruct as forcibly as a happy one. The mystery of providence, which has "often puzled the *Understanding*, and discomposed the *Temper* of the Wisest and Best of Men," lies in the prosperity God allows "*impious* and *flagitious* Men" while "*good* and *upright* Men are often overwhelmed with *Poverty* and *Distress*." Scorning the simplified resolution of a fortunate conclusion, Blackmore argues that Job instructs the reader that providence cannot be adequately comprehended by the mind of man and that, instead of attempting to "reflect on the narrow and broken, as well as obscure *Prospect*" which we have of God's plan, he should "contemplate the *Works* of *God's Creation*, of which our selves are so small a Part." Also, since Job was ignorant of the later revelations to Moses and the Jewish prophets, his story shows what "great *Advances* may be made in *Vertue* by a diligent attendance to the *Dictates* of our *Natural Light*."

Next to the excellence of its moral and the opportunity it provided for natural theology, Blackmore most admired the "richness" of Job, especially its "bold and surprizing Metaphors." Everyone agreed on the efficacy of similes to "raise Admiration" in the heroic poem; but Dryden's opinion in the dedication of the *Aeneis* that "similitudes and descriptions, when drawn into an unreasonable length, must need nauseate the reader" is representative of the taste of an age reacting to the audacity of metaphysical exuberance. Had Virgil lived to revise his work, Dryden says, he would certainly have contracted some of his similes. Blackmore, on the contrary, although he avoids repetition, determines to amplify the original text, rendering the metaphors even more surprising. The thickly conceited, grandiose style which critics have so frequently denigrated in Blackmore's *Paraphrase* was, if not wise, at least deliberate. In anticipation of this sort of censure, he protests in the preface against the sectarian English literary taste which cannot relish the wild irregularity of style which so evidently pleased the Jews.

Agreeing with Cowley that the scriptures furnish the most noble subjects, Blackmore concludes his innovative preface with the hope that his paraphrases will be some improvement in respect to "*Perspecuity* and *Coherence*" over the earlier versions by "Mr. *Sandys*, a *Gentleman* of *great Merit*."[62] Thus Blackmore invites an interesting comparison between his paraphrases and Sandys's. A contrast of both writers' rendering of Habakkuk 3:4 illustrates Blackmore's tendency to amplity the original and to improve on Sandys's sometimes harsh versification:

> King James version: And *his* [God's] brightness was as the light;
> he had horns *coming* out of his hand: and there *was*
> the hiding of his power.
>
> Sandys (1638): His glory shone,
> Which fill'd the heav'ns themselves with brighter rays,
> And all the earth replenish'd with His praise.
> His brightness as the sun's; His fingers streams
> Of light project; His power hid in those beams.[63]
>
> Blackmore (1700):
> Torrents of Glory dazling bright,
> Too fierce and keen for Human sight
> Broke from th' immense Abyss of uncreated light.
> Ev'n from his Hands a bright Eruption came,
> A pointed Efflux of Immortal Flame.
> Transcendant Splendor did th' Almighty shroud,
> No Less than did the thick surrounding Cloud.
> His being thus lay hidden either Way,
> In too much Darkness, or in too much Day.[64]

Blackmore's conscious elaboration does much to explain why his version of Job is four times as long as Sandys's.

Blackmore's *Job*, like Sandys's, is in couplets, despite the increasing disapproval of rhyme in epic.[65] With greater emphasis, Blackmore continued his practice from the *Arthurs* of employing run-on lines and great variation in the placing of caesuras to add variety to his couplets, devices he recommends in his *Essays* in order to "avoid Monotony and Uniformity."[66] Again, popular opinion disagreed with Blackmore, believing that rhyme and run-on worked to cross purposes.[67] Certainly Blackmore's enthusiasm in this respect leads him into awkwardness, as when God asks Satan:

> In thy Way
> And toilsome Course, Ambitious Spirit, say
> Hast thou observ'd good *Job*, my Servant, one
> In Righteousness and Piety, by none
> Thro' all the wide Terrestrial World out-done? (p. 3)

Notwithstanding, the greatest defects of *Job* are neither its exhausting amplification nor its frequently infelicitous versification but its audacity of metaphor. "Lowring Clouds" which spit "their ruddy Vomit thro' the Air" recall the more horrific descriptions in his earlier epics. When Job describes his ulcerated flesh as "cloath'd with Worms" the lines suggest the influence of the grotesque strain in metaphysical religious verse. The infractions against good taste which Pope cites again and again in *Peri Bathous* usually proceed from Blackmore's wringing a metaphor to death. No better illustration of this unpruned excrescence exists than his anthropomorphic paraphrase of part of Psalm 104:

> King James Version: He looketh on the earth, and it trembleth:
> he toucheth the hills, and they smoke.
>
> Blackmore: If on the Earth he does in Anger look,
> It trembles at the terrible Rebuke.
> It from its strong Foundations starts for fear,
> And twisting Gripes its working Entrails tear.
> The Mountains shiver, and their Heads incline
> At the reproof of Majesty Divine.
> The Hills forget they're fixt, and in their fright
> Of all their weight they strip themselves for flight.
> The Rocks from off their Marble Pillars break,
> And which they us'd to give, a Refuge seek.
> The Woods with Terror wing'd outstrip the Wind,
> And leave the heavy, panting Hills behind.
> All Nature troubled and in deep distress,
> Of God's Displeasure does her Fear express. (pp. 229–30)

As in too many passages of *Job*, Blackmore's admitted ingenuity simply wanders into absurdity or exhausts itself in tedious length.

Not that *Job* is without passages of poetry. Eliphaz's vision of man creates the same melancholy mood found in Edward Young's *Night Thoughts* or in Pope's "lurking principle of death" in *An Essay on Man:*

> A worthless Wight that triumphs for a Day,
> Whose Habitation is a House of Clay.
> Whose Fort of Life is founded in the Dust
> Which quickly falls, and disappoints his Trust,
> Tho' but a gnawing Worm the Work assails,
> Or but a Silly Moth the Fabrick scales.
> Each hour the sap'd Foundation feels decay,
> And Life ev'n in its blooming fades away,
> Made to its own devouring Flames a Prey. (p. 17)

As if to balance the bathos of his description of clouds as God's "floating Bottles," Blackmore describes how God "studs the Sable Night with Silver Stars." Something of the charmed movement of Marvell's "Bermudas" animates the lines when God

> moulds, and whitens in the Air the Snow,
> And with its Fleeces spreads the Earth below. (p. 160)

And Newton authentically fires Blackmore's imagination when

> the Lord of Nature in the Air
> Hangs evening Clouds, his Sable Canvas, where
> His Pencil dipt in Heav'nly Colours, made
> Of intercepted Sunbeams mixt with Shade,
> Of temper'd Ether, and refracted Light,
> Paints his fair Rainbow, charming to the Sight. (p. 161)

It is painfully obvious that Blackmore's metaphorical method left him open to censure from more disciplined critics like Alexander Pope; but it is also possible to wonder if without descriptions of a God who in forming the morning

> the rich Metal beats, and then with care
> Unfolds the Golden leaves to gild the Fields of Air (p. 169)

the subsequent century could have produced Christopher Smart's *Song to David.*

After all that can be said in defense of *Job* has been said, however, the fact remains that Blackmore's preface is more engaging than his poem. The modern reader is perhaps apt to turn Job's wife's ejaculation—"How much thy pious dullness I detest!" (p. 8)—against Sir Richard himself and yawn with Bildad when he asks Job

> When wilt thou finish thy prolix Discourse,
> Sounding indeed enough, but void of Force? (p. 76)

Such factiousness would have caused trouble in the weeks after Blackmore's *Paraphrase* appeared, for literary tempers were high. Elizabeth Thomas reported to a friend that in attempting to buy Blackmore's book she had "committed an unlucky Blunder" in the bookseller's, "for instead of asking for his *Paraphrase,* I enquired for his *Satire* on JOB, which mightily offended some Friends of Sir *Richard's* that were in the Shop." She protests her innocence though admitting that the book "has been most terribly handled at Parnassus."[68]

Typical of this terrible handling is the anonymous *The Devil, A Wife, and a Poet. A Satyr Occasion'd by a late Paraphrase on the Book of Job.* In the poem Job's wife advises Satan to mangle Job's poem and thereby break his spirit. Satan convinces Blackmore to render Job's "easie style" in the most strained and "lewd Jargon." Shown Blackmore's *Paraphrase* Job curses God and dies.[69] Brown, as always, kept the fires of Blackmore's defamation well fanned. The project for a commendatory volume on *Job* failing, Brown wrote "A Merry Interview by Moon-light, betwixt a Ghost and the City-Bard" which, printed separately, he planned to bind with the unsold volumes of *Commendatory Verses.* In the "Interview" Blackmore is taxed for the cruelty shown "poor *Habakkuk*" and the "almost *hellish* Anguish" Job endures because of the physician's paraphrase:

> Were he now *living,* and thy *Theme,*
> He cou'd not help, but must blaspheme.[70]

With a similar maliciousness in *Amusements Serious and Comical,* Brown instructs a visitor to London what he must do if he is to dine with Blackmore "or sit within ten yards of him, up one Pair of Stairs at *Garraway's* Coffee-house." "You must,"

Brown says, "cry, *Sir* Richard, *your Paraphrase upon Job outdoes your* Arthurs; but for your dear Health's sake, don't say, in Dulness."[71]

Blackmore, as Elizabeth Thomas' letter suggests, had defenders, most notably Samuel Wesley. Wesley, another who urged "conformity with a predominately middle-class ideal,"[72] had been linked with Blackmore in *Commendatory Verses* as another poet who disgraces his pious themes. Blackmore is advised: "Who hates not *Wes[le]y*, may Thy Works esteem" (*CV* 18). The first edition of Wesley's *Life of our Blessed Lord and Savior Jesus Christ: An Heroick Poem* appeared two years before *Prince Arthur* and probably influenced Arthur's disgression on Christ in that poem. Further, Wesley had verse paraphrases of the Old and New Testaments in progress when *Job* appeared. Consequently, it is not surprising that when his *Epistle To A Friend Concerning Poetry* appeared on April 25 it contained a defense of Blackmore. In the poem Wesley reveres Dryden's ability but deplores the atmosphere created by the wits. He, unlike Dennis, finds passion in Blackmore's *Prince Arthur*, especially in Elda's pathetic plea for her husband's life. Blackmore's subject and his style are well chosen and

> Each *Page* is big with *Virgil's Manly Thought,*
> *To follow him too near's a glorious Fault.*[73]

Whether Wesley's failure to say anything about his friend's *Job* is conscious reticence or simply the result of a publisher's deadline is impossible to say; however, the barbs Blackmore sustained did not deter Wesley from publishing his own paraphrases in 1701 and 1704.

Blackmore's poem encouraged others. Another rector, Daniel Baker of Norfolk, praises Blackmore's version in the preface to his own *History of Job: A Sacred Poem in Five Books* (1706). And still another rector, Christopher Pitt, paraphrased Job and the Psalms. In 1710 William Broome, yet another clergyman, tried his hand at improving the same Habakkuk verses rendered by Sandys and Blackmore. William Coward published his 326-page epic *Abramideis, or the Faithful Patriarch Exemplified in the Lives of Abraham, Isaac, Jacob, and Joseph: An Heroic Poem* in 1705; and both John Henley's *Esther* (1714) and Aaron Hill's *Gideon* (1741) were in the same vein. All of which suggests that the failure of *A Paraphrase on the Book of Job* may have stimulated others to attempt the Biblical epic which would lead to the pious reformation in modern poetry which Blackmore desired.

VI *Dryden's Death*

Dryden did not contribute to *Commendatory Verses,* but he had not been idle in the months following the publication of Blackmore's *Satyr against Wit;* and when his *Fables Ancient and Modern* appeared in early March, it contained several attacks on the City Bard. Because publication follows publication so rapidly during this period—*Commendatory Verses* on February 27 or 28, *Job* on February 29, Dryden's *Fables* on March 5—careful attention to chronology is vital. Clearly the wits knew enough of Blackmore's forthcoming *Paraphrase* to ridicule it before its publication. Similarly, Blackmore probably knew something of the contents of Dryden's *Fables* before the volume was issued. By March 20, 1699, when Dryden received the contract for the *Fables,* his publisher, Jacob Tonson, already had three-quarters of the verses in his possession.[74] Tonson was also Blackmore's publisher. He had issued *King Arthur* in 1697 and was working about the time he concluded Dryden's contract in printing Blackmore's *Short History of the Last Parliament.* Furthermore, by December 1699 Dryden is complaining that "My Book is printing, and my Bookseller makes no hast."[75] Consequently, even without considering the possible activities of the "turncoat" editor of *Discommendatory Verses,* Blackmore could not have had much difficulty in gaining a prepublication look at the *Fables.* Actually, however, all Blackmore had to know for his preface to *Job* was that Dryden had translated passages from Ovid, information which would have been common knowledge in literary circles throughout the previous year.

For in the *Job* preface, Blackmore challenges Dryden again. Knowing that the *Fables* would be published within the week, Blackmore characterizes such translation of the classics as at best "a pardonable sort of Idleness" and asks that *Job* be compared with Dryden's *Aeneas,* the Christian with the pagan. Most obviously intended to annoy Dryden is Blackmore's reference to Sandys at the conclusion of the preface. Dryden, in the persona of Neander, had praised Sandys's *Paraphrase upon the Psalms* in

Of Dramatic Poesy,[76] but much more recently he had criticized Sandys's *Ovid's Metamorphosis* as deficient in the perfections of poetry. Because Sandys lived in an age which "neither knew good verse, nor loved it . . . all their translations want to be translated into English."[77] In the preface to the *Fables* Dryden says that he believes he has given his retranslations of Ovid "the same turn of verse which they had in the original; and this, I may say, without vanity, is not the talent of every poet. He who has arrived the nearest to it, is the ingenious and learned Sandys, the best versifier of the former age."[78] It is also the ambition to "supply some Defects" in the paraphrases of the meritorious Mr. Sandys that prompted Blackmore to complete his *Job.* Consequently, Blackmore is not only categorizing Dryden's forthcoming translations of Ovid as pagan and therefore trivial but is also inviting comparison between his improvement on Sandys and Dryden's own.

When *Job* appeared on Thursday, the last day of February, 1700, it was too late for Dryden to revise his own preface before the *Fables* went on sale the following Tuesday. The success of *A Satyr against Wit* had obviously irritated Dryden, for despite his insistence in the postscript to the *Aeneis* that Blackmore "had it not in his power" to defame him, he felt some rebuttal was called for in the preface to the *Fables.* Consequently, Dryden chides Blackmore for having "written scurrilously" against him without any more provocation than his having been "a little hard on Blackmore's fanatic patrons" in *Absalom and Achitophel.* With heavy irony he resolves to speak civilly of Blackmore's epic "because nothing ill is to be spoken of the dead." For the first time, Dryden accuses Blackmore of plagiarism: "I will only say that it was not for this noble Knight that I drew the plan of an epic poem on King Arthur in my preface to the translation of Juvenal. . . . Yet from the preface he plainly took his hint; for he began immediately upon the story, though he had the baseness not to acknowledge his benefactor, but instead of it to traduce me in a libel." After speaking more gently of Collier and again recanting "all thoughts and expressions of mine which can be truly argued of obscenity, profaneness, or immorality," Dryden concludes his last preface by denouncing Blackmore and Luke Milbourne as only distinguished from the other "scoundrels" who have written against him "by being remembered to their infamy."[79] Both enemies also receive rough treatment in the best poem included in the *Fables,* that "To my Honour'd Kinsman, JOHN DRIDEN." Blackmore appears lampooned as Maurus ["Moorish"] the physician who

> sweeps whole Parishes, and Peoples ev'ry Grave.
> And no more Mercy to Mankind will use,
> Than when he robb'd and murder'd *Maro's* Muse.[80]

Maurus reappears at greater length in the prologue to *The Pilgrim,* first performed on April 29. Dryden's last words against Blackmore are his bitterest. Apparently dissatisfied with the feeble offerings in *Commendatory Verses,* Dryden sharpens the same jokes the wits had run over and over. Blackmore's slipshod union of the functions of physician and poet is ridiculed:

> At leisure Hours, in Epique Song he deals.
> Writes to the rumbling of his Coaches Wheels,
> Prescribes in hast, and seldom kills by Rule,
> But rides Triumphant between Stool and Stool.[81]

Libelously ignoring Blackmore's accomplishments at Oxford, Dryden damns his lastest poem:

> Quack *Maurus,* tho' he never took Degrees
> In either of our Universities;
> Yet to be shown by some kind Wit he looks,
> Because he plai'd the fool and writ Three Books.
> But if he wou'd be worth a Poet's Pen,
> He must be more a Fool, and write again:
> For all the former Fustian stuff he wrote,
> Was Dead-born Doggrel, or is quite forgot;
> His Man of *Uz,* stript of his *Hebrew* Robe,
> Is just the Proverb, and *As poor as* Job.
> One wou'd have thought he wou'd no lower Jog;
> But *Arthur* was a Level, *Job's* a Bog.
> There, tho' he crept, yet still he kept in sight;
> But here, he flounders in, and sinks down right.

Blackmore is not "shown" in *The Pilgrim,* Dryden explains, because of the difficulty of doing justice to his multifarious character.

> We know not by what Name we should Arraign him,

For no one Category can contain him;
A Pedant, Canting Preacher, and a Quack,
Are Load enough to break one Asses Back.[82]

Dryden did not survive to see Blackmore "shown" in Burnaby's *Reform'd Wife*. A few days before the revised second edition of the play was published, he died.

Dryden's prologue, spoken by Colley Cibber, was to a revision of Fletcher's play by Vanbrugh to be presented to raise money for his friend Dryden. Ironically, Dryden died on the night of May 1, the evening of the play's third night, the performance from which Dryden was to receive the proceeds. The prologue has nothing to do with the play; and it is tempting to speculate why he elected to reply to Blackmore on this occasion. Perhaps, realizing that no writer with talent sufficient to dispose of Blackmore had come forward in his defense, he felt the need to effectively vanquish the doctor himself.

Whatever his motivation, Dryden spent his last days defaming Blackmore. On April 11 he wrote a friend that he had finished the *Secular Masque*, to be presented with *The Pilgrim*, and lacked only the prologue and epilogue. In rehearsal Vanbrugh gave the epilogue to Cibber for memorization; and Cibber reports in his *Apology* that it was upon hearing his recitation of the epilogue that Dryden entrusted him with the prologue.[83] Cibber's account suggests that the prologue was written after the epilogue, thus making his attack on Blackmore Dryden's last poem. Blackmore, for his part, observed Dryden's injunction that nothing ill should be spoken of the dead. When he mentioned Dryden after his death it was invariably with respect. For his part, Tom Brown quipped that Dryden's punishment in the underworld would be to "get Sir Richard Blackmore's translation of Job by heart."

VII A New Session of the Poets, Occasion'd by the Death of Mr. Dryden

In Brown's *Letters from the Dead to the Living* (1702) the ghost of Dryden tells of the "execrable smell" generated by someone uttering verses from Blackmore's *Arthurs*. Fortunately a newcomer from London clears the air with the recitation of a few "Commendatory Verses."[84] To help eradicate the scent still lingering on earth, a bantering burlesque criticism entitled *Homer and Virgil Not to be Compar'd with the TWO ARTHURS* appeared in mid-June of 1700. The passages of satire are strained but the serious criticisms interspersed in the 165-page attack are occasionally interesting and just. Although it has never been suggested, Pope almost certainly drew on *Homer and Virgil* in preparing *Peri Bathous.* The book is a catalogue of Blackmore's worst passages together with sarcastic ridicule of individual lines. As in the *Bathous,* Blackmore's "itch of Writing" proceeds from an illness in the brain which leads him to inflate metaphors in a manner similar to his description of Job's admirers, an example also cited by Pope:

> A *Waving Sea* of *Heads* was round me *spred,*
> And still *fresh Streams* the gazing *Deluge* fed.[85]

The anonymous author ridicules the "pathetic" scene of Elda pleading with Arthur to spare her husband's life which Samuel Wesley had praised a little over a month earlier; and he recommends "Mr. *Dennis's* excellent Treatise" as the best autopsy of *Prince Arthur.* Blackmore offends by his use of "impure" diction, by admitting words improper to the nobility of epic. To have the gates of heaven "jarring," for example, "supposes the Hinges not well oyl'd." To the opposite extreme, Blackmore's sublime hyperbole does "violence to Reason and Common Sense." Also deferring to Longinus, the author anticipates Pope by considering the various "manners" of Sir Richard's poetry, perhaps most typically the *"boisterous* or *creeping* manner of Writing."[86] At one moment indisciminately ridiculing the idea of the fury Persecution being "it self a Hell"—ignorant as he is of Blackmore's imitation of Milton's characterization of Satan—and astutely objecting to "high strains of *wild Conceits"* at another, the author finds Blackmore's epics a mixture of *"low trifling* Expressions" and "over-heated and intoxicated . . . *raging Metaphors* and *extravagant Non-sense."* In essence, he finds Blackmore *"Dulness"* personified. The only greater offenders are his "Modern Admirers" who can be relied on to judge worse than even Blackmore can write. Against infection by "the nauseous Encomiums" lavished on the City Bard, the author recommends an antidote of verses by Dryden and Garth.[87]

Dryden dead, there was a need to decide the succession of Parnassus; and little time elapsed before another physician-poet, Daniel Kenrick, published *A New Session of the Poets.* Into the mold of this popular genre[88] Kenrick tosses many of London's leading poets and poetasters. Obeying Apollo's summons are that master of "dangling Dogrel" Tom D'Urfey and the "late-bruis'd" Tom Brown as well as Congreve, Southerne, Tate, and Samuel Garth. Dennis is severely rebuked as a member of the tribe of carping critics:

> This peevish Race will take a World of Pains,
> To Shew that both the *Arthurs* had no Brains;
> And labour hard to bring Authentic Proof,
> That he that wrote Wit's Satyr was an Oaf.[89]

Lest his censure of Dennis suggest a sympathy for Blackmore's verse, Kenrick quickly brings in the author of the two *Arthurs:*

> lo! a busy Bard came pressing on,
> And cleft the Crowd, and elbow'd every one;
> And that the Judge his Name might understand,
> He brought a British Hero in each Hand,
> Who with him in a Coach, their Birth-place rode,
> And, being alighted, thus address'd the God:
> I, bright *Apollo,* come, said he, to sue
> For what the World long since allow'd my due:
> God's who no Envy have like moral Men,
> May Justice do the Labours of my Pen:
> Nor yet by Human Pow'rs have I been slighted,
> For if I am not Laureated, I'm Knighted.
> Then, putting hand beneath the Tufted Robe,
> Pull'd out a hopeful Paraphrase on *Job.*
> Enough, replied the Deity, enough:
> Long since I've seen thy sad Romantick Stuff:
> Thy Doughty *Arthurs* ev'ry where are known. . . .
> In which thy Rhymes a constant Cadence keep,
> At once they make us smile, and make us sleep:[90]
> And he that can in *Job* six Pages view,
> Ought to possess your Prophet's Patience too.

Should he award the laurel to Blackmore, Apollo further explains, Dryden would rise from his recent grave to right the act:

The injur'd Shade himself would Justice do,
And Epilogue, and Prologue thee anew:
Put up thy Pen, and Noble Verse give o'er,
Quack, and kill on, but murder me no more.[91]

A New Session of the Poets was printed for A. Baldwin in Warwick-Lane. On the first of November the same bookseller published an anonymous reply in the form of *An Epistle To Sr. Richard Blackmore, Occasion'd by The New Session of the POETS.*[92] Acknowledging that whatever merit his poem possesses is due to the influence of Blackmore's "Immortal Song," the author laments that poets have degenerated from singing the praises of God and his creation to writing lewd plays and lampoons. He praises Blackmore for dignifying the epic but also for being versatile enough to stoop to satire when necessary to chastise the wits:

You neither soar too high, nor creep too low;
'Tis natural all, and not attain'd by Force,
You guide with steddy Reins th' unruly Horse;
Whilst those who neither Rule nor Distance keep,
Like *Icarus*, descend into the Deep.
To move their Rubbish you your self demean,
Yet cannot this *Augean Stable* clean.

Dryden burns in hell, the flames fed by his own impious compositions. Like the devil, "Malicious, Envious, and Uncivil," Dryden remained contemptible to the last:

His dying *Epilogue* with Curses cramm'd,
Has both the *Arthurs*, and their Author damn'd.[93]

Garth's arrangements for Dryden's body to lie in state at the Royal College of Physicians are satirized, as is his failure to write a true heroic poem. In addition to the standard shafts against "leud" Dennis and "libelous" Tom Brown, Prior is dismissed as a sychophant and his patron Charles Montagu, Earl of Halifax, censured for financing an elaborate tomb for Dryden, "fresh Laurels" for his "Impious Head."[94] This suggests that Blackmore knew nothing of the *Epistle* before its publication, for he had praised both Prior and Montagu extravagantly in *A Satyr against Wit*[95] and neither man had joined in the *Commendatory* attack.

Assured that Sir Richard, "the beamy God of Wit," will prove superior to any stratagem hatched by the wits at Will's, the anonymous author concludes with a scatological simile that further disassociates him from Blackmore. The huntsman Dryden dead, it remains for Blackmore to

> engage his Pack of Hounds.
> So have I seen an *English* Mastiff pass
> Along the Streets with a Majestick Grace;
> The little Dogs come barking from their Cell,
> And whine and growl with a confounded Yell;
> The num'rous Crowd on the bold Mastiff stare,
> And Think each minute he the Curs will tear,
> When he who with his Jaws might have undone 'em,
> Lift up his Leg, and only piss'd upon 'em.[96]

The "num'rous Crowd" which the author of *An Epistle to Sr. Richard Blackmore* mentions must have been composed of bookbuyers. For although Blackmore took no further action against the wits after Dryden's death, the booksellers had the inhabitants of the lower slopes of Parnassas keep up the appearance of warfare long after the chiefs had quit the field. The obligatory slights continued. Sir Richard is a wretched physician[97] and a witless satirist;[98] but his greatest failure is the "rumbling verse" of his heroics,[99] the "heavy Flights of Bl[ackmore]'s humble muse."[100] Pretending to fear Blackmore's prestige as an "Idol of the Mob,"[101] writers warred courageously against his reputation. "I have writ *Prince Arthur* and *King Arthur,"* Abel Boyer has Blackmore say. "Am I not then equal to *Homer,* and superior to *Virgil?"* Utilizing Blackmore's metaphor in *A Satyr against Wit,* Boyer responds: "No, *B[lackmo]re,* we judge of *Poetry* as we do of *Metals,* not by the *Lump,* but the intrinsick Value. New cast your Poems, purge 'em of their Dross, reduce 'em to the Bulk of the *Dispensary,* and if then they weigh in the Balance with *that,* we will allow you a Place among the First-Rate *Heroick Poets."*[102] Others argued in defense of Sir Richard. The author of *The Court* maintains that only the British Pindar, Blackmore, commands the power to chronicle William's exploits;[103] and Edward Bysshe's *Art of English Poetry* abounds with more "sublime" passages from Blackmore's epics than from any authors other than Milton and Dryden—and the excerpts from Dryden are almost always from his translations rather than his original works.[104]

But it was his enemies who bawled loudest and longest. Tom Brown proved indefatigable, even in death. The most amusing of his numerous attacks on Blackmore are "A Lent-Entertainment" and an interview Brown and his Indian friend have with the City Bard in the "London" section of *Amusements Serious and Comical, Calculated for the Meridian of London.* Appended to the 1702 second edition of *Commendatory Verses,* "A Lent-Entertainment" summons the ghost of Maevius, archetype of wretched writers, to appear to Blackmore in a scene which suggests the opening of *The Dunciad.* Before the end of the poem, Blackmore's supreme dullness antagonizes even the ghost, who casts Sir Richard his withered bays with the words:

> Know, I am *Maevius,* that of old,
> In *Thoughts* sublime, and *Matter* bold,
> Did every *versifying* Ass,
> By a Bar's length at least, *surpass;*
> And only am out-done by you
> In lofty *Noise* and *Nonsense* too.[105]

In *Amusements,* Brown's friend's sudden illness precipitates a visit to Blackmore, that "Worshipful Graduate in the noble Art of Manslaughter." Sir Richard startles the Indian out of his lethargy by reciting battle scenes from his folio *Prince Arthur.*[106] Even his death in June of 1704 could not entirely undo Tom Brown. His publishers apparently continued to update his jibes at Blackmore; and subsequent editions of *Amusements* speak of the "invincible opiate" of Sir Richard's *Eliza* despite the fact that Brown had descended to his eternal reward a full year before *Eliza* appeared. Furthermore, the frontispiece of the first volume of the 1707 edition of Brown's *Works* show an ill-humored individual scrawling the words "Satyr agt Wit" on a paper before him. To the side of Blackmore is a satyr holding a portrait of the late Thomas and pointing gleefully at the physician-poet.[107]

On the eighth of August following Brown's death, a new session of the poets convened in a poem which bears, even in its title, signs of Brown's influence.[108] *The Tryal of Skill: or, A New Session of the Poets. Calculated for the Meridian of Parnassus* dismisses one aspiring poetaster after another. Appropriately, Blackmore follows Dennis:

> Sir *Richard* rejoic'd at his Critick's Rebuke,
> Stood up with the Volumes he writ,
> And desir'd of the Bench, they would please next to look
> On his *Arthurs*, and *Satyr against Wit.*
>
> But a Goddess that sat there to give him a Rub,
> Told him, he his Addresses might spare,
> And a Man that had tir'd out the *Patience of Job*
> Would Infallibly be tiresome to theirs.
>
> Yet nothing abash'd he went on with his Tale,
> And harangu'd in Defence of his Lays,
> Declaring that what went off best in the Sale,
> Best deserv'd their Opinion and Praise.

Blackmore's publishers enter and substantiate that his verses sell; but Apollo, "enrag'd with his Bombast," condemns Blackmore

> For attempting with Nonsense to Murder the Court,
> As he did his poor *Patients* with *Pills.*[109]

Even such exhausted wit assumes something like potency if repeated often enough. The repetitious din of the same outworn insults is sometimes sufficient to influence a reader's opinion, much as we buy one tub of butter rather than another while mindlessly whistling its advertising jingle. The sheer volume of the wits' ridicule must have infected Blackmore's reputation in a way that had little to do with the quality of his poetry. Although it is easy to agree with the critic who, after a careful study of Blackmore's war with Will's, determined that the wits would have been wiser to leave Sir Richard alone,[110] the fact remains that the infamy which his name enjoys in literary circles to this day had its genesis in the rare felicity of rhymes like "pills" and "kills." Believing that the "unremitted enmity" on the part of the wits was "provoked more by his virtue than his dulness," Johnson tried to rehabilitate Blackmore's memory in *The Lives of the English Poets.*[111] The rehabilitation was, of course, unsuccessful.

Contempt is contagious. By Johnson's time Blackmore had ceased to be a poet and had become the Maevius of the English Augustan age.

CHAPTER 4

The Town Poet

While I so near, so long the Hero view,
And Hints suggest to be improv'd by you,
My fading Flame does in my Veins renew,
An inward Impulse does me almost choak,
Urging your muse I do my own provoke,
Until my Fires all terminate in Smoak.

The Flight of the Pretender (1708)

I A Hymn to the Light of the World

THE call in the preface to *Job* for "some good Genius" to write a Christian epic established Blackmore among the pious as a champion of poetry. In opposition to the lewd scurrility of the theater or Covent Garden he proposed the writing of original and energetic religious verse. Advocating "a most rational and praise-worthy Enthusiasm," Blackmore recognized the creative spirituality essential to poetry of the highest caliber; and he exercised his considerable influence to encourage fellow poets to attempt those heights.[1]

Blackmore's own guiding star was Milton. The failure of the first critics to recognize Milton's unmistakable influence on *Prince Arthur* suggests that even Dennis, Milton's subsequent champion, was far less familiar with *Paradise Lost* than Blackmore. In 1702, Bysshe, discussing versification, offered juxtapositions which suggested Milton's pervasive influence. Some words, he explains, may be of either two or three syllables as in the following:

From Diamond Quarries hewn, and Rocks of Gold. Milt.

A Mount of Rocky Diamond did rise. Blac.

But if a vowel precedes a liquid, it may not be cut off. "And therefore it is a fault in some Poets to make, for Example, *Sonorous* of two Syllables, as in this Verse

> *With Son'rous Metals wak'd the drowsie Day.* Blac.

which always ought to be of three; as in this,

> *Sonorous Metals blowing Martial Sounds.* Milt."[2]

Verbal resemblances, however, are infrequent and less important in Blackmore's poetry than the influence of Milton's sublime conceptions, his ideas of heaven or hell, of chaos and creation.

It is not surprising, then, that during the Christmas season of 1702 Blackmore emulated Milton's "On The Morning of Christ's Nativity" with the publication of *A Hymn to the Light of the World. With a Short Description of the Cartons of Raphael Urbin, In the Gallery at Hampton-Court.*[3] Characterized, as is Milton's poem, as a hymn, Blackmore's poem actually abandons Milton's regular stanzaic pattern to produce an irregular ode, a form appropriate to the sublimity of the subject. Adopting Milton's image of Christ as "Light unsufferable," Blackmore echoes just enough of his mentor's diction to make his source unmistakable. Twelve folio pages into the poem, for instance, Blackmore's "Blest be the Day, be blest the happy Morn" recalls for the reader Milton's opening line: "This is the month, and this the happy morn." The resemblance established, Blackmore plays grandiose variations on Miltonic ideas. The sun which, ashamed of his "inferior flame," hides his head in Milton's seventh stanza becomes the lover of Blackmore's poem:

> In all his Glory let the Sun,
> From his Rooms of State sublime,
> As an eager Bridegroom run
> To wed this Day, the fairest Child of Time.
> Nor let the Sons of Art, in Planets wise,
> With long, far-seeing, Astrologic Eyes,
> Be able now to trace
> One Speck or Spot in all his splendid Face.
> Let no outragious Winds the Seas molest,
> Let Storms, their Fury sooth'd, in Caverns rest.

Let no black Cloud, no sullen Vapour rise,
To trouble or pollute the Skies.
Let not a Frown appear
Upon one Brow, or on one Face a Tear. (p. 13)

When he deserts Milton's influence, the verses become less adventurously harmonious but more interesting. The almost metaphysical description of circulation as essential to life reminds the reader of Blackmore's profession:

Then the warm Blood did from its Goal, the Heart,
To run its purple Ring with vigor start:
Then Infant Life began to play,
To bound and leap along th' Arterial Way;
And carry'd on the circling Tide,
Did thro' its winding Labyrinths and veiny Mazes glide. (p 5)

His metaphorical description of Man's position in the chain of being recalls Pope's more polished and predictable "Isthmus of a Middle State":

Thus half Immortal, and half Mortal, He,
To Angels and to Brutes ally'd,
A true AEquator is design'd by Thee,
In halves the whole Creation to divide. (p. 5)

Hoxie Neale Fairchild characterizes Blackmore as "flat when he is simple and ungainly when he soars."[4] *A Hymn to the Light of the World* is on tiptoes for all fifteen pages and the freedom of the ode form invites airy bombast. When compared with other religious odes of the period, however, Blackmore's nativity ode does have passages of originality, energy, and lyricism which make the reader lament that Blackmore did not uniformly employ his file.

The last third of the volume contains Blackmore's couplet descriptions of the Raphael cartoons, now in the Victoria and Albert Museum. As Physician in Ordinary Blackmore had been assigned accommodations at Hampton Court for himself and his servant for years;[5] but it was during the winter of 1701-1702 that Blackmore most frequently passed the famous pictures hanging in the King's Gallery. Despairing of his health even before his fall in February, the king demanded much of Sir Richard's time.

After William's death, Blackmore successfully petitioned for additional compensation, arguing that during the winter he had been "principally entrusted" with the king's health and "that whilst his Ma^{ty} resided at Hampton Court he constantly attended him once a Week."[6]

Blackmore saw the cartoons weekly not long after the publication of an anonymous *Advice to a Painter* revived that favorite poetic genre to accompany an engraving of the five Kentish petitioners who had angered Parliament by supporting the king's military policies; and this may have suggested Blackmore's adaptation of the genre. Generally undistinguished, the verses describing the cartoons sometimes dip to the heavy-handed alliteration of a line such as "Aloud for Alms the crawling Cripples cry'd" (p 19). Interested primarily in exhortation, Blackmore emphasizes the didactic aspect of each of Raphael's biblical history paintings.

The parallel between poetry and painting interested Blackmore and provides the title to two issues of *The Lay Monk* in January 1713. In paper 31, three members of the "lay Monastery" are, by the sight of a rainbow, led into a discussion of Newton's optics and "Nature's Skill in Painting."[7] Noting that although the resemblance of the "Sister Arts" is a commonplace, very little of a specific nature has been said of the relationship between poetry and painting, one of the "monks" asserts that "the Painter is a Poet to the Eye, and the Poet a Painter to the Ear." He sees relationships between Dutch "Grotesque" painting (i.e., Brueghel, Teniers, Hals) and "humorous Ballads, Farce and Burlesque Verse"; between landscapes and pastorals; but most conspicuously between epic or tragedy and history painting. In this regard, he praises both Raphael's "Epick Imagination" and Virgil's "masterly and admirable Painting."[8]

The discussion continues in paper 32 for Wednesday, January 27. After observing that the "masters of the Pencil" often borrow ideas and emotions from the poets, the speakers recommend the cartoons of Raphael as able not only to move the passions but also able to inspire "generous Sentiments" and convey "Moral and Divine Instructions."[9] The essay concludes with an observation that must have reflected Blackmore's feelings when, attacked so vehemently after his *Paraphrase on the Book of Job,* he imitated Milton in the ode which accompanied the descriptions of Raphael. The speaker muses that in poetry, as in painting, it is only "after the passage of time" that the true value of a work is adequately recognized. Milton, for instance, "now acknowledg'd to be the most admirable Production of *British* Genius, lay many years, to the great Dishonour of that Age, unread and little respected." Perhaps Blackmore consciously compared his own situation with Milton's when he noted that "when disinterested Posterity holds the Balance of Justice, to weigh the real Worth of a Poem, it will first refine and purify it from all the allay cast in by Malevolence and Detraction; as on the other hand it will efface all ungenuine and adventitious Beauties imparted to it by the Indulgence of Friends, or the Zeal of a designing Party."[10]

Even in the wake of *Job* not all was "Malevolence and Detraction," for to many Blackmore seemed the personification of pious inclinations in poetry, politics, and science. In 1704 he was asked to contribute to *A Collection of Divine Hymns,* a volume dedicated to Sir Richard Blackmore as "a Zealous Friend to Religion" who has "retriev'd the Honour of Poetry, and rescu'd the Muses from that vile Drudgery they've of late Years been Condemn'd to, and convinc'd all unprejudic'd Readers, that the best Poetry, and Manly Sense, are very consistent; and that Wit never appears so Illustrious, as when she borrows her Themes from Virtue and Religion."[11] In the preface to *Horae Lyricae* (1706), Isaac Watts similarly praised Blackmore for having disproved Boileau's objection to Christian poetry with his *Arthurs,* "large and labored" works which display "all the shining colors of profuse and florid diction."[12] Watts' high opinion indicates that Blackmore was revered by dissenters; and the fact that Nahum Tate calls him the "British Elijah"[13] in a periodical Queen Anne suggested for the "promoting of Religion and Virtue" shows that he stood high among members of the Established Church as well.

II "*So Vast a* Genius"

The verdict of time not yet disentangled from party perversity and the "plaudits of his own coffee-house satellites . . . sweet in his ears,"[14] Blackmore undertook to grace English letters with another heroic poem. Advertised in mid-July 1705, *Eliza: An Epic Poem* rumbled out the tale of Spain's machinations against Elizabeth and Protestantism in ten tedious books. Incensed at Elizabeth's support of the Reformed Netherlands, Satan calls his hellish counsel and is advised by the hideous goddess Bigotry to have Philip of Spain attack England thereby forcing the recall of Elizabeth's troops under the command of Sir Francis Vere in the low countries. With the support of the Pope and of malcontent Catholics and supporters of Mary Stuart in England, Philip prepares for an invasion while treacherously offering peace. Between land and sea battles, Vere tells his ally, Maurice of Nassau, the story of Elizabeth's life (Book V); Elizabeth hears a lengthy sermon on the "awful Depths of Providence Divine" at St. Paul's (Book VII); Gabriel shows her the new Jerusalem and a Pisgah-sight of the future of reformed religion which includes the exploits of John Churchill, Duke of Marlborough, and the piety of the "new Eliza," Queen Anne (Book VIII); and the mourners for Vere's fallen son Albon are treated to an almost unending disquisition on death at his funeral (Book IX). A plot to poison Vere foiled, the epic ends with Vere victorious over all Catholic opposition.

Again Blackmore's allegory is transparent. The "Great Campaign" (p 304) he sings is Churchill's war on the Continent. Many of the military metaphors doubtless derive from the battlefield engravings which sold so furiously following Blenheim. Satan hastens to hell

> As when, a Town beseig'd, a flaming Bomb
> Discharg'd from some capacious Mortar's Womb,
> On its destructive Message swiftly flies,
> Inflames the Air, and terrifies the Skies. (p 9)

Predictably, Blackmore's friends are praised, Congreve and Prior for their "distinguish'd Wit" (p. 183), the physician Edward Tyson for his work with the mentally ill (p. 202). As citizen of London, Blackmore's rhetoric swells with pride at the sight of the "num'rous Ships" crowding the city with commerce:

> the *Boyant* Groves at Anchor ride.
> Where *British* oaks, and high *Norwegian* Pines
> Reer'd their contiguous Heads in thicker Lines,
> Than when before they on the Mountains stood,
> And throng'd each other in the shady Wood. (p. 59)

Likewise, meditation on providence or death never failed to stimulate Blackmore to song, an obvious didacticism which most theorists of epic condemned. In *Eliza,* however, Blackmore's sound is most originally adjusted to his sense when he assumes the pulpit:

Thou dost, O Death! a peaceful Harbour lie
Upon the Margin of Eternity;
Where the rough Waves of Time's impetuous Tide
Their Motion loose, and quietly subside. (p. 247)

Although Johnson was not strictly correct in saying that this product of Blackmore's "teeming" brain dropped dead-born from the press,[15] *Eliza* attracted contemporary comment not so much as an heroic poem but as an attack on Sir Richard's professional enemy, the celebrated and eccentric Dr. John Radcliffe. Noted for his erratic behavior, his Roman Catholic sympathies, and his overweening pride, Radcliffe was immediately identified as the Portuguese physician Lopez who contracts to poison Eliza in Blackmore's poem:

A Man of unrecorded Insolence,
Ill-manner'd, loose, and noisy without Sense.
Defaming all, in his own Praises loud,
Vain without Skill, and without Merit proud.
He with Contempt the greatest Subject us'd,
And mad with Pride, e'en Kings and Queens abus'd.
(pp 259-60)

Eager to be appointed chief physician to the Queen, Lopez importunes Vere for patronage but is refused. Bitter, Lopez resolves to murder Vere. His own intemperate tongue gives him away, however; and he leaves the poem in a state of lunacy.

There was enough truth in the characterization of Lopez to make it humiliating for Radcliffe. He had been chief physician to Anne when she was Princess but offended her irreparably in 1694 by refusing to attend her one evening while he was drinking, brutally dismissing her complaints as nothing more than a fit of vapors.[16] When Anne became queen, Radcliffe lobbied assiduously to be appointed to his old position, even attempting to engage the Duchess of Marlborough in his support. By that time, however, Anne had a stronger reason for disliking Radcliffe. One of Elizabeth's visions of the future in *Eliza* is the death of Anne's son "in a burning Fever" for which "Some the

Disease, Physicians some accuse" (p. 222). Radcliffe, summoned by Anne only after repeated urging by Sarah, Duchess of Marlborough, blamed the doctors. The young duke of Gloucester had been unskillfully treated for smallpox when he only suffered from a rash, Radcliffe pronounced upon arriving, and would consequently die the following day regardless of what anyone did. Radcliffe's gruffness and his insolent criticism of his fellow physicians antagonized Anne, already distraught by her son's condition. In 1703 Radcliffe alienated the Duchess of Marlborough by refusing to visit her only son when he fell ill with smallpox at Cambridge. The queen sent her own physicians to attend the ailing Marquis of Blandford; but Sarah, believing in Radcliffe's ability, hurried to London to persuade him in person. Radcliffe refused, explaining, "Madam, I should only put you to a great Expence to no Purpose, for you have nothing to do for his Lordship now, but to send down an Undertaker, to take care of his Funeral; for I can assure your Grace, he is dead by this time, of a Distemper call'd *The Doctor.*"[17]

Radcliffe's biographer, William Pittis, intends *"The Doctor"* to point clearly to Blackmore, who was attending the Duchess of Marlborough and her family about this time.[18] Pittis also indicts Blackmore as one of the physicians who prescribed the Duke of Gloucester to death.[19] This, however, is only another round in Pittis's continuing retaliation against Sir Richard for the Lopez portrait in *Eliza.* Abundant contemporary evidence proves that Blackmore was not among the doctors Anne consulted during her son's illness.[20] Almost certainly subsidized by Radcliffe's famous generosity, Pittis began his war against Blackmore two weeks after the appearance of *Eliza* in the shortlived periodical the *Whipping Post.* The July 31, eighth issue drags the malefactor Blackmore before the bar for writing his latest epic or, as the bench characterizes *Eliza,* his "Apozem rather; the Doctor design'd it for a Sleepy Potion for such as cannot take Physick."[21] In the ninth issue Blackmore is "Censur'd by way of Reprimand for calling a Collection of Couplets tag'd with Rhimes an *Epick Poem,* that was full of nothing but Tautologys and Repetitions, that was neither Methodical nor Concise, but had Periods and Smiles long enough to Tyre the very Lungs of a Pedant, and Kill an Audience at an *Evenings Lecture;* that had nothing in it Beautiful but what was stoln, and nothing deform'd, and *Mal'apropos* but was his own."[22]

Pittis denounces the "Barbarous Description of *Lopez*" in the ninth issue. Within a month after the publication of *Eliza* three proposed rebuttals to Blackmore's attack on Radcliffe were advertised in Defoe's *Review*, none of which ever appeared.[23] Anne subsequently made Sir Richard one of her Physicians in Ordinary; and her continued enmity to Radcliffe became the nation's when Anne died. Summoned to the queen's deathbed, Radcliffe, suffering from gout himself, refused to attend her. After Anne's death, he was denounced for his unpatriotic conduct and threats were made on his life.[24] Radcliffe followed the queen a few months later, leaving Blackmore in possession of the field. Ironically, however, with Anne's death and George's accession Garth replaced Blackmore as court physician.

III Advice to the Poets

Eliza rode (or floundered on) the crest of British jubilation over Marlborough's victory at Blenheim the previous August, the first serious defeat the French had suffered in battle since Louis XIV came to the throne and the first resounding success for an English general since the Middle Ages.[25] Although there was dissension among the Tories, Marlborough's own party, the Whigs indulged their genuine enthusiasm without regard for party allegiance. At Godolphin's instigation, the Whig Addison published his popular *Campaign* at roughly the same time *Eliza* appeared. The High Church Tories retaliated immediately with John Philips's ineffectual *Blenheim* but could do nothing to discourage Churchill's increasing prestige.

The war droned on without excitement until late May 1706, when, at Ramillies, a few miles from Namur, Marlborough decisively defeated the French and the Bavarians, entered and seized Brussels, and accepted the surrender of the great fortress of Antwerp. The railings around St. Paul's hung heavy with the tributes of English pens. One anonymous writer, however, noticed that the author of *Eliza* had not celebrated the victory and in *An Epistle to Sir Richard Blackmore* urged him to do so. Seeing the offerings of so many other poets, the author asks:

> Oh *Blackmore!* Why do'st *thou alone* refuse
> To grace *Ramillia* with thy noble Muse . . .? (p. 1)

Blackmore need not continue to grieve for William since he "will *ever* in thy *Arthur* live," graced with laurels which like Blackmore's own "will never fade." Yet *Eliza* proves that

> So vast a *Genius* and so large a Mind
> Can never to *One Heroe* be confin'd. (p. 2)

Though poets as skillful as Prior or as poor as Defoe, who

> Execrably bad,
> Throws out a Hasty *Poem,* wrote like Mad (p. 3),

laud Marlborough's victory, the nation still wants the sublime strains, the "true *Specimen* of Wit," of which only Blackmore is capable.[26]

Two months to the day after the battle of Ramillies and less than a week after the anonymous *Epistle,* Blackmore's response appeared as *Advice to the Poets.*[27] Twice the length of Addison's *Campaign,* Blackmore's poem imitates Addison's just enough to seem complimentary, as when Addison's characterization of the enemy troops, "The dread of *Europe,* and the pride of *France*" (1. 294), alters slightly to "The Plague of *Europe,* and the Pride of *France*" (p. 8). The "advice" promised in the title is Blackmore's suggestion that all the best English poets pool their individual excellencies to write an epic adequate to the majesty of Anne and the valor of her warrior general.[28] This ingenious hyperbole allows Blackmore to compliment poets like Prior, Congreve, Granville, Walsh, and John Hughes while hymning the virtues of his hero and heroine. Dismissing his own *Eliza* as "unfinish'd," "crude," and useless as a model (p. 12), he recommends to the assembled poets study of the ancients and use of a Christian hero who unites the virtues of Aeneas and Achilles and is consequently fit to give "an allegoric View" of Marlborough. Remembering his journey through France, Blackmore suggests an episode in which a foreigner in Paris meditates disdainfully on the decay of Louis's greatness (pp. 14-22).

In singing the "One Month so full of Miracles," Blackmore is no worse than Addison. But, his advice ended, Blackmore literally is lifted by airy bombast out of sight:

'Tis done. I've compass'd my ambitious Aim,
The Hero's Fire restores the Poet's Flame.
The Inspiration comes, my Bosom glows,
I strive with strong Enthusiastic Throws.
Oh! I am all in Rapture, all on Fire,
Give me, to ease the Muse's Pangs, the Lyre. (p. 26)

Transported through the "beauteous Order" of the heavenly spheres, Blackmore hears loud acclamations of applause as seraphs sublimely hymn Churchill's Christian triumph.

Although predominately panegyric, *Advice to the Poets* does attack John Philips, who had merited Blackmore's dislike by his opposition to Addison and his profanation of Milton in the wonderfully clever "Splendid Shilling." With *Blenheim* clearly in mind, Blackmore castigates Philips as a "vain Pretender to the Song sublime":

All who can raise a Shed, must not presume
To frame a Palace, or erect a Dome.
No more let *Milton's* Imitator dare
Torture our Language, to torment our Ear
With Numbers harsher than the Din of War.[29]

Despite its length, Blackmore's poem was popular; and a second edition was quickly called for. A Tory defense of Philips appeared at once under the title *A Panegyric Epistle* dedicated "To S. R— B— on his most Incomparable Incomprehensible Poem, Called *Advice to the Poets.*" The song Blackmore heard in his superterrestrial rounds is ludicrously quoted out of context as "a Taste of Angels Verse." All the battalions of superannuated insults are drawn out to support the rejection of "our heav'nly Bard" while "Great Milton's Imitator" is lauded as the equal of his master.[30] Philips' defense continued even after his death with attacks on Blackmore's "quintessential Dullness" by Leonard Welsted[31] and Edmund Smith.[32]

An anonymous author whose weary muse chugs out such exclamations as "O glorious clank of Arms" attacked both Blackmore and Philips in another panegyric on the Great Campaign, *The British Warriour.*[33] Blackmore's ecstatic ascent to heaven in *Advice to the Poets* is ridiculed as "lampooning the Stars" and his praise of Churchill disparaged as "a swoln and windy Timpany of Words" which sinks the hero "beneath the

Lays of Chivy-Chase."[34] Damning the "labour'd Volum" of Blackmore's "sturdy Verse," the author wishes: "Oh that his Muse was delicate as loud!" (p. 4).

Much more successful is the ridicule of *The Flight of the Pretender, With Advice to the Poets,* a burlesque described on the title page as in the "Arthurical,-Jobical, -Elizabethecal Style and Phrase of the sublime POET MAURUS."[35] Issued by Henry Hills, the same unscrupulous publisher who pirated two of Blackmore's later poems, *The Flight of the Pretender* borrows lines from *Advice to the Poets* to fashion a mock-heroic account of the Old Pretender's unpropitious attempt to land an army in Scotland. The style of the "Voluminous" Blackmore has been chosen to compliment the dignity of the subject, the preface informs the reader: "no Persons Enthusiastick Genious and blustring Expressions coming up to such a high Undertaking, except those of *Maurus,* it was thought fit to make use of his noble Flights and Expressions to describe the egregious Flight of this Pretender." Blackmore, of course, is treated as the chief illegitimate Pretender in poetry.

Page numbers in the margin refer the reader to the relevant passages of Blackmore's poem, and except when the author deviates to ridicule the real Pretender, the parody is very close. Where Blackmore advises the poets to

> Let *Mantuan* Judgment, and *Horatian* Words,
> And all the noble Fire which *Greece* affords,
> With all the Beauties which in *Spencer* shine,
> To form their Diction's Dignity, combine:
> Let all the Charms of Sound, and Strength of Sense,
> Let all the Pride and Force of Eloquence . . . (p. 15),

the author of *The Flight of the Pretender* modifies the passage to describe more adequately Blackmore's own style:

> Let my own Judgment and *Tom. Durfey's* Words
> And all the Fire which *Grubbias Street* affords,
> With all the Beauties which in *Flecknoe* shine,
> To form their Diction's Dignity, combine:
> Let sound that seldom pleasing is with Sense,
> Let all the Emptiness of Eloquence. . . . (p. 4)

When Blackmore asks what glories England may expect in the

Autumn from such "a luxuriant Harvest of Renown" (p. 25) in the spring, his metaphor is made ludicrously literal in the parody:

For if the *Spring* such *Pease* and *Cherries* gave,
What *Pipins* may we in the *Autumn* have. (p. 6)

When, contemplating Marlborough's exploits, Blackmore in *Advice to the Poets* becomes infused with "a Portion of the noble Fire," *The Flight of the Pretender* has all his fire "terminate in Smoak." The cleverest variations occur when Blackmore is wafted to heaven, in an already much-abused "sublime" scene. It is Blackmore's scientific preoccupation which betrays him, as

Thro' the steep Gulph I to the Stars ascend.
Stars, which I now behold vast Orbs of Light,
Only by Distance little to the Sight.
All Suns of equal Bulk, and equal Flame
With that, which rules the World from whence I came. (p. 27)

becomes

Diving in Gulphs, I to the Stars ascend.
I'm now pursuing Stars, and having caught 'em.
Find them to be much bigger than I thought 'em. (p. 7)

The Flight of the Pretender was published in 1708, a great year for Marlborough on the Continent. With the victory of Oudenarde and the capture of Lille, Ghent and Bruges capitulated, leaving the road to Paris open. Only the "crystal chains" of winter stalled the march into France. Undeterred by the ridicule of anonymous hacks, Blackmore celebrated the good news in "A Sequel to the Advice to the Poets" entitled *Instructions to Vander Bank*, a famous Belgian tapestry weaver.[36] Somewhat more restrained than *Advice to the Poets*, the poem is essentially its earlier cousin rejuvenated with the names of Marlborough's most recent conquests. Twice pirated by Henry Hills, Blackmore's poem should not be dismissed as popular only because of the contemporary adulation of Marlborough, since it was included in 1717 in *A Collection of the Best English Poetry*. Unfortunately, however, the taste which relished such verbal history painting seldom survives today and was shifting even in Blackmore's day. *Instructions to Vander Bank* was advertised in the *Daily Courant* for March 14. On April 14, in *Tatler* No. 3, Steele dealt facetiously with Blackmore's offerings to the outmoded genre, probably thereby hastening the decline of "advice" poetry. Steele apologized for his jest in a subsequent number of the *Tatler*.[37]

IV The Kit-Cats

Although not adverse to good-humored raillery, Steele and his friend Addison almost always spoke respectfully of Sir Richard in print. Steele had contributed to *Commendatory Verses* in response to Blackmore's plea in *A Satyr against Wit* that God guard poor Addison from infection at Will's. But that momentary antagonism was unnatural to men who so stoutly ascribed to moral theater, Whig politics, and the ideal of the Christian hero. What part Blackmore played in the early years of the Whig Kit-Cat Club, which both Steele and Addison frequented, is obscure; but clearly his best poem of this otherwise lean period, *The Kit-Cats,* is an attempt to reconcile temporary differences within the group which Horace Walpole described as "the patriots that saved Britain."

Always uneasy beneath his crown, the publisher Jacob Tonson[38] was apparently expelled from his own club on January 4, 1704. The event attracted enough notoriety to send hawkers scurrying into the streets with broadsheet advertisements for a poem to "be speedily publish'd" on the subject of *Jacob's Revenge.*[39] The poem never appeared; but *The Kit-Cats,* not published until four years later, was Blackmore's privately circulated attempt to laugh the factions of the club back together again. Probably Sir Richard was formally a member of the club at this time, before he became Physician in Ordinary to Anne. In any event, it was Tonson who had published Blackmore's nativity ode the previous year.

Building on the mock-heroic achievement of "Mac Flecknoe" and *The Dispensary,*[40] *The Kit-Cats* tells of the growing renown of the club under Tonson's leadership and the attempt of those opposed to the rule of "Wit and Sense" to have their patron Dulness destroy Tonson's influence. The poem is consistently humorous, as when the tavern where the Kit-Cats congregate is described.

Here Politicians us'd to recreate
Their Lungs exhausted with their long Debate,
In setling, or perplexing Points of State.
In Pleasure here they pass the wearing Night,
And the hard Labours of the Day recite . . .
What wretched Speeches t'other Party made,
How weak, and how insipid things were said
By all their leading Men, but by their own
What Miracles of Eloquence were shown,
What Flames of Fire, what Thunder-bolts were thrown![41]

Blackmore is at his best, however, when, remembering Spenser's House of Morpheus, he describes the lake which surrounds the abode of Dulness:

A lazy Lake, as *Lethe,* black and deep,
Secure from Storms, extended lies asleep.
Young vig'rous Winds, which heavy Tempests bear,
With fruitless Toil shove at this stagnant Air;
Their Breath all spent, they from their Labour cease,
And leave th' unweildy Fogs to rest in Peace.
The Beasts that come for Water, at the Brink,
Benumn'd stand nodding, and forget to drink;
The Birds by luckless Fortune hither brought,
Fall down and sleeping on the Waters float. (p. 10)

The Temple of Dulness itself is made of mud with niches housing the animals sacred to the God, owls and asses.[42] Leaden Dulness yawns beneath a wreath of poppies as

Sleek pamper'd Priests beneath the Altar snore,
And stretcht at Ease their stupid God adore. (p. 11)

Everything is contrived to "Blunt the sharp Edge of Thought, and kindly cloud the Brain." The emissaries dispatched to importune Dulness bear "pond'rous Loads" of books as offerings to the sleepy god. Blackmore glances at an old, pathetic enemy:

The Scribling Rakes sent the poor Devil *Brown,*
Who doom'd to starve, yet fated to believe
He shall in Eating Circumstances live,
Does with a Stomack empty, as his Head,
Write in a Garret to the Shops for Bread.[43]

The petition interrupted by the emissaries' irresistible sleepiness, the poem concludes with Dulness's prophecy of the coming "great Event," the eventual overthrown of Tonson, the Kit-Cats, and all wit and learning in the English isle.

Blackmore's poem suggests that he was part of Addison's Whig circle during the great years of Marlborough's campaign. It also proves Blackmore's ability to write excellent humorous verse. But, more importantly, *The Kit-Cats* proved to be the cause of genuine greatness in another. For it is impossible to believe that Pope's *Dunciad* or his Cave of Spleen in *The Rape of the Lock* would have been as they are without the earlier effort of his prime dunce, Sir Richard Blackmore.[44] Despite its delayed publication, the poem must have been popular, for the industrious Henry Hills pirated two editions of the poem, the original publisher of which had been none other than the abominable Edmund Curll, as yet a mere novice in such nefarious arts.

CHAPTER 5

Science Rendered Sublime

Natura Codex est Dei.
St. Bernard

The works of Nature everywhere sufficiently evidence a Deity.
John Locke

I The Nature of Man

DESPITE the distrust of "all Hypotheses" which Blackmore shared with Newton and Locke, Molyneux's judgment that he was pehaps uniquely capable of writing "a natural history of the great and admirable phenomena of the universe"[1] lingered with Blackmore until he finally published his first original philosophic poem, *The Nature of Man,* in April 1711.

His travels abroad and the diversity of men that war or trade drew to the great port of London as well as his inevitable interest as a physician stimulated Blackmore to study the effects of climate on personality and intelligence. The hypothesis of climatic influence is as old as Aristotle and had enjoyed rejuvenated interest in the many seventeenth-century British editions of Giovanni Botero's *Relations of the Most Famous Kingdomes and Commonwealths thorowout the World.*[2] Blackmore's interest in the inequalities of nature which influenced man probably received early impetus from William's Chaplain-in-Ordinary, Thomas Burnet, whose *Sacred Theory of the Earth* attributed the chaotic state of the world since the fall to man's sin. Prior's *Solomon* examined these same inequalities from the torrid to the frozen zones; and although *Solomon* was not published until 1718, it was completed by 1708 and Blackmore, as an ardent admirer of Prior's, probably examined the poem in manuscript. Additionally, Blackmore's friend Dr.

Edward Tyson had written provocatively of the relation between man and the Orang-outang in the chain of being,[3] a topic Blackmore comments on in *The Lay-Monk*.

In the first of the three Books of *The Nature of Man* Blackmore finds the "Disparity of the intellectual Faculties, Dispositions, and Passions of Men" due to their situation relative to the sun, a temperate clime being more advantageous even to "moral Improvements" than such areas of extreme cold or heat as the tropics:

Where Sun-burnt Nations of a Swarthy Skin
Are sully'd o'er with blacker Clouds within.
Their Spirits suffer by too hot a Ray,
And their dry Brain grows dark with too much Day.[4]

The Hottentot, for example, is so "void of Sense"

That 'tis disputed, if his doubtful Soul
Augment the Humane or the Brutal Roll. (p. 7)

Blackmore anticipates *Spectator* No. 389 in dismissing the atheistic argument that such unschooled human nature has no notion of God:

Know, hardy Atheists, who insulting say—
Some populous Realms to Gods no Homage pay;
And therefore Nature's universal Law
Imprints not on the Mind Religion's Awe;
That those, who no superior Being own,
Are more from Beasts by shape, than Reason known. (p. 31)

Books two and three turn from religious to political argument as the distinctive characteristics of the European countries are described and the causes of a "great and worthy Race of Men" are enumerated. Blackmore sees an unmistakable relationship between English liberty and the prosperity which allows the British to "wear India's Gems, and drink Burgandia's Wine." Constitutional monarchy provides the government most congenial to liberty, poetry, and prosperity; and although, like organisms, all states eventually die, good government retards the inevitable. *The Nature of Man* concludes patriotically with a panegyric on the true religion and vibrant culture sustained in England though the rule of "fair Liberty."

II *Physicotheology*

Nothing in the mundane *Nature of Man* prepares a reader for Blackmore's greatest and most popular poem published ten months later as *Creation. A Philosophical Poem. In Seven Books.* Most knowledgeable critics have concurred with Johnson that "whoever judges of [*Creation*] by any other of Blackmore's performances will do it injury."[5] Southey thought its diction and numbers so superior to Blackmore's epics that *Creation* seemed "the work of another mind."[6] "Far superior to his epics,"[7] *Creation* is "from any viewpoint, indeed, his most ambitious and most successful work."[8] Modern critics, conditioned to expect something dismal from Blackmore, have "unjustly dismissed . . . the encyclopedia of physico-theology."[9] Initiating the period of greatest influence of physicotheological ideas in English poetry, *Creation* is the best example of early eighteenth-century praise of God's handiwork.[10] Beyond its artistic success, Blackmore's poem provides a "perfect mine of historically significant ideas"[11] which makes it one of the most "important philosophical poems of the century."[12]

Physicotheology is the use of the scientific examination of nature to establish and raise admiration for the existence and providence of God. Far from feeling any "discord between the aesthetic intuitions of mankind and the mechanism of science,"[13] the English Augustan poets embraced the subtleties of "Natural Knowledge" as the best evidence of the supernatural and the most formidable answer to the atomism of Epicurus and the mechanism of Hobbes.[14] Most men regarded Descartes, Spinoza, Gassendi, and Hobbes as latter-day disciples of Epicurus. Thus if Epicurus were answered effectively, the systems of the modern "atheists" would crumble, being built on the same hypothesis of the chance concatenation of atoms.

The chief spokesman for Epicurean thought was, of course, Lucretius, one of the "best philosophers and the supreme poets of Rome" according to Sir William Temple. This "profound oracle of wit and sense," according to the libertine Bruce in the opening scene of Thomas Shadwell's *The Virtuoso*, "reconcil'st philosophy with verse and dost almost alone demonstrate that poetry and good sense may go together."[15] Popular with non-Latinists in the frequently reprinted verse translation by Thomas Creech[16] or the powerful passages done into English by Dryden,

De Rerum Natura was recommended as second only to the *Aeneid* in Joseph Trapp's scholarly *Praelectiones Poeticae* (1711) and Thomas Tickell's *De poesi didactica* (1711). Only the most discriminating literary men—Dryden, Blackmore, Prior, and Swift—distinguished between Lucretius's poem as a great work of art on the one hand and a doubtful piece of philosophy on the other.[17] For the majority the polish of Lucretius's verses served to make the poison more palatable and, therefore, all the more dangerous to their souls' health.

In consequence, clergymen and poets alike turned to the great advances of seventeenth-century science to refute the "absurd Mechanism" of the Epicurean School.[18] In *The Usefulnesse of Experimental Natural Philosophy* (1663), Robert Boyle praises science as an incentive to devotion since experimentation and observation "especially with the aid of such instruments as the telescope and microscope, reveal the power, wisdom, and goodness of God as seen in his marvellously contrived creations." How "rapt into an Extasie of Astonishment and Admiration" had Pliny been had he viewed a common drop of water through one of our microscopes, John Ray speculated in *The Wisdom of God Manifested in the Works of Creation* (1691). Is not the study of nature the true "preparative to Divinity?" he urged in assailing the Lucretian doctrine of creation by chance. Following the lead of Henry More, Ralph Cudworth, George Wilkins, Edward Stillingfleet, Thomas Sprat, Joseph Glanvill, Walter Charleton, as well as Boyle, Samuel Parker similarly illustrates the wisdom of God from the natural world in his polemic against Epicurus, *A Demonstration of the Divine Authority of the Law of Nature* (1681).

One beauty of Christianity, as Locke suggests in *The Reasonableness of Christianity* (1695), is its conformity to reason, the laws of nature reflecting as they do the mind of God. "God both endowed mankind," Bentley argues in his third Boyle Lecture, *A Confutation of Atheism from the Structure and Origin of Human Bodies,* "with power and abilities, which we call natural light, and reason, and common sense; by the due use of which we cannot miss of the discovery of his being."[19] "Natural Revelation" proceeds inevitably from the mind's attention to natural phenomena. All the arguments for the existence of God, Bentley says in his sixth lecture, derive from one of three sources: the study of "organical bodies of the various animals and the immaterial souls of men"; the observation of inanimate nature and the cosmos; or human testimony of divine communication or intervention in human affairs. Because the atheist dismisses the last as unreliable, Bentley confutes his enemies with modern discoveries in psychology, physiology, physics, and astronomy, a methodology which elicited Newton's praise.[20] Similarly, William Molyneux, who, through Locke, encouraged Blackmore's epic on these "admirable phenomena," thinks that "one argument drawn from the Order, Beauty, and Design of Things is more forcible against Atheism" than any number of "metaphysical" proofs, especially if buttressed by the discoveries of the new science. The telescope and microscope are particularly fertile, Molyneux suggests, in evincing "the *Power* and *Wisdom* of an *Almighty Creator*" and indispensable in "admiring the vast Extent, Order and Beauty of the Creation."[21]

Bentley's intelligent religious use of Newton's laws of gravitation and motion and the scientist Molyneux's solicitude for an aesthetic appreciation of nature are evidences of the enthusiastic interrelationship between science and the liberal arts which the rapid development and specialization of the various branches of science made increasingly more difficult after Blackmore's death.[22] The physicotheological handbooks, such as Ray's *Wisdom of God,* digest contemporary science and theology in a manner sufficiently simplified to be readily comprehended by laymen who possessed no specialized knowledge. Such popular compendiums intentionally resemble those Biblical passages, especially in Job and the Psalms, which celebrate the wonders of nature. The physicotheologists drew upon metaphors and illustrations from science to continue this ancient celebration of God's glory. Blackmore's *Paraphrase* is the obverse, the utilization of the new science in a Biblical context. Inspired by Blackmore's blemished work, Edward Young goes further and actually appends scientific notes to his *Paraphrase on Part of the Book of Job* (1719).

With contemporary theology, the physicotheologists reject the debilitating theories of the decay and the imperfection of nature. Instead the emphasis falls on the spiritual and scientific progress possible through empirical observations. The Fall no longer haunts John Ray as it had Thomas Burnet. Nature is no longer regarded as the reflection of man's sin but as the "finished and unimprovable product of divine wisdom, omnipotence, and benevolence."[23] To Ray the body is no penitential prison house but the most "curious," subtle, and admirable "Machine" produced by the divine artificer.[24]

This optimistic attitude is even more pervasive in John Edwards' 418-page *Demonstration of the Existence and Providence of God, From The Contemplation of the Visible Structure of the Greater and Lesser World. In Two Parts. The First, Showing the Excellent Contrivance of the Heavens, Earth, Sea, etc. The Second, the Wonderful Formation of the Body of Man.*[25] Adopting Bentley's division to refute Descartes "Mechanick Principles" and the "Modishness of the Copernican Notion,"[26] Edwards follows the argument from design which he finds in Job and the "hymns of David." Contrary to what the "Theorist" Burnet suggests, "the Shape of the Earth at this day is not irregular and deformed" but bespeaks an omnipotent architect. In the first Book, Edwards finds the rainbow and the flea equally "the Workmanship of Divinity."[27] In examining the most "excellent and perfect" body of man, he praises "the excellent Fabrick of the Ear" and the "Divine Artistry" of the stomach and the lower intestines; he makes apologies for the unjust accusations of impiety frequently lodged against physicians; and he concludes the whole with the reflection that "an *Anatomy Lecture* is a Preparative to one of *Divinity:* And whilest [man] views and considers the Exactness of the *Humane Fabrick,* he is thence effectually provok'd to acknowledge, revere, and worship the *Divine Architect.*"[28]

The most popular handbook of this type was written by the otherwise undistinguished vicar of Upminster, William Derham, a virtuoso collector of birds and insects, a student of astronomy as well as of the habits of wasps, a cleric interested in meteorology, bird-migration, "mechanics," and the deathwatch beetle.[29] A fellow of the Royal Society for the Improving of Natural Knowledge, Derham was invited to deliver the Boyle Lectures in 1711 and 1712. His lectures proved so popular that they were issued in 1713 as *Physico-Theology, or a Demonstration of the Being and Attributes of God from his Works of Creation.* Exciting adoration of God through admiration of his supreme artistry, Derham argues that the world is "a Work too grand for any thing less than a God to make." "Let us cast our Eyes here and there," he urges, "let us ransack all the Globe, let us with the greatest accuracy inspect every Part thereof, search out the inmost Secrets of any of the Creatures; let us examine them with all our Gauges, measure them with our nicest Rules, pry into them with our Microscopes, and most exquisite Instruments, still we find them to bear Testimony to their infinite Workman."[30] In 1715, Derham's "survey of the Terraqueous globe" was supplemented by an examination of the heavens in *Astro-theology;* and he intended to write still another volume filled with similar scientific data on the sea which his dedicated service to his parishioners in both his capacities as physician and priest prevented.

Perhaps, even lacking an *Aqua-Theology,* a broad outline of the primary religious arguments marshaled by the advocates of the new science are sufficiently clear: (1) "vast immensity." The telescope has opened up avenues to the heavens which, as Newton's laws demonstrate, are orderly and harmonious despite their awesome grandeur. The sublimity of a plurality of worlds suggests the magnificence as well as the omnipotence of God's wisdom; (2) "the peopled grass." The minute world opened by the microscope testifies to the abundance of God's creation. Loving a "plentitude" of life forms, He has housed "green myriads" in a drop of ditch water. This boundless fertility, these "numberless kinds of living creatures" as Addison says in *Spectator* No. 519, almost stupefy the mind when one considers that the entire universe nurtures such a rich complexity of life forms; (3) how "curiously" wrought. The microscope further demonstrates the incredible delicacy of God's creation, a complexity of "parts" as far beyond the imagination as the ability of any mortal craftsman. The human body, particularly, bespeaks an artisan able to activate "secret springs" of sensation and reflection inconceivable to the mind of man.

The realization of the immensity, the fecundity, and the complexity of nature impressed the early eighteenth century, as it had Job, with the vanity of deifying human reason, since man's humble portion of light so clearly paled in the presence of an infinity of suns. Further, to adapt Newton's characterization, the humility which science made appropriate to men playing with pebbles on the shore of an undiscovered, vast, and sounding sea, made any questioning of God's providence dwindle to impertinence. At the same time, science offered the adventure of unraveling the mysteries of nature, a study which inevitably led either to awe or to verification of God's wisdom or both. The creation was truly the dial plate of the divine mind, empirical evidence of His wisdom and will. Thus divinity and science were "preparative" to one another. Their marriage occurred in the various volumes of physicotheology, the progeny of which were the multitude of poems which worked through nature up to nature's God.

III *"Sings the Sacred Source, Whence All Things Came"*

Although John Reynolds's *Death's Vision, represented in a Philosophical Sacred Poem* (1709) has been described as the first scientific poem of the century,[31] Reynolds himself defers in his preface to Blackmore as well as to Lucretius, Cowley, and More. Certainly poems dealing with the Mosaic hexaemeral tradition were common in English verse. Sylvester's popular translation of Du Bartas's *Holy Days and Weeks,* hostile to Lucretius, was especially popular in the seventeenth century. *Paradise Lost* is the most famous of the hexaemeral poems but less ambitious efforts such as Traherne's *Meditations on the Six Days of the Creation* (published 1717) testify to the vigor of the genre.

As early as 1695, in *Prince Arthur,* Blackmore had utilized modern science to raise admiration in his narrative of the creation; and this was something comparatively new. But it was not until 1712 with *Creation* that the first comprehensive scientific celebration of nature appeared.[32] Perhaps prompted to timely publication by the success of Derham's Boyle Lectures, *Creation* owes its genesis, as Majorie Hope Nicolson suggests,[33] to Blackmore's desire to oppose the growing power of "atomism"; and it appropriately became the inspiration and model for many subsequent poems attacking the influence of Epicurus, Gassendi, and Hobbes.

As his preface indicates, Blackmore wishes to cast the arguments for God's existence and providence into as attractive a form as Lucretius had Epicurean atomism. He quite consciously thinks of himself as a Christian Lucretius, codifying the gains of physicotheology for his own age. And it is to make this contrast more forceful that Blackmore frequently appropriates and modifies to his purpose "the design, the method, and the poetic details of Lucretius."[34]

Invoking St. Paul's tendency to "deduce the cause from the effect, and from the creation infer the Creator," Blackmore concurs with Locke in banishing those "metaphorical terms, altogether unbecoming philosophical and judicious inquiries" which argue for an innate idea of God. Although the mind is "endued" with the power to perceive God's existence from the evidence of an external world, Blackmore finds it "too difficult" to comprehend "how ideas can exist in the mind without and before perception."[35] Consequently, *Creation* presents only "a religion of natural reason"[36] with which deists would find little to quarrel. Blackmore makes clear in the preface, however, that deists who maintain that God "showed no wisdom, design, or prudence, in the formation, and no care or providence, in the government of the world" are atheists despite their lip service to a divine being. "Such notions of a Deity," he insists, "lay the axe to the root of all religion." As in his *Paraphrase of Job,* the question of providence seems almost the only important concern. In Latitudinarian fashion, Blackmore decries the religious disquiet generated by mere "erroneous opinions" over dogma and ardently defends unorthodox philosophers whose doctrines "the common people are not able to examine or comprehend" (pp. 326–27). Atheism, he maintains, derives from a lethargy of thought rather than from too much knowledge; and philosophy, like science, is a true handmaiden of religion.

The most "inveterate enemy of religion" is the implacable Epicurus, propagated in the present age by Gassendi, Hobbes, and Spinoza. Surprisingly, Blackmore also accuses Aristotle of "atheism," arguing that Aristotle's contention that the "progression and duration" of the world is independent of the gods amounts to a denial of providence (p. 328). He judges the spread of irreligion in England as due to the "loose" Restoration manners engendered in reaction to "the former fanatical strictness" of Cromwell's reign. The aristocratic morality of honor popular in the Restoration Blackmore finds "an idle chimera" when abstracted from religion. Anticipating some ridicule for his efforts, he returns momentarily to the subject of *A Satyr against Wit.* "Wit and pleasantry" are charming qualifications unless misapplied; and he asks the reader to distinguish carefully "between raillery and argument" (pp. 329–31).

Blackmore apologizes for a poem that might otherwise seem "impertinent and unnecessary" by pointing out that while the existence and providence of God have been "abundantly demonstrated" by previous authors they wrote, often in Latin, for a "learned" audience and their prose, consequently, seems too frequently "obscure, dry, and disagreeable." Blackmore justifies his choice of verse as more engaging and easier to retain, arguing that "the Epicurean philosophy had not lived so long, nor been so much esteemed, had it not been kept alive and propagated by the famous poem of Lucretius." Rarely using any "terms of art," Blackmore hopes he has achieved an "easy and familiar expression" which will, in his paraphrase of the *Specator*, "bring philosophy out of the secret recesses of the schools, and strip it of its uncouth and mysterious dress, that it may become agreeable, and admitted to a general conversation" (pp. 331–32).

The method of *Creation* is determined by Blackmore's two aims: "to demonstrate the self-existence of an Eternal Mind from the created and dependent existence of the universe" (p. 332) and to prove "that no hypothesis hitherto invented in favour of impiety has the least strength" (p. 335). He uses science to increase religious awe, to destroy heathen arguments, and to verify that, as Locke and Newton assumed, God is as much an indispensable hypothesis for the astronomer and the physician as for the cleric. In demonstrating "the unreasonableness of irreligious principles,"[37] Blackmore usually describes a natural phenomenon, considers contending hypotheses which purport to explain the phenomenon, usually in order of their increasing adequacy, and finally dismisses all explanations as insufficient to answer the ultimate questions involved.

Arguing teleologically in Book I, Blackmore describes the "marks of wisdom, choice, and art, which appear in the visible world." The situation and cohesion of the earth strike Blackmore as irrefutable evidence of design. Considering the "stupid" atom, he asks rhetorically:

> What charms could these terrestrial vagrants see
> In this one point of all immensity. . . ? (p. 340)

If asked how the atoms are activated, the atheists lamely answer, "The nature of the thing is so." Others who, with more appearance of deliberation,

> ascribe this one determin'd course
> Of pondrous things to gravitating force,

Refer us to a quality occult,
To senseless words. . . . (p. 340) [38]

Similarly, those who invoke "magnetic power" merely substitute empty phrases for explanations while the mystery remains as awesome as ever, evidence of "how dark is human reason" when struggling with the profundities of nature.

In his preface Blackmore warned the "judicious reader" not to expect the "ornaments of poetical eloquence" in the "philosophical and argumentative" portions of the poem, believing that metaphor and description would "darken and enfeeble the argument" (p. 332). In his descriptions of the "finish'd beauty" of earth, however, Blackmore allows his muse more latitude, as when, in a passage describing the "economy" of nature which prevents our globe from growing "a wilderness of sand," he anticipates Shelley's powerful image of Mt. Blanc:

The waters still their circling course maintain,
Flow down in rivers, and return in rain. . . .
The mountains more sublime in ether rise,
Transfix the clouds, and tower amidst the skies;
The snowy fleeces, which their heads involve,
Still stay in part, and still in part dissolve;
Torrents and loud impetuous cataracts,
Through roads abrupt, and rude unfashion'd tracts,
Roll down the lofty mountain's channell'd sides,
And to the vale convey their foaming tides;
At length, to make their various currents one,
The congregated floods together run;
These confluent streams make some great river's head,
By stores still melting and descending fed. (p. 343)

Those who would explain the formation of "the spacious hollow, where the waves reside" or how the ocean is salted to prevent putrefaction have recourse only to "a cant of words" when they ignore the "wise contriver" who "season'd all the sea" (p. 344).

After hymning the blessings of religion as a rebuttal to Lucretius' aspersions,[39] Book II celebrates the efforts of "th' Artificer Divine" in creating the awesome harmony of the cosmos:

In beauteous order all the orbs advance
. . . in their mazy complicated dance. (p. 346)

Anticipating Thomson, Blackmore describes the change of seasons as the sun progresses through the zodiac. Often the resemblances are closer than Thomson scholars would lead one to expect, as when following the chemical processes of winter the warm winds of spring

> Ferment the glebe, and genial spirits loose,
> Which lay imprison'd in the stiffen'd ground,
> Congeal'd with cold, in frosty fetters bound. (p. 346)

When he allows himself the latitude, even Blackmore's "scientific" images are frequently charming, as when the summer sun

> tinctures rubies with their rosy hue,
> And on the sapphire spreads a heavenly blue. (p. 347)

Ranging through the "wide inextricable maze" of the solar system and beyond to "this wide machine, the universe," Blackmore celebrates the wonders of light, which by its spreading radiance "reveals/All Nature's face" yet "still itself conceals." Mighty as our system seems to the inquiring mind, Blackmore emphasizes, the telescope tells us it is "but one of thousands," a plurality of worlds severed by "spacious voids of liquid sky":

> All these illustrious worlds, and many more,
> Which by the tube astronomers explore;
> And millions which the eye can ne'er descry,
> Lost in the wilds of vast immensity;
> Are suns, are centres, whose superior sway
> Planets of various magnitude obey. (p. 349)

Book II concludes with Blackmore expatiating on "this wide field of wonders" that comprises our world, from the pores of tree roots to the "wondrous web" of air.

Until "vain Philosophy" nurtured abstract theorists who

> imagine'd realms of science rule,
> With idle toil form visionary schemes,
> And wage eternal war for rival dreams (p. 351),

man pursued useful knowledge, Blackmore says in the third Book. The "Lucretian tribe," however, "presum'd to soar" beyond the realms of human wit and searched nature in such a way as to lose sight of "th' Almighty Cause." Whereas natural man is ravished into respect for the wisdom which produced "the long coherent chain of things," the Lucretian finds only atoms and the void. Contemptuously, Blackmore demands of Lucretius how "constant order" could result from the chance concatenation of atoms. Without an efficient and a final cause, he argues, the absurd possibilities are endless:

The forest oak might bear the blushing rose,
And fragrant myrtles thrive in Russian snows;
The fair pomegranate might adorn the pine,
The grape the bramble, and the sloe the vine;
Fish from the plains, birds from the floods, might rise,
And lowing herds break from the starry skies. (p.353)

Book III is Blackmore's vindication of God's wisdom and benevolence in the face of the atomists' objection to "the pretended unartful contrivance of the world." Granting that God might have created an environment more hospitable to man than the "sad and moving spectacle of woe" which a world with earthquakes and plague sometimes presents, Blackmore insists that nature's "exhaustless energy" generates "perfections different in degree," for God values variety, a plentitude productive of richer beauties than man's feeble conception of perfect order. By "different parts" God makes "one whole complete" and his concern is with a multiplicity of galaxies not with man's anthropomorphic pettiness:

Now to the universal whole advert;
The Earth regard as of that whole a part. (p. 353)

Of the "numerous kinds of life" with which God's bounty filled the universe, man is but one. To mortify his pride, presumptuous man need only survey the heavens:

We may pronounce each orb sustains a race
Of living things, adapted to the place.
Were the refulgent parts, and most refin'd,
Only to serve the dark and base design'd?
Were all the stars, whose beauteous realms of light,
At distance only hung to shine by night,
And with their twinkling beams to please our sight? (p. 354)

Though a "mean" part of the whole, earth nonetheless "has all perfections which the place demands":

> Were to your view the universe display'd,
> And all the scenes of Nature open laid;
> Could you their place, proportion, harmony,
> Their beauty, order, and dependence, see,
> You'd grant our globe had all the marks of art,
> All the perfection due to such a part. (p. 354)

The very "imperfections" are what assure man's free will and render the world a vale of soul-making. The greatest earthly evil, death, the fear of which the Lucretian fights against in vain, loses its terror when viewed from a Christian perspective. Hope, rather than the fear Hobbes proposed, is the origin of religion, Blackmore argues. And although man cannot know all the uses of the universe, he certainly knows more than the sceptics admit. Even granting the Epicureans' assertion that the earth is imperfect, it does not follow that wisdom and design are entirely absent, as they insist. Even the atomists cannot doubt the remarkable ingenuity presupposed by the growth of a plant or the "fine texture of a fibrous nerve." Human nature is such, in any case, that regardless what kind of world God had fashioned man's "wanton wit" would have discovered something to blame.

Blackmore's debate with the atomists is conducted as an heroic combat in which his final opponent is in some ways the most interesting. The Book ends with his refutation of Spinoza's pantheism. Blackmore responds to the pantheist with ridicule of a religion which "saves the name while it subverts the thing:"

> "The lucid orbs, the earth, the air, the main,
> With every different being they contain,
> Are one prodigious aggregated God,
> Of whom each sand is part, each stone and clod;
> Supreme perfections in each insect shine,
> Each shrub is sacred, and each weed divine."[40]
> Sages, no longer Egypt's sons despise,
> For their cheap gods, and savoury deities!
> No more their coarse divinities revile!
> To leeks, to onions, to the crocodile,
> You might your humble adorations pay,
> Were you not gods yourselves, as well as they. (p. 357)

Agreeing with Lucretius that no man is happy who has not conquered the fear of death, Blackmore in Book IV argues that theism rather than the atomism of Epicurus provides the only effective consolation. Utilizing modern science to show the primitive nature of Epicurean physics, Blackmore refutes atomism point by point, concluding it impossible that

> all the rolling globes, and spacious skies,
> From happy hits of heedless atoms rise. (p. 363)

Book V, arguing repeatedly from the necessity for a self-existent first cause, refutes the Aristotelian fatalists who assert the eternity of the world. Borrowing his arguments in part from Lucretius, Blackmore demonstrates the universal mutability of nature while stressing "necessary existence"—i.e., a state of being which cannot be conceived not to exist—as the requisite characteristic of permanance. As do all temporal existences, even the sun has its duration:

> should the Sun of finite bulk sustain,
> In every age, the loss of but a grain;
> If we suppose those ages infinite,
> Could there remain one particle of light? (p. 365)

The abstract concept of "Fate" is dismissed as an invitation to equivocation and a self-contradiction. The Book ends, rather incongruously, with patriotic praise of Marlborough and England under Queen Anne.

The sixth Book celebrates God's most meticulous creation—the wondrous body of man. As an experienced physician, Blackmore draws upon a sophisticated knowledge of anatomy unavailable to most other physicotheologists whether they wrote in prose or verse. Thus, Book VI, despite the curious, sometimes comic reaction a modern reader feels, is the most original part of the poem and provides an especially vivid insight into early-eighteenth-century scientific enthusiasm. Others, of course, had repeatedly written of the human body as God's greatest earthly glory; but Blackmore was able to unite this inspiration with a thorough knowledge of medicine. Just as Books IV and V reverse Lucretius' arguments in *De Rerum Natura* (II and III) that the soul is mortal but the world of atoms immortal, so in this Book

Blackmore refines the crude explanation of bodily functions in Book IV of *De Rerum Natura* not to attack all teleological theories of nature but instead to prove the providence of God.

To the Lucretian notion that man was spontaneously generated from the earth much as insects are, Blackmore opposes the modern microscopic discovery that fertilized eggs, too minute for the unaided eye to see, are necessary even for the generation of insects. Ignoring his own injunction in the preface to distinguish between raillery and rational argument, Blackmore finds the idea of a well-irrigated field producing a "crop of reasoning creatures" too absurd not to belabor:

> tell us, Epicurus, why the field
> Did never since one human harvest yield?
> And why we never see one ripening birth
> Heave in the glebe, and struggle thro' the earth? (p. 370)

Why has some country lumpkin, plowing his fields, never discovered "soft-bones" or "unfashion'd veins" much as he might unearth an immature turnip.

There are no attempts at the ludicrous, however, when Blackmore begins to hymn the human body in questions reminiscent of God's chastisement of Job:

> When first the womb did the crude embryo hold,
> What shap'd the parts? what did the limbs unfold?
> O'er the whole work in secret did preside,
> Give quickening vigour, and each motion guide?
> What kindled in the dark the vital flame,
> And, ere the heart was form'd, push'd on the reddening stream?
> Then for the heart the aptest fibres strung?
> And in the breast th' impulsive engine hung?
> Say, what the various bones so wisely wrought?
> How was their frame to such perfection brought?
> What did their figures for their uses fit,
> Their numbers fix, and joints adapted knit;
> And made them all in that just order stand,
> Which motion, strength, and ornament, demand?
> What for the sinews spun so strong a thread,
> The curious loom to weave the muscles spread;
> Did the nice strings of tended membranes drill,
> And perforate the nerve with so much skill,
> Then with the active stream the dark recesses fill?

The purple mazes of the veins display'd,
And all th' arterial pipes in order laid,
What gave the bounding current to the blood,
And to and fro convey'd the restless flood? (p. 371)

It is easy for our age to smile at what we perceive to be the inappropriateness of metaphorically describing God as the potter of the embryo, the weaver of the muscles, or the plumber who lays the "arterial pipes." Wrenching lines out of context, Pope schools us in such absurdities in *Peri Bathous.* Clearly, however, Blackmore's intention is not to vulgarize a sublime subject by intruding "base" ideas but to emphasize the absolute difference between fashioning the cleverest clockwork and the simplest organic existence, the absolute difference between turning a pot and animating human clay.

Despite all apologies, however, the fact remains that the revolutions of taste since Blackmore's time have dwindled some of his fire into farce. From his survey of a heart which "entertains the purple guest" to nerves that as "watchful sentinels at every gate,/At every passage, to the senses wait," *Creation* has potential comedy far more deeply interfused than Blackmore foresaw. For a modern reader he is perhaps at his worst in describing digestion:

See, how the human animal is fed,
How nourishment is wrought, and how convey'd:
The mouth, with proper faculties endued,
First entertains, and then divides, the food;
Two adverse rows of teeth the meat prepare,
On which the glands fermenting juice confer;
Nature has various tender muscles plac'd,
By which the artful gullet is embrac'd;
Some the long funnel's curious mouth extend,
Through which ingested meats with ease descend;
Other confederate pairs for Nature's use
Contract the fibres, and the twitch produce,
Which gently pushes on the grateful food
To the wide stomach, by its hollow road. (p. 373)

Although descriptions of "artful gullets" devouring "grateful food" make Blackmore one of the most vulnerable of English poets, a fair evaluation of Book VI would emphasize his considerable creativity in celebrating a subject which the modern reader may judge ill-adapted for poetry. Again, the ages intervene. Perhaps what Blackmore perceived as a "field of Miracles," the physiology of the human body, seems today more mundane than it must have to eighteenth-century Englishmen who in the lines of the body traced the lineaments of the divine mind.

The final Book turns from the body to the mind, drawing heavily on Locke's *Essay Concerning Human Understanding.* Locke was a friend of Blackmore's, the man who conveyed Molyneux's encouragement that he write *Creation* in the first place. Nothing is easier to imagine than Blackmore and Locke, both Whigs, both men of medicine, passing the evenings in discussion and clarification of the psychology of the *Essay.*

Although Blackmore's description of sensation and reflection shows a clear understanding of his friend's work, Book VII is more than versified Locke. It is a celebration of the mystery as well as the design of instinct in animals and reason in man. Over and over again Blackmore emphasizes the elusive nature of human understanding, so complex and yet so resistant to analysis into constituent parts. Psychologists who analyze the intellect with "anatomic art" murder to dissect, "dividing the things that are in nature join'd." God's greatest wonders inevitably remain beyond the reach of human reason:

> For what enlighten'd reasoner can declare
> What human will and understanding are?
> What science from those objects can we frame
> Of which we little know, besides the name? (p. 379)

After a celebration of the free will which makes morality possible, *Creation* concludes with a hymn to the "omniscient Architect" who with equal art can suggest a scruple or create a world.

IV *The British Lucretius*

If *Creation* lacks the majesty of Milton, it has, as one critic points out, "sublime moments far removed from the pedestrian and long-winded epics on which Blackmore's literary reputation unfortunately seems to be based."[41] Blackmore's debt to

Lucretius, reminiscent of his debt to Virgil in *Prince Arthur*, functions both as artistic catalyst and discipline in *Creation*. Most important, however, Blackmore knew his material. Unlike most poets he really understood the implications of Newton's *Opticks*.[42] He saw clearly the distinction between how a man "sees" and how he "perceives," the problem which had dogged Kepler, Descartes, Molyneux, Locke, and Newton and which served as a point of departure for Berkeley.[43] And, of course, his expertise as a physician enabled him to survey the "wonders of man's body never before so clearly understood."[44] In *The Grounds of Criticism in Poetry*, to which Blackmore subscribed, John Dennis had argued that "Natural Philosophy" or science is "absolutely necessary to a Poet, not only that he may adorn his Poem with the useful Knowledge it affords, but because the more he knows the immense Phaenomena of the Universe, the more he will be sure to admire them."[45]

As Dennis suggests, the age was poised for such a poem; and Blackmore was prepared as no other poet to produce it. Despite occasional snipings,[46] the public immediately acclaimed his British *De Rerum Natura*. Barely a month after the appearance of *Creation*, Addison digressed from his discussion of Milton in *Spectator* No. 339 to recommend Blackmore's poem as a work which "was undertaken with so good an Intention, and is executed with so great a Mastery, that it deserves to be looked upon as one of the most useful and noble Productions in our English Verse. The Reader cannot but be pleased to find the Depths of Philosophy enlivened with all the Charms of Poetry, and to see so great a Strength of Reason, amidst so beautiful a Redundancy of Imagination. The Author has shewn us that Design in all the Works of Nature, which necessarily leads us to the knowledge of its first Cause."[47] Emphasizing the many "Demonstrations of a Supreme Being, and of his transcendent Wisdom, Power, and Goodness" to be found in a careful study of the human body, Addison again recommends *Creation* in *Spectator* No. 543 later the same year. In Sir Richard's poem, Addison says, "the Anatomy of the Human Body is described with great Perspicuity and Elegance."[48]

Aided by Addison's enthusiastic recommendation,[49] *Creation* became by far the most popular of Blackmore's works. A second edition was called for the same year and a third in 1713. In all *Creation* went through sixteen editions. Everyone read it.

Stephen Switzer, relishing its "natural sublimity," advised those interested in gardening to study "the Seraphick Pen of Blackmore."[50] In *The Character of a Fine Gentleman,* Thomas Foxton's perfect gentleman, Serino, found *Creation* second only to Milton.[51] The young sentimentalist Henry Needler added his praise in "To Sir Richard Blackmore, On His Poem, entitled, Creation":

> guided by thy tuneful Voice, I stray
> Thro' Radiant Worlds, and Fields of Native Day,
> Wafted from Orb to Orb, unweary'd fly
> Thro' the blue Regions of the yielding Sky,
> See how the Spheres in Stated Courses roll,
> And view the just Composure of the Whole![52]

Needler especially admires Blackmore's treatment of the human body,[53] and lauds him as the modern Orpheus, the singer of nature's deepest secrets. Predictably, the influence of *Creation* on contemporary physicotheological poetry was profound and includes, only to mention the most ambitious works, Richard Collins' *Nature Display'd* (1727), David Mallet's *Excursion* (1728), Samuel Edward's *The Copernican System* (1728), Richard Gambol's *The Beauties of the Universe* (1732), Henry Baker's *The Universe* (probably1734), Henry Brooke's *Universal Beauty* (1735), and, of course, James Thomson's *Seasons.* Blackmore's poem continued to be read throughout the century and probably influenced Erasmus Darwin's *Botanic Garden* (1791).[54]

John Dennis spoke for the majority of his fellow men, therefore, when he contended that Blackmore had graced English letters with a philosophic poem superior to any written by the ancients. "We have lately been entertained and instructed," he wrote, "by an admirable Philosophical Poem which has equall'd that of LUCRETIUS, in the Beauty of its Versification, and infinitely surpass'd it, in the Solidity and Strength of its Reasoning."[55] Even most of those who, following Dennis's earlier lead, had judged Blackmore's heroic poems realistically were ready without reservation to acclaim him the British Lucretius. In the second dialogue of Charles Gildon's *The Complete Art of Poetry,* when Mr. Lamode declares that despite his traditional university education he finds "the *Arthurs* as good as *Homer*, or *Virgil*," Morisina doubts that even Sir Richard would concur with the popular taste in ranking his epics above the ancients: "I am very confident, that the *admirable* Author of *the Creation*, has too much *Judgment*, and too much *Modesty*, to have any such Thoughts himself. Let it suffice, that the Author of the *Arthurs* has the Glory of excelling *Lucretius*, it is a Palm gain'd only by him; but leave the Soveraignty of *Homer* untouch'd even by *Milton* himself."[56] *Creation* escaped the ignominy suffered by Blackmore's other epics; and by mid-century when the *Arthurs* survived only as gargantuan examples of lulling lumber, *Creation* was pronounced in Theophilus Cibber's *Lives of the Poets* as having "now deservedly become a classic."[57]

Creation was included in his edition of the *English Poets* at Johnson's recommendation. In his "Life of Blackmore" Johnson deals harshly with Blackmore's "languid, sluggish, and lifeless" prose and his hasty, grandiose poems. "Having formed a magnificent design," Johnson criticizes, "he was careless of particular and subordinate elegances; he studied no niceties of versification; he waited for no felicities of fancy; but caught his first thoughts in the first words in which they were presented: nor does it appear that he saw beyond his own performances, or had ever elevated his views to that ideal perfection which every genius born to excell is condemned always to pursue, and never overtake."[58] This harshness makes Johnson's extravagent praise of *Creation* all the more remarkable. Had he written nothing else, Johnson contends, *Creation* alone "would have transmitted him to posterity among the first favorites of the English Muse."[59] Praising its union of "philosophical judgment and poetical spirit," Johnson finds more circumspection in *Creation* than in Blackmore's other works: "it wants neither harmony of numbers, accuracy of thought, nor elegance of diction: it has either been written with great care, or, what cannot be imagined of so long a work, with such felicity as made care less necessary."[60]

Johnson's support insured that *Creation* would, for a time at least, as Sir John Hawkins says, live "in the esteem of every judicious reader."[61] "Let Dr. Johnson," Cowper wrote, "only speak as favourably of me as he has spoken of Blackmore (who, though he shines in his *Creation*, has written more absurdities in verse than any writer of our country), and my success will be secured."[62] Cowper's editor, the poet Robert Southey, praised

Johnson's inclusion of *Creation* in the *English Poets* and had some part in perpetuating esteem for Blackmore's poem into the nineteenth century.[63]

All, however, was not praise even for Blackmore's best work. Capitalizing on Sir Richard's popularity, John Gay surreptitiously parodied devices in Blackmore's *Creation* and in the "Song of Mopas" from *Prince Arthur* in his "Saturday" song of Bowzybeus in *The Shepherd's Week*.[64] In the preface to his own *Creation* in 1720, Aaron Hill notes that Milton, Cowley, and Blackmore have all "tried their Strength in this celestial Bow; Sir *Richard* may be said indeed to have shot *farthest*, but too often beside the Mark; he . . . is too minute, and particular, and rather labours to oppress us with every Image he cou'd raise, than to refresh and enliven us, with the noblest and most differing. He is also too unmindful of the Dignity of his Subject, and diminishes it by mean, and contemptible Metaphors."[65] Lord Hervey informed Lady Mary Wortley Montagu that she should only expect yawns should she deign to examine Blackmore's tiresome *Creation*. Eventually the current of contempt bore down this as it had Blackmore's other works. Near the close of the nineteenth century Leslie Stephen commented on what had become a curious artifact from another culture. "Blackmore's *Creation*," he noted, "gives a system of natural theology in several thousand lines of blank verse, of which no phrase has survived, though Johnson's orthodoxy caused a reprint of the portentous mass in collections of English poets."[66] Stephen's dismissal of Blackmore's "blank verse" poem proves it was no longer necessary even to glance at the heroic couplets of *Creation* to denigrate its "portentous mass." The heyday of physicotheology was over.

V The Lay-Monk

As early as 1695, even before the publication of *Prince Arthur*, Blackmore was involved with Addison and other Oxford graduates on a translation of Herodotus for the bookseller Jacob Tonson.[67] During the war of the wits Addison demurred from criticizing Sir Richard even though his private correspondence shows he shared the flippant attitude of the circle at Will's coffeehouse. In the winter of 1701 Addison wrote from Geneva that he had written a "Rhiming Epistle" while crossing the Alps, a feat as extraordinary in its way as writing "an Heroic poeme in a Hackney Coach." He resuscitated the same joke two years later when, affected by news of his father's death, he wrote from Amsterdam that it was impossible for him to write unless he had "bin possest with such a muse as Dr. Blackmore that could make a couple of Heroic poemes in a Hackney-Coach and a Coffy-house."[68] Addison's private ridicule of Blackmore was little more than a fashionable affectation, however; and their mutual interests and enthusiasms insured an amicable relationship. Addison praised *Creation* and Blackmore tried to convince his friend Dennis to deal gently with *Cato*.

Like the rest of London, Blackmore admired Addison's periodical journalism and was consequently disappointed when *The Guardian* ceased publication on October 1, 1713, to allow Steele to publish the political *Englishman*. Blackmore approached John Hughes with a proposal for a new periodical, encouraging him to enlist Addison's aid. Hughes was close to both men, looking to Blackmore as his model in moral verse and to Addison as his guide in prose. It was through Addison's auspices that he had become one of the most important minor contributors to *The Tatler* and *The Spectator*. When Hughes suggested the new venture to Addison, he politely declined, pleading the need to rest and "lay in fewel for a future work." "I beg you will present my most sincere respects," Addison adds, "to Sir Richard Blackmore, and that you will add my sister's, who is now with me, and very much his humble servant."[69] Despite Addison's encouragement, Hughes also elected to set the project aside.

Sir Richard was more tenacious. A month later, on November 11, he wrote Hughes that *The Lay-Monk*, already twice advertised, was shortly to make its triweekly appearance. "I believe," he continued, "the tenderness of your friendship, joined with your diffidence of success, begins to put you in pain, and make you sweat for me."[70] Sir Richard's resolve overcame Hughes's fear of failure and he joined to contribute all the Friday papers.[71]

When the first number appeared on November 16, it was clear that *The Lay-Monk* was essentially the same periodical that Hughes had proposed to Addison as the *Register*. Sir Eustace Locker, convinced of the virtues of a retired life "to inspire the Soul with generous Sentiments and Divine Passions, to augment and refine our Ideas, and elevate the Mind to the greatest

Heights of Science and Vertue," invites a fraternity of learned men to meet regularly at his country house. There they are to read papers in turn, political subjects only excluded. Besides Sir Eustace, a country gentleman who pursues metaphysical speculations without pedantry, the fraternity includes: Mr. Johnson, a critic suited exactly to Pope's taste who eschews a "mechanical Manner" and values both ancient and modern writers on the basis of their intrinsic worth; Sir Arthur Wimbleton, a middle-age gentleman much versed in history and given to the invention of fables and apologues; Ned Freeman, a gallant with a taste for scholarship; Jacob Ravenscroft, secretary of the fraternity and self-described as "a Pythagorean," transmigrated through the world; and Dr. Lacon, the fraternity member most like Blackmore. Dr. Lacon is a physician whose timely inheritance allows him to leave "a Profession so full of Care and Anxiety; a Profession that obliges a Man to converse perpetually with melancholy Objects, exhausts him with wakeful Nights and laborious Days, and makes Submission to Passion and Impertinence, and mean Condescensions, hard to be born by Men of Sense and Spirit, so often necessary."

The papers themselves allow Blackmore to advance his varied interests, from freedom of the will (37) to the fecundity of nature (19). Scholastic subtleties are censured (2); and Epicurus (20) and Lucretius (19) are opposed and the omnipotence of God demonstrated by arguments accessible to any literate eighteenth-century Briton. Four papers are devoted to that peculiarly English malady, the spleen (22, 26, 34, 35). Many papers reflect Blackmore's scientific interests. Dr. Lacon, discussing the variety and gradation of animal life marvels that "a little Pepper-Corn is crouded, like a populous City, with Inhabitants." "Nothing is more surprizing and delightful," he notes, "than to observe the Scale or gradual Ascent from Minerals to Plants, from Plants to Animals, and from Animals to human Nature" (5). The fifth *Lay-Monk* presents the general reading public for the first time with Blackmore's friend Edward Tyson's conclusion that of all animals the Orang-Outang "has the Honour of bearing the nearest Resemblance to human Nature." In the fortieth paper, the wonder of light, a favorite subject of Blackmore, is celebrated—its speed, imagistic power, and fertile heat. Blackmore insists that goodness rather than knowledge is our final goal (8) and this predisposition determines his emphasis in the scientific papers. Those who fail to rise from a contemplation of nature to a reverence for nature's God are dismissed as shallow virtuosos. Such a one is Sir Gregory Bookworm, described in the eighth *Lay-Monk* as a "Grammatical Blockhead" who avidly collects all Aristotle's commentators but avoids the popular Archbishop Tillotson. "His conversation," Blackmore writes humorously, "at first turn'd upon the surprizing Curiosities and wonderful Productions of Nature, which he exemplify'd in the admirable Structure and Variety of Cockle-shells; and the numerous Kinds of Grass, which, as I remember, he said were Four-score. He next expatiated on the History of Mushrooms, and the Properties of that peculiar Worm or Insect bred in this dubious Species, whose Volatile Salt, as he said, made such an agreeable Sauce."

The Lay-Monk ended publication with the fortieth number on February 15, 1714. Despite the fact that the periodical was increasing in popularity, Hughes wrote, Blackmore had grown weary and chose to conclude the club.[72] How many copies each issue sold is unknown, but five years later Charles Gildon spoke of *The Lay-Monk* as a success.[73] Clearly the venture might have continued, for when, shortly after *The Lay-Monk* ceased publication, the essays were collected as *The Lay-Monastery*, two editions were called for within the year. The charm and interest of several of the essays survive even today. Robert J. Allen finds *The Lay-Monk* "one of the most interesting of all the imitations of *The Spectator*"[74] and Walter Graham concurs.[75] Probably Blackmore simply did not have the leisure to continue *The Lay-Monk*. In January he had turned sixty, but unlike his imaginary Dr. Lacon he had not been freed from "the wakeful Nights and laborious Days" which his private practice and an ailing queen necessitated.

CHAPTER 6

Last Days in London

With a huge Mountain-load of Heroical Lumber,
Which from *Tonson* to *Curl* ev'ry Press had groan'd under;
Came *Blackmore*, and cry'd, look! all these are my Lays,
But at present I beg you'd but read my *Essays*.
John Sheffield, "The Election of a Poet Laureat" (1719)

I *Alexander Pope's "Most Humble Service"*

BLACKMORE was sixty years old when he attended Queen Anne during her final illness and was at the height of his medical and literary success. James Yonge, a fellow surgeon, speaks of him as "my celebrated great acquaintance,"[1] meaning not only that Sir Richard was rising to new positions of authority in the Royal College but also that *Creation* had reestablished his reputation in literary circles and among the public at large. Additionally, Blackmore was now highly regarded as a popularizer of the effect of nature on the mind of man.[2] Freed by Anne's death from the arduous honors of a Physician in Ordinary, the aging Sir Richard continued to write essays toward a volume, a less taxing format than the thrice-weekly periodical. And he resolved to collect his shorter poems in a more enduring form than their initial single issues.

During these same years a young poet was coming to the maturity of his artistic powers. In his adolescence Alexander Pope had tried his inexperienced genius as an heroic poet. "My epic poem," he later told Joseph Spence, "was two years in hand (from[my] thirteenth into fifteenth [year]). . . . It was better planned than Blackmore's *Prince Arthur*, but as slavish an imitation of the ancients."[3] Guided by his older friend George Granville, however, Pope grew scornful of those "who driven with ungovernable fire" burlesque the art form they pretend to reverence. In the fourth note to his *Essay Upon Unnatural Flights in Poetry* (1701), Granville struck indirectly at Blackmore as one famed for "extravagant flight." As his letters prove, Pope imbibed the same contempt and quickly made himself master of the usual coffeehouse conceits.[4] It was almost automatic, therefore, when he published *An Essay on Criticism* in May of 1711, for Pope to include Blackmore as a foil to Dryden, drawing upon Dryden's own words in the "Preface" to the *Fables*:

> Might he return, and bless once more our Eyes,
> New *Blackmores* and new *Milbourns* must arise.
> (ll. 461-62)[5]

Blackmore, of course, need not have arisen in such a case; he was still very much around, a superannuated absurdity to those, like Granville and Pope, who thought of him only as an impediment to the fortunes of a man greater than himself. The success of *Creation*, however, caused Pope to pull up short and substitute Shadwell for Blackmore, another antagonist of Dryden who, unlike Sir Richard, was safely in his grave. Pope studied *Creation* carefully, as is evident from *An Essay on Man*, and even imitated some of Blackmore's better lines in the 1714 edition of *The Rape of the Lock*.[6] Two months after Blackmore and John Hughes desisted from publishing *The Lay Monk*, Pope wrote Hughes asking for assistance in promoting subscriptions to his translation of Homer. The letter concludes with a request that Hughes make Pope's "most humble service acceptable to Sir Richard Blackmore."[7]

Setting the question of expedient hypocrisy aside, it is clear that Pope's contempt for Blackmore had only gone underground to better accommodate Blackmore's resurgence of popularity and to avoid antagonizing potential subscribers to his *Iliad* who might also be admirers of the City Bard. Two months after his letter to Hughes, Pope was already busily collecting specimens of atrocious verse for the Scriblerian *Peri Bathous*. On June 26, Arbuthnot reported to Swift that Pope had been "collecting high flights of poetry, which are very good, they are to be solemn nonsense."[8] As Pope's notes to *Peri Bathous* indicate, the citations from *Prince Arthur* are taken from the latest and "most correct" edition, the fourth edition issued early in 1714. Thus while offering his "most humble service" in public, in private Pope was mining Blackmore's epic for ludicrous gems to adorn the projected Scriblerian treatise.

Furthermore, as a recent critic notes, Pope's *Guardian* No. 78, which he later incorporates as Chapter 15 of *Peri Bathous*, surreptitiously ridicules Blackmore rather than Le Bossu as Pope's contemporaries assumed.[9] Building on Steele's clever raillery of Blackmore's advice poems in *Tatler* No. 3, Pope offers his "Receit, to make an Epick Poem," a method assuring success "*without a Genius*, nay without Learning or much Reading."[10] Although Pope never mentions Blackmore specifically there are numerous clues that Sir Richard has already mastered the art of making an epic poem. When Pope recommends "ancient Geography" as useful in creating an impression of deep learning, the target is clearly Blackmore's habit of appending a lengthy geographical index to his epics. In the preface to *King Arthur* Blackmore defers to Culverius as the authority on historical names, the same source Pope recommends to his fledgling heroic poet. [11] Similarly, a fable is readily available in "any old Poem, History-books, Romance, or Legend." Pope specifically recommends "Geffry of Monmouth," to whom Blackmore owed his fable in both *Arthurs* as he acknowledged in the preface to *King Arthur*. "If you have need of Devils," Pope advises, "draw them out of *Milton's Paradise*, and extract your Spirits from *Tasso*." Again, Blackmore borrows from both men, praising Milton in the *King Arthur* preface as a "very Extraordinary Genius." The recipe for a description of an exceptionally violent tempest suggests the storm which opens *Prince Arthur*, a passage from which Pope drew lines for *Peri Bathous*. The archaic diction, useful for a "venerable Air of Antiquity," which Pope suggests, glances at Blackmore's Spenserian proclivities; and the final sentences of the satire are delightfully appropriate to the too frequent bombastic passages in Blackmore's epics: "I must not conclude, without cautioning all Writers without Genius in one material Point; which is, never to be afraid of having *too much Fire* in their Works. I should advise rather to take their warmest Thoughts, and spread them abroad upon Paper; for they are observed to cool before they are read."[12]

It is both delightful and a trifle disillusioning to imagine the meetings of the Scriblerians during the final, uncertain months of the queen's ministry. Swift was out of London; Harley and Bolingbroke were too busy with political matters to attend with any regularity. But since Arbuthnot and Blackmore attended the queen almost daily, Pope and Gay could depend upon Arbuthnot to supply fresh ancedotes concerning the bedside manner of his fellow Physician in Ordinary. The covert nature of the contempt they shared for the Whiggish Sir Richard was the salt that made them relish it all the more.

II "*Read My* Essays"

If Blackmore recognized the ridicule in *Guardian* No. 78, he took it with excellent humor, for he not only subscribed to Pope's expensive translation of Homer but praised it in *Essays upon Several Subjects*, which appeared in early March of 1716.[13] Of the essays, that "Upon Epick Poetry" is the most innovative and was the most popular with Blackmore's contemporaries. Organized upon Le Bossu's plan, the almost two-hundred-page "essay" opposes uncritical subservience either to the "rules" or to the practice of ancient authors. Blackmore argues that the hero need not be engaged in "some eminent Action" and contends that only such dogmatic preconceptions could have blinded critics to the recognition that Adam is the hero of *Paradise Lost*. In fact, he specifically argues that a woman may properly be "the Principal Person of an Epick." Blackmore sees no necessity for "poetic justice," insisting that an epic may end effectively with misfortune falling to the major characters. As for style, he advocates rhyme but dislikes the monotony of closed couplets, he commends occasional "Roughness in the true Sublime," and he urges creative "metaphysical Abstraction" in forming metaphors.[14] The coffeehouse critics followed Addison's lead in "commending and approving" the essay on epic but, as one contemporary diary attests, the rest "were not so well liked."[15]

The "rest" included essays upon wit, false virtue, the immortality of the soul, the laws of nature, and the origin of civil power. Partly physiological speculation and partly denunciation of profane theater, the discussion of wit praises the proper use of wit in the *Tatler* and *Spectator*, contrasting the proper exercise of that spirited faculty with the "pernicious" and "audacious" misuse of wit in *A Tale of a Tub*. Had Swift's satire "been publish'd in a Pagan or Popish Nation," Blackmore insists, "no doubt but the Author would have receiv'd the Punishment he deserv'd. But the Fate of this impious Buffoon is very different."[16] Blackmore sees Swift's preferment to the Deanery of St. Patrick's as a travesty of true religion. In his zeal against what he judged to be the misuse of wit in *A Tale of a Tub*, Blackmore aroused two opposed camps against him. The friends of Swift, of course, could not but feel that this relic of King William's days had had some hand in hardening Anne's heart against Swift and had, consequently, not only kept Swift from an English bishopric but had played a part in insuring his Irish exile. Arbuthnot was certainly in a good position to know one way or the other. At the same time that the Scriblerians were aroused, Addison's supporters, while pleased with Blackmore's commendation, were less enthusiastic over his insistence in the preface to the volume that even the "fine Raillery and Satire" of the *Spectators* "tho admirable in their kind, never reclaim'd one vicious Man, or made one Fool depart from his Folly."[17] In defending the high seriousness of the majority of his essays, Blackmore, perhaps unconsciously, trivializes the moral influence of the *Spectator*, an influence which Addison prided himself on.

Only the "Language of the Heart," Blackmore insists, will move men to reformation. Consequently, he not only eschews wit but also the "Technical" style which sometimes characterized his treatment of divine subjects in earlier works and made them "obnoxious to Censure." Similarly, he vows to avoid the style which typifies the lettered gentlemen, for "the soft and gentle Persuasions and well-bred Address of a meer elegant Writer will make no more Impression on their [the readers'] Minds, than the Descent of a Feather upon the Ground, or a gentle Breeze upon a Rock."[18] Nor is the sophisticated wit of *The Tatler* or *The Spectator* useful. "One may as well charge a Gyant with a Bull-rush," he writes later, "or play upon a Conflagration with a Syringe, as attempt to make a wise and vertuous Nation with pleasant Humour and facetious Fancies."[19]

The "Language of the Heart" which Blackmore adopted for his nonliterary essays suggests that the physician-poet had studied the human heart only in specimen jars, for his style is usually cold and inert. The dreary drone is only occasionally relieved by passages of genuine insight and interest. His discussion of human perception in "An Essay upon the Immortality of the Soul" and his suggestions of the correspondences between moral laws and religious injunctions raise the reader's expectation to a level which the most of the essays disappoint.[20] The *Essays* received, as they merited, a mixed reception. Despite Blackmore's resolution to avoid "the manner of the Gown,"[21] his essays seem to have been most warmly received at Oxford. When, in April 1717, Thomas Hearne visited the Master of University College he found a Fellow of Magdalen with him. "The Master was reading . . . a passage out of one of the volumes of of sir Richard Blackmore's Essays, and thence he took occasion to extoll sir Richard's writings in a most extravagant manner. . . ."[22]

Why Blackmore chose to attack Swift as an "impious Buffoon" just when his star seemed to have waned is impossible to say. Perhaps the "Essay upon Wit" was written earlier while Swift was still active for Harley's ministry and a chief antagonist of Marlborough. Blackmore did have some justification for being soured on the subject of Swift aside from his alleged impiety. In *A Tale of a Tub* Swift takes a fashionable jab at Blackmore's habit of writing to the rumbling of his coach's wheels: "Ask an *Author* how his last Piece hath succeeded; *Why, truly he thanks his Stars, the World has been very favourable, and he has not the least Reason to complain: And yet, By G—,* He writ it in a Week at Bits and Starts, when he could steal an Hour from his urgent Affairs; as it is a hundred to one, you may see farther in the Preface, to which he refers you. . . ."[23] Although Swift uses no names, the preface is clearly that of *King Arthur.* Elsewhere Swift inveighs against "paultry *Scribblers*" who perniciously counterfeit continuations of successful works. The narrator of *A Tale of a Tub* foresees that "as soon as I lay down my Pen, this nimble *Operator* will have stole it, and treat me as inhumanely as he hath already done Dr. Bl— re. . . ."[24] Swift, of course, is mocking the inferior quality of Blackmore's second *Arthur.*

In the *Battle of the Books* he transmutes one of Blackmore's most horrific Spenserian episodes in *King Arthur* into the solicitation of the goddess Criticism by Momus.[25] However, perhaps because of Swift's dislike of Dryden, Blackmore is treated as gently as Swift's estimate of his ponderous style allows. When Lucan appears, slaughtering his cohorts, Blackmore, "a famous *Modern* (but one of the *Mercenaries*) strenously opposed himself, and darted a Javelin with a strong Hand, which falling short of its Mark, stuck deep in the Earth." Lucan responds with a lance which Aesculapius deflects. Perceiving that Blackmore merits the protection of a god, Lucan desists from battle and the two warriors exchange appropriate gifts: "*Lucan* then bestowed the *Modern a Pair of Spurs*, and *Bl-ckm-re* gave *Lucan* a *Bridle.*"[26] After the *Battle of the Books*, Swift joined Lucan in his truce with Sir Richard. Only much later in *On Poetry: A Rapsody* does Blackmore hitch into a rhyme which recalls the satire of Will's Coffeehouse at the turn of the century:

> How few have reach'd the *low Sublime?*
> For when our high-born *Howard* dy'd,
> Blackmore alone his Place supply'd. . . . (11. 370–72)

After Blackmore's gratuituous attack, although Swift was unwilling to enter such an unequal battle, Pope was eager to engage. The *Essays* had been sold jointly by J. Pemberton and Edmund Curll, the "thorough bookselling Rogue" who Swift tells Pope "is better qualified to vex an author, than all his contemporary scriblers in Critick or Satire, not only by stolen Copies of what was incorrect or unfit for the publick, but by downright laying of other mens dulness at your door."[27] Curll had repeatedly offended Pope or his friends in both these respects; and when Curll unscrupulously published a volume of *Court Poems* on March 26, only three weeks after Blackmore's sober *Essays* appeared, Pope went into action. Curll's title page intimated that the *Court Poems* were by Gay, "a Lady of Quality," and "the Judicious Translator of Homer," the last two being transparent references to Lady Mary Wortley Montagu and Pope, whose second volume of the *Iliad* had been published two days earlier, on Saturday, March 24.

Diminutive and consequently unable to administer the drubbing Curll's audacity deserved, Pope hit upon a more subtle revenge. The story of Pope's administration of the emetic to the infamous bookseller is delightfully set forth in *A Full and True Account of a Horrid and Barbarous Revenge by Poison, On the Body of Mr. Edmund Curll* and is too well known to be repeated here.[28] Events moved quickly. *Court Poems* appeared on Monday; on Wednesday Pope gave Curll the emetic; and by Saturday, March 31, just in time for April Fool's Day, *A Full and True Account* was being insultingly hawked along Fleetstreet outside Curll's shop, the Dial and Bible. In the pamphlet, Blackmore is Curll's physician as well as his insurance against damnation. Pope implies that Curll published Blackmore's *Essays* partly because ("God bless Sir *Richard*") he "takes no Copy Money" but also because their pious tone compensates for some of Curll's other volumes. On his deathbed he exclaims: "Heaven pardon me for publishing the *Trials of Sodomy* in an *Elzevir* Letter; but I humbly hope, my printing Sir *Richard Bl[ackmo]re's* Essays will attone for them." Except for complimentary copies, Curll notes, "near the whole Impression" of the *Essays* still lay heavy on his shelves.[29]

Undismayed, Curll responded with several burlesque advertisements in *The Flying-Post* asking for contributions to a volume to be called *Homer Defended*, a "Detection of the many Errors committed by Mr. *Pope*, in his pretended Translation, of Homer," a device reminiscent of Tom Brown's call for discommendatory verses on Blackmore's *Job*. This kind of retaliation Pope must certainly have expected; but the events which bring Blackmore back into the squabble show Curll at his most resourceful. Pope had attacked Curll like a man who did not need to fear the exposure of any sin of his own. However, Pope had lewdly burlesqued Thomas Sternhold's version of the first Psalm and had indiscreetly allowed copies to go abroad. Curll knew that Pope was extremely sensitive to suspicions of his piety. And, sure enough, the *Flying-Post* for June 28–30 announced publication of Pope's burlesque as "A *Roman Catholick* Version of the First Psalm; for the Use of a Young *Lady*. By Mr. POPE. Printed for R. Burleigh in Amen Corner."[30] Despite the smokescreen of the non-existent Mrs. Burleigh, the two-penny sheet was, predictably, published by Edmund Curll. The burlesque created a sensation; less pious souls than Sir Richard were shocked and the outrage over Mr. Pope's "prophane Ballad" continued long and loud despite Pope's repeated and "hypocritical"[31] disavowal of any hand in the poem. Blackmore reacted to the Psalm both by criticizing its author in the draft of a essay for a second volume and by disassociating himself from Curll. When the second volume of *Essays* appeared the following year, Bettesworth had replaced Curll as Blackmore's publisher. He blamed Curll as much for publishing the burlesque as Pope for writing it.

The chronology at this point is somewhat complicated. The few references to Blackmore in Pope's *Full and True Account* had been good-humored and without disrespect, gentlemanly gibing much less vitriolic than Blackmore's cirticism of Swift.

Despite his secret contempt, Pope continued to show some deference toward Sir Richard. The situation altered radically, however, when Pope discovered that Blackmore, champion of piety, intended to print a condemnation of his burlesque in the second volume of his *Essays.* It is, of course, supposition that Pope knew of Blackmore's criticism in 1716 since the second edition of the *Essays* did not appear until late March of 1717. Yet in the preface to the 1717 edition Blackmore clearly indicates that the "Essay upon Writing" in which Pope is criticized was actually printed, although not bound, some time before the preface to the volume was ever written. Consequently, he finds it necessary in the preface to amend some comments he had made in the essay. Since the corrections are relevant to Addison's *Freeholder* No. 40 of May 7, 1716, the "Essay upon Writing" had to have been completed after that date but presumably before January 1717, when *Three Hours After Marriage* was performed, for the preface of Blackmore's second edition contains criticism of that dramatic satire which should otherwise logically occur with the other criticism of Pope in the body of the essay. Since, as is discussed below, it seems likely that "An Essay upon Writing" was composed partially as a heated response to *Freeholder* No. 40, Pope probably knew soon after Curll's publication of the burlesque Psalm that Sir Richard's ponderous but influential rhetoric was to be trained on him.

If Pope realized that Blackmore's views might really damage his reputation with some readers, so did the intrepid Curll, who over and over again pirated Blackmore's paragraph on Pope's Psalm as "A Character of Mr. Pope's Profane Writings. By Sir Richard Blackmore Kt. M.D."[32] Whether Pope actually saw the relevant passage prior to publication of the 1717 *Essays*, the controversial atmosphere following Curll's issue of the Psalm almost insured that Pope would get wind of the gist of the passage from typesetters' gossip or elsewhere. Pope's own publisher, Bernard Lintott, who had helped Pope poison Curll, would conceivably have been a help in this respect.

Blackmore's brief criticism makes Pope sound like the chief threat to king and country. Lumped with "a petulant Set of Writers, who have no way to Popularity and Fame but by making their Court to the Vices and Follies of the age, from a rooted and inflexible Enmity to Piety and Vertue, and immortal Hatred to all good Men," Pope is finally singled out by Blackmore as worthy of special comment. "I cannot," he writes, "but here take notice, that one of these Champions of Vice is the reputed Author of a detestable Paper, that has lately been handed about in Manuscript, and now appears in Print, in which the godless Author has burlesqu'd the *First Psalm of David* in so obscene and profane a manner, that perhaps no Age ever saw such an insolent Affront offer'd to the establish'd Religion of their Country, and this, good Heaven! with Impunity. A Sad Demonstration this, of the low Ebb to which the *British* Vertue is reduc'd in these degenerate Times."[33]

Pope, for his part, rallied his friends to ridicule Blackmore both in response to his characterization of the Dean of St. Patrick's as "an impious Buffoon" and in anticipation of his own denigration in the forthcoming second volume of the *Essays.* Swift responded to Pope as one unperturbed, considering enemies like Curll and Blackmore as "Tools as necessary for a good writer, as pen, ink, and paper."[34] Gay, as Pope reports, "broke forth in a courageous couplet or two upon Sir *Richard Bl*——,"[35] a reference to the short portrait of Maurus near the conclusion of *An Epistle to the Right Honourable the Earl of Burlington.*[36] A far more ambitious condemnation appeared in *A Letter to the Knight of the Sable Shield* by Pope's friend Elijah Fenton. The old rhymes are dredged up from discommendatory days to defame an author

> who knows with equal skill
> To make a poem and a pill.

In Fenton's satire a balding Sir Richard laments that Jacob Tonson thinks it profitable to gull the tasteless town by reissuing his epics, an event certain to draw ridicule from all the wags about town. In fact, Tonson, who had published the first three editions of *Creation*, had recently capitalized on Blackmore's new popularity by publishing pocket editions of *Prince Arthur* (1714) and *Job* (1716). Since these are the editions from which Pope edited material for *Peri Bathous,* it is reasonable to assume he had some part in motivating Fenton's poem, which presumably appeared shortly after the pocket *Paraphrase on Job* in late June, 1716.[37]

Pope had reason to be especially irritated in late June. Not only had Curll just added to the furor by publishing the Psalm burlesque; but Pope was still smarting from another of the unspeakable bookseller's inspirations. The *Flying-Post* for May 31 announced the publication (anonymously) of John Dennis's caustic *True Character of Mr. Pope, and His Writings.* Issued under the false imprint of Sarah Popping, the pamphlet was, of course, part of Curll's continuing retaliation. The facts, moreover, suggest that the enmity between Pope and Blackmore may have been largely the ingenious product of Curll's covert machinations. Significantly, *A True Character* exaggerates the number and the intensity of Pope's previous attacks on Blackmore. Aside from the good-humored account of Curll's emetic, Pope's only other publicly perceived stab at Blackmore had been the quickly deleted couplet in *An Essay on Criticism.* Yet Dennis alleges that Pope has attacked none of his friends or benefactors "so often, or with so much ridiculous, impotent Malice, as Sir *Richard Blackmore*; who is Estimable for a thousand good and great Qualities. And what time has he chosen to do this? Why, just after that Gentleman had laid very great Obligations on him; and just after he had oblig'd the World with so many Editions of his Excellent *Poem* upon *CREATION*, which *Poem* alone is worth all the *Folios*, that this Libeller [Pope] will ever write, and which will render its Author [Blackmore] the Delight and Admiration of Posterity."[38] By "great Obligations" Dennis may refer to the praise of Pope's *Iliad* in Blackmore's *Essays* or to aid he may have afforded in soliciting subscriptions in the City. Or he may have simply wished, as Curll did, to brand Pope as an ingrate, ready to betray to ridicule those most kindly disposed toward him. Whatever the intention, however, Dennis's *A True Character* certainly fomented trouble. Years later in notes to the *Dunciad Variorum* (II, 258), Pope still felt it necessary to exonerate himself from this charge of ingratitude to Blackmore.

As distinguished from those he influenced, Pope himself published nothing against Blackmore until late November or early December 1716, by which time he must have known of Blackmore's condemnation of the burlesque Psalm, printed but awaiting a preface and sufficient additional material to fill out a volume. At that time, Pope anonymously issued *A Further Account of the Most Deplorable Condition of Mr. Edmund Curll, Bookseller.*[39] Curll is still Pope's central character but now abuse of Blackmore has become a major theme. His physiological discussion of wit is cited from the *Essays* only to be ridiculed as medical jargon.[40] Pope hints that the *Essays* sell so slowly that Curll willingly takes less than their full price.[41] As the *Account* ends Curll is disconcerted as "a whole Pile of *Essays* on a sudden fell on his Head; the Shock of which in an Instant brought back his Dilirium. He immediately rose up, overturn'd the Close-Stool, and beshit the *Essays*," which, Pope concludes, "may probably occasion a *second Edition.*"[42]

III *Addison's "Reasonable Freedom"*

Pope's most surprising recruit to the anti-Blackmore forces may have been Joseph Addison. Although the clandestine nature of the goings on between Pope and Addison after Tickell's abortive rival translation of the *Iliad* tends to shroud all the facts in some degree of mystery, certain things are clear enough to allow some tentative suggestions. On the first of May Curll attempted to bring Addison and his fellow denizens of Button's Coffeehouse into the campaign against Pope by publishing "To the Ingenious Mr. Moore, Author of the Celebrated Worm-Power" and attributing it to Pope. The last lines of this crude poem were designed to irritate the Buttonians:

Ev'n Button's wits to worms shall turn,
Who maggots were before.

Perhaps because he saw through Curll's intent or perhaps because Pope had let him examine the Atticus portrait, Addison refused to be seduced into the argument.

Instead, just a week after the poem appeared, Addison graciously complimented Pope's *Iliad* in *Freeholder* No. 40 (7 May 1716). More importantly, Addison used the same issue of the *Freeholder* to characterize the superannuated author, a transparent portrait of Sir Richard Blackmore. "There is not a more melancholy Object in the Learned World," Addison insists, "than a Man who has written himself down." Suggesting the contrast between *Creation* and Blackmore's recent *Essays*, Addison continues: "As the Publick is more disposed to censure than to praise, his Readers will ridicule him for his last Works, when they have forgot to applaud those which preceded them.

In this case, where a Man has lost his Spirit by old Age and Infirmity, one could wish that his Friends and Relations would keep him from the use of Pen, Ink, and Paper. . . ." Equally insulting is Addison's suggestion that Blackmore's age makes dullness inevitable, for "neither his own Strength of Mind, nor those Parts of Life which are commonly unobserved, will furnish him with sufficient Materials to be at the same time both pleasing and voluminous. We find even in the outward Dress of Poetry, that Men, who write much without taking Breath, very often return to the same Phrases and Forms of Expression, as well as to the same Manner of Thinking."

The suggestion that Blackmore was senile and consequently that nothing he wrote should be considered seriously eventually became the opinion of the town to the extent that, according to Thomas Hearne, he was looked upon as "a sort of madman." This, of course, eventually served Pope's purpose; but Addison's primary motivation was probably Blackmore's insistence in the *Essays* that even excellent polite raillery such as was to be found in the *Tatler* and *Spectator* was morally impotent. Addison was too clever to rebut Blackmore's contention in *Freeholder* No. 40; but he returned to the subject two weeks later in *Freeholder* No.45 (25 May 1716). "I have lately read," Addison begins, "with much Pleasure, the Essays upon several Subjects published by Sir *Richard Blackmore*; and though I agree with him in many of his excellent observations, I cannot but take that reasonable Freedom, which he himself makes use of, with regard to other Writers, to dissent from him in some few particulars." Addison goes on to argue for the moral efficacy of his own periodical journalism. The "reasonable Freedom" Blackmore takes with fellow writers probably refers to his condemnation of Swift, which makes it all the more amusing that Swift misread the tone of Addison's opening to *Freeholder* No. 45 and noted in the margin that "I admire to see such praises from this Author to so insipid a Scoundrel, whom I know he despised."[43]

Blackmore did not misread the tone of *Freeholder* No. 45 nor did he fail to make proper application of the portrait in the fortieth number. Had he been more perceptive or suspicious, Blackmore might have wondered at Addison's duplicity earlier. It was Addison, of course, who had published Pope's covert ridicule of Sir Richard in *Guardian* No. 78 (10 June 1713), just at the time when Blackmore was using his influence with John Dennis to have the critic moderate his attack on *Cato*,[44] a pet production about which Addison was especially sensitive. Moreover, Addison invited Blackmore to come to Bilton for a visit in the fall of the same year, 1713.[45] Blackmore had all the more reason to be surprised at Addison's devastating insinuations in *Freeholder* No. 40 because all of his references to Addison in the *Essays* were complimentary, even excessively so; and *Cato* is singled out for special praise repeatedly,[46] a judgment which Dennis still disagrees with vehemently in "To Sir Richard Blackmore, on the Moral and Conclusion of an Epick Poem."[47]

Although Blackmore characterizes his disagreement with Addison's *Freeholder* No. 40 as a "friendly Debate," he defends himself vigorously. To Addison's charge that a writer's poorer works efface the fame of his earlier efforts, Blackmore asks "Did *Paradise Regain'd* destroy the Reputation of *Paradise Lost*?"[48] In a subsection of "An Essay upon Writing" entitled "Of the proper Age of Man for Writing," Blackmore refutes Addison by maintaining that mature wisdom is essential to the best poetry and that genius continues into the sixties (Blackmore's own age) if health is not impaired. To Addison's suggestion that age abates a writer's strength, Blackmore responds that such is true only of "weakly and washy Wits" but that the best writers "have no less the Strength of the Axe, than the Edge of the Razor."[49] And far from being a sign of protracted dullness, voluminous writing, if not deficient in other respects, is a proof of vitality. As was explained earlier, the "Essay upon Writing," which contains the reply to Addison as well as the criticism of Pope, was printed prior to the preface of the 1717 volume in which it appeared. In the interval between the printing of the essay and the printing of the preface which introduces and comments on each essay included in volume two, Addison must have attempted to convince Blackmore that the aging author in *Freeholder* No. 40 was not intended as a portrait of Sir Richard, for in the preface to the 1717 volume Blackmore says that he "misinterpreted" Addison's essay. Consequently, the preface treats the whole matter more temperately than does "An Essay upon Writing."

By the time the second volume of *Essays* was advertised in the *Evening-Post* for March 26-28, Blackmore did share some common literary ground with the Addisonian circle—they both deplored the Gay-Pope-Arbuthnot dramatic satire *Three Hours*

After Marriage which had run for seven consecutive nights in January. The characterizations of the several doctors in the play may have chagrined Blackmore and he may have vicariously suffered for his friend Dennis as the absurd Sir Tremendous; but it was the frequent obscenities which most offended Sir Richard and the wits at Button's. At the height of the outcry against Pope's part in the play,[50] Blackmore added his voice to the pack. "SINCE the ESSAY upon WRITING was printed, tho no[t] publish'd," he notes in the preface, "a New Comedy has been acted, so empty of Wit and Sense and so redundant in shameless Immorality, that perhaps no Dramatick Representation did ever so much disgrace the Stage or affront a *British* Audience. The Author and his two Friends, who, as he affirms, gave him their Assistance, and therefore must have approv'd this obscene Piece, have not only discover'd their own vitiated Judgment, but with an arrogant Assurance have taken it for granted that the Nation has the same degenerate and corrupt Taste."[51] If compared with John Durant Breval's *Confederates,* which the industrious Curll published only a few days after Blackmore's *Essays* went on sale, Sir Richard's comments seem, for all their vehemence, the objections of a gentleman. The Alexander Pope that Blackmore paints may be a bad influence on polite letters but he is scarcely Breval's deformed coward.[52] It was precisely because Blackmore was anything but a Grub Street hack laboring in the limbo of Curll's approval that he represented such a threat to Pope's reputation. However many readers slighted Blackmore's epic pretensions, few doubted his integrity. And therein lay his danger to Pope. In the 1717 edition of *An Essay on Criticism* Shadwell was banished and Blackmore restored to his rightful eminence.

The remainder of the essays in Blackmore's 1717 volume, on atheism, the spleen, future felicity, and divine love, creep by at a very petty pace. "An Essay upon Future Felicity" may interest those concerned with the development of the idea of progress but promises little to anyone else. The essay on atheism predictably denounces Epicurus' sensual conception of the greatest good and agrees with Locke that such atheists cannot properly be responsible citizens. Perhaps Blackmore's democratic bias is most evident in the style of "An Essay upon Divine Love," which he remarks "is not calculated for Persons of great Erudition, polite Literature, and superior Conversation" but for members of "the 'Middle Rank, who {in} their Number, Industry, and Vertue are so considerable a Part of Mankind."[53]

Blackmore is speaking of poetasters who pander to the vanity or vice of a degenerate public when he characterizes their work as ephemeral in "An Essay upon Writing"; but his words, Pope might say, turn almost of themselves on their pious author and accuse his own *Essays:* "All Authors must not expect," Blackmore warns, "that their Labours will be transmitted to Posterity, and that they shall offend and persecute the Ages to come as they do this, by their weak, or their loose and detestable Pens: tho the Species of ill Writers, by an uninterrupted Succession, will continue as long as the Press is imploy'd, yet following Ages will suffer by Individuals of their own Production."[54]

IV *"All These Are My Lays"*

Still smarting from Addison's indictment, Blackmore nonetheless went ahead with the publication of *A Collection of Poems on Various Subjects* the following year. Many of the poems are reprinted from previous editions or from larger collections in which they appeared anonymously and all are, relative to his epics, short, for Blackmore, somewhat peevishly, finds the modern taste "too impatient to undergo the Labour of long Reading."[55] "It has been objected to me," he also notes, probably in reference to *Freeholder* No. 40, "that I have already writ too much, and therefore should now spare the Press."[56] The public apparently does not share that opinion, he responds, since his works continue to sell.

Dismayed in his preface by the feeble quality of contemporary Christian lyrics, Blackmore has unalloyed praise only for Isaac Watts; but he continues to insist on the potential of Christian themes. Ironically, Blackmore's own religious lyrics are the poorest part of the poems which appear for the first time in the 1718 volume. Better is "Cremes," a social satire in the Horatian mode. The country bumpkin Cremes receives the advice of an experienced sinner as to the vices which are essential to success in the city. Cremes is instructed to "shake off your pious Rust" and

> Learn with Delight Religion to explode,
> As idle Cant, as Fancy, or as Fraud;

As an ignoble, feeble Passion, fit
For giddy Women, not for Men of Wit.[57]

Always inspired by the thought of the tomb, Blackmore writes best in the vein of reflective morality. In "On Fame" he argues that even that last noble infirmity loses its relish in the dust:

And yet their Atomes scatter'd by the Wind,
Thro' the wide Void, or to the Tomb confin'd,
Of all we say, unconscious Still remain,
They taste no Pleasure, as they feel no Pain.
Do's *Maro* smile, when we extol his Lays?
Or *Tully* listen in his Urn to Praise?[58]

Interestingly, in "The Retirement," a choice poem similar to John Pomfret's, Blackmore announces his desire to move away from London:

At a fit Distance from this noisy Town
A small neat Box would all my Wishes crown.[59]

The pun on the Essex village of Boxted seems too neat to be accidental. Perhaps in 1718 Blackmore had already purchased his retreat and was making future preparations to leave the house in Earl's Court, Kensington, to which he moved from Cheapside at about this time.[60]

The town was simply satiated with new tomes from Sir Richard. The *Poems* failed to sell. No second edition was called for; and five years later enough unsold copies survived to make it profitable for one of Blackmore's publishers, John Walthoe, to advertise them at a reduced rate in the *British Journal* (September 21, 1723). This is not to suggest that Blackmore did not continue a champion to the advocates of divine poetry. There were many who would rather praise him than read him. "You have . . . by your Writing," the 1719 edition of *A Collection of Divine Hymns* said of Blackmore, "retriev'd the Honour of Poetry, and rescu'd the Muses from that vile Drudgery they've of late years been Condemn'd to."[61] The volume is dedicated to Blackmore. Watts wanted to praise Blackmore publicly in the preface to his *Imitation of the Psalms of David* published the same year; but Blackmore, probably afraid that Watts would become a target for Pope's circle, dissuaded him from doing so. Instead, Watts personally inscribed the complimentary volume he presented Sir Richard on January 9, 1719.[62]

Meanwhile Nicholas Rowe, the poet laureate whose plays Blackmore praised lavishly in volume one of the *Essays,* died. Arbuthnot wrote Swift in December 1718 that "Mr. Rowe the Poet Laureat is dead and has left a Damn'd jade of a pegasus," a reference to Laurence Eusden, who was to succeed Rowe two weeks after Arbuthnot's letter. Remembering the spurs in *The Battle of the Books,* Arbuthnot opines that Eusden will have "more need of Lucan's present than Sir Richard Blackmore."[63] Rowe's death inevitably occasioned another session of the poets, this time under the supervision of the Duke of Buckingham, John Sheffield, in *The Election of a Poet Laureat* (1719). Needless to say, Sir Richard leads the aspirants:

> With a huge Mountain-load of Heroical Lumber,
> Which from *Tonson* to *Curl* ev'ry Press had groan'd under;
> Came *Blackmore,* and cry'd, lŏok! all these are my Lays,
> But at present I beg you'd but read my *Essays.*

But no one pays any attention, and the aging physician is soon shuffled aside by younger poets.

V *New "Huge Mountain-Loads"*

Blackmore was weary of literary controversy, though not of literature. During the intervals of his professional career after publication of his collected *Poems,* he was busied with completion of a project which he had begun twenty years earlier—the translation of the Psalms. When finished, probably in early 1720, Blackmore sent copies of the complete text to most or all of the Anglican bishops and archbishops with a request for their support in having the translation adopted for use in the churches. The Archbishops and Bishops of London, Winchester, Worcester, Ely, Chichester, Llandaff, Hereford, Norwich, Rochester, Oxford, St. David's, St. Asaph, Bangor, Peterborough, Bristol, Lichfield, and Coventry all responded with support for Blackmore's version, attesting to the King that it "has such an Agreement with the *Original Hebrew,* such Clearness and Purity of *English Stile,* and is so well adapted to the Capacity and Affections of the Common People" that it should be adopted.[64]

Armed with this formidable support, Blackmore officially petitioned the Lords Justices on October 27 to sanction his translation; and a royal licence was granted. The printing, commissioned by the Company of Stationers, was undertaken by John March. The number of copies must have been large, for a letter written to the secretary of the Society for the Propagation of the Gospel, suggests that it took John March several months to print and bind "the Whole Number of 'em."[65] Despite a preface which gives intelligent guidelines for scriptural versification, Blackmore's Psalms, though occasional passages may soar or sink, mostly creep their dull way along. Consequently, they never caught on in the parish churches; and their first edition was also their last. In 1724 the Society for the Propagation of the Gospel requested Blackmore to make a selection of his Psalms which might be printed inexpensively and used in rural parishes. Sir Richard responded enthusiastically; but, probably because of the Bishop of London's objection "to ye use of Private Compositions in Pub. Worship," the project never reached fruition.[66]

While manuscripts of the *New Version of the Psalms* were passing from prelate to prelate, Blackmore, using *Creation* as a model, turned his attention to a poem defending the divinity of Christ. Increasingly convinced that Arianism rather than Epicureanism posed the greatest threat to the established church, Blackmore used the intervals when he was working on his new poem to frame prose objections to the "fashionable heresy," as he characterizes it. In *Just Prejudices Against the Arian Hypothesis,* Blackmore argues that "the Arian Scheme shakes and subverts the Christian Institution; nor will it be possible for all the Wit of Man to uphold it, if the Divinity of Christ be given up."[67] Since toleration of Arians within the Church of England encourages the infection, he urges those who cannot ascribe to Christ's divinity to separate themselves from the Church.

One of the most influential opponents of the Arians, Joseph Pyke, praised Blackmore's stand and even made use of one of his arguments against toleration in *An Impartial View* printed the same year.[68] In an extended rebuttal to Pyke, a Dissenter, Thomas Morgan, sneered in passing at Blackmore's arguments.[69] In the interim, however, Blackmore had responded to objections that his stand was intolerant by publishing the more militant *Modern Arians Unmask'd,* in which the Arians are characterized as pernicious hypocrites, at once subscribing to and undermining the articles of faith.[70] Morgan, who had dismissed Blackmore with a few paragraphs in his *Refutation,* now perceived the doctor as a more formidable adversary and published *A Letter to Sir Richard Blackmore; Occasioned by his Book, intituled Modern Arians Unmask'd,* a work of interest here chiefly because of its false claim that Blackmore had once been an ardent Dissenter himself.[71] Doubtless Morgan was honestly misled by Blackmore's earlier latitudinarian stand and by his popularity as a pious poet among the Dissenters themselves.

Blackmore did not respond to Morgan directly. However, his poem in defense of Christ spoke to the purpose when it appeared the same year as *Redemption: A Divine Poem.*[72] The work itself, a 355-page couplet complement to *Creation,* is sandwiched between an interesting preface and the lyric "Hymn to Christ the Redeemer," which is sonorous enough to have inspired Thomson's hymn to the God of nature at the close of *The Seasons.*[73] Showing how congenial Blackmore found Dennis's aesthetics, the preface celebrates the "harmonious Dependence" of passion and reason. As he has demonstrated in *Creation,* Blackmore insists, it is "by Reason we may know God, but it is by Love that we must enjoy Him." A "most rational and praise-worthy Enthusiasm," Blackmore finds essential to great poetry. Unfortunately, despite its ambitious scope, *Redemption* is animated only infrequently by this "praise-worthy" fire. Certainly for the modern reader, uninterested in Arianism, the poem seems everlasting in the pejorative sense. Too frequently the little lightnings of its verse paragraphs terminate in smoke. Addison would have agreed with a modern critic that *Redemption* is "an old man's work."[74] By contrast, *Creation* is a work of genius. The pious theme of *Redemption* made it immune from literary criticism, so that its publication was received silently, without praise or blame.

On October 22, 1722, Blackmore resigned as an Elect, informing the Royal College of Physicians that he was retiring to Essex. Although he was to devote the reminder of his life to the composition of medical treatises, Blackmore concluded his days as a London physician after nearly thirty-five years of prosperous practice. After his retirement he published only one other literary work, *Alfred. An Epick Poem. In Twelve Books* in September 1723, a year after he moved to Boxted. Probably his heart was not in it. *Alfred* had been "ready for the Press" for over three years;[75] and yet Blackmore had delayed publication, possibly to avoid the inevitable aspersions that would follow its appearance were he still in London. Since *Alfred* is dedicated to Prince Frederick of Hanover, Blackmore knew that his literary enemies would insinuate that Sir Richard's lastest allegorical epic was simply another plea for appointment as Physician in Ordinary. And, in fact, in the preface, Blackmore insists that he had more to do with Frederick's grandfather's accession than had hitherto been recognized.[76]

The 450-plus pages of *Alfred* are as labored as long; and, apart from one unpublished American doctoral dissertation, there does not seem to be any evidence that anyone, even in Blackmore's own day, read his final epic. Benevolence, as Johnson so aptly says, was ashamed to favour, and malice was weary of insulting.[77] Even his friend Isaac Watts, who in the preface to *Horae Lyricae* had praised the two *Arthurs*, consigned *Alfred* to silence. "Pray tell me, Sir," he wrote William Duncombe six years after Blackmore's death, "whether Sir R. Blackmore's preface to his *Alfred* does not convince you that a Christian poet has happier advantages than a pagan? His *prefaces* are certainly better in their kind than his *poems*, as several gentlemen of good taste have acknowledged."[78]

The preface which Watts admired justifies the use of Christian machinery in epic and dismisses the "absurd and monstrous notion" that pagan theology is appropriate for a modern epic. Although many of his arguments are repeated from the preface to *Job* and "An Essay upon Epick Poetry," Blackmore's rebuttal to Boileau's objection to Christian machinery is thorough and effective.[79] "Thus," he says in summation, "revealed Religion by affording a real and substantial Ground and Reason of Disagreement and Opposition between the Machines, that is, good and bad Angels, and by administering great Plenty of lofty and wonderful Images, various Matter for beautiful Episodes, frequent Occasions of surprising Allusions, and every Thing that conduces to the Symmetry, Decoration and Dignity of the Poem, so that it may prove delightful, marvellous, and instructive, appears perfectly accommodated to all the Purposes of an Heroick Writing."[80]

Blackmore makes several other interesting and sometimes unorthodox observations in the preface. He disapproves of the modern tendency to eschew anything remotely sententious in epic as inappropriately preachy;[81] and he defends the "less musical and more diffusive" style of British epic poets when compared to the ancients by contrasting English with the classical languages. He also argues against a uniformly sublime style in epic as often inappropriate to the context (transitions, delivery of messages, etc.) or to the content ("low and vulgar Subjects"). "As it is not necessary," Blackmore concludes, "that the whole Poem should be active, but only a predominant Part, so I affirm that the Sublime Stile is preserved if it be found in all the lofty Subjects, tho, not in many others where it is not demanded; and it would be very absurd to act otherwise, for that would vitiate the Stile and swell it with a Tympany or empty Luxury of improper and pompous Expression."[82]

Beyond the preface, however, lay a desert into which few were intrepid enough to wander. If whole passages of *Alfred* were, in Blackmore's phrase, "obnoxious to Censure" there were no critics to find those errors out. In the absence of critical comment, one suspects that Thomas Hearne's reaction was fairly typical. On July 25 he recorded in his diary: "Yesterday going into a Shop, I saw an 8 vo Book just published, intitled, *Alfred*, A Poem in XII Books. The Author, Sir Richard Blackmore, a great Writer upon all Subjects, so that he is looked upon as a sort of Madman. He formerly writ a Poem in fol., called *Prince Arthur*, to flatter the Prince of Orange, and then he writ one called *Eliza*, to flatter Q. Anne, and now this is to flatter the Hanover Family; such is the poor Spirit of the Man."[83] Fallen away from the fat days of folio publication, *Alfred* suffered the additional indignity of selling so slowly that the bookseller advertised it in the *Daily Courant* as "just published" on the 19th of September, two months after Hearne's vision of *Alfred* had moved him to his *sic transit* meditations. Such decrepitude doubly impressed Hearne because he remembered that Blackmore "when of Edm. Hall (where he had his Education) was a great Tutor, and much respected, as I have often heard, for he left that place some years before I was matriculated."[84]

Undeterred by *Alfred's* natal mortality, Blackmore assiduously labored on his medical treatises for the benefit of fellow physicians and common readers alike. Before he died, as Johnson observes, there was scarcely any distemper of dreadful name which Sir Richard had not taught his readers to oppose.[85] The "affected contempt of the ancients" and the "supercilious derision of transmitted knowledge" which Johnson believed he had discovered by his admittedly "transient glances" at the medical volumes are really evidences of Blackmore's enlightened empiricism. As Blackmore explained in the preface to his treatise on consumption, he "honoured and esteemed all Men of superior Literature and Erudition" and only disparaged "false or superficial Learning, that signifies nothing for the Service of Mankind."[86]

In the years of retirement preceding his death, Blackmore served mankind with works on medicine and morality.[87] "While the distributors of literary fame were endeavouring to depreciate and degrade him," Johnson notes, "he either despised or defied them, wrote on as he had written before, and never turned aside to quiet them by civility or repress them by confutation."[88] While Blackmore was still in London Giles Jacob had described him as "an Excellent *Physician*, and a good Poet."[89] When he died on October 9, 1729, his old antagonist Abel Boyer wrote of him as "an eminent Physician but a very indifferent Poet."[90] In praise of Blackmore's endurance, it should be noted that even while his reputation declined his literary chariot rumbled on and that its wheels were only silenced at the grave.

CHAPTER 7

The Homer of the Bathous

'Tis true, Sir Richard was a Poet, but he is not placed by the best judges at the top head.

Thomas Hearne (22 November 1734)

An universal Genius rises not in an Age; but when he rises, Armies rise in him! he pours forth five or six Epick Poems with greater Facility, than five or six Pages can be produc'd by an elaborate and servile Copyer after Nature or the Ancients.

Alexander Pope, *Peri Bathous* (1728)

It is perhaps uniquely appropriate to perform a postmortem on the reputation of an author who so many enemies insisted never gave birth to a single living line. Whether, as Johnson thought, Blackmore merited the unremitting enmity of the wits "more by his virtue than his dullness"[1] is probably a fruitless inquiry. For wherever justice lies, the rough treatment Sir Richard received after he retired from London, the abuse he suffered or ignored in silence, is the whole extant history of the physician-poet for most students of literary history. Perhaps no other poet was so successfully "amber'd o'er" for posterity; and, predictably, prime credit belongs to Alexander Pope.

I *Prior to Death, Damnation*

Blackmore exists for the modern reader primarily as the father of the low sublime in Pope's brilliant *Peri Bathous;* and the generation of that work as it relates to satire of Sir Richard is an interesting and untold episode in Pope's literary career. Always eclectic, Pope had almost instinctively assimilated contempt for Blackmore from the Restoration wits who were his earliest friends and advocates in London literary society. His consanguinity with Dryden made that great man's enemies his dunces,[2] as the *Essay on Criticism* couplet suggests. Even as late as November of 1716 Pope clearly demonstrates a feel for the kind of ridicule heaped on Sir Richard over fifteen years earlier. In writing to the Earl of Burlington, Pope imagines a scene in which his publisher chides him for not composing while riding horseback: "there's Sir *Richard* in that rumbling old Chariot of his, between *Fleet-ditch* and *St. Giles* pound shall make you a half a *Job*.'"[3] If it was accidentally Blackmore's association with Curll that led to Pope's harassment there is yet something more inevitable in their antagonism. It is as if Pope had inherited from Dryden the commission to scourge Blackmore from the slopes of Parnassus.

The requisite tools awaited his genius. *Commendatory Verses* provided a rich harvest of sinking or opiate metaphors for *Peri Bathous*. Blackmore himself perceptively cited Tillotson's observation that "the gravest Book that ever was written, may be made ridiculous, by applying the Sayings of it to a foolish purpose."[4] This device, so successful in the *Bathous*, began in Blackmore's case with Tom Brown's "Epitome of a Poem" in *Commendatory Verses* and was improved upon in the "Arthurical,—Jobical,—Elizabethecal Style and Phrase" of the anonymous *Flight of the Pretender*. Most like the *Bathous*, however, is the 165-page prose *Homer and Virgil Not to be Compar'd with the Two ARTHURS*, which appeared shortly after the publication of *Job* in 1700. The anonymous author variously cites offensive passages from the two *Arthurs* and *Job* and comments on their absurdity. The author of *Homer and Virgil* preempts Pope by citing some of the same short passages included in the *Bathous*.[5]

Other resemblances, as well, suggest that Pope borrowed many of his ideas from the anonymous tract. The author of *Homer and Virgil* juxtaposes Longinus's expectations for sublime poetry and Blackmore's mundane practice. Pope's *Peri Bathous*, of course, imitates Longinus's *On the Sublime*. In *Homer and Virgil*, "The itch of Writing [which] lies in the Brain" is not to be cured by any medicines whatsoever (p. 78). Poetry in *Peri Bathous* is similarly described as "a *natural* or *morbid Secretion from the Brain*" (p. 12). The medical metaphors which Pope's editors have eruditely sought to explain by reference to Plato or Elizabethan humours psychology[6] almost certainly derive from the ridicule of Blackmore as physician-poet in the preceding four pages of *Homer and Virgil* (pp. 75–78). Chapter XII of *Peri Bathous,* "Of Expression, *and the several Sorts of Style of the present* Age," cleverly develops the gallery of "Manners" of writing in *Homer and Virgil.* "The Florid" of *Peri Bathous,* for instance, imitates "the *bold Kind*" in *Homer and Virgil,* where one finds "the *Colours* glaring, and laid on in *heaps*" (p. 117). The "*boisterous*" style in *Homer and Virgil* (p. 119) similarly suggests Pope's "PERT *Stile.*" Both critics object to Blackmore's absurd hyperbole as doing "Violence to Reason and Common Sense" (p. 116). Too frequently Sir Richard's "Mind is over-heated and intoxicated by *raging Metaphors* and *extravagant Non-sense*" (p. 138) leavened with "a Just *Mixture* of *Dulness*" and "*low trifling* Expressions" (p. 139).[7]

From Arbuthnot's report it is clear that Pope was doing some collecting of quotes as early as 1714, probably following the appearance of the fourth edition of *Prince Arthur,* which Pope repeatedly cites. Other concerns, however, caused Pope to set the Scriblerian project aside, and no reference to the *Bathous* survives until a few months before its publication in March 1728. Although hitherto unnoticed, Aaron Hill figures prominently during the middle years of this hiatus in the evolution of Pope's treatise. Inclined by a similar disposition in himself to be cynical regarding Pope's sincerity and general moral fervor, Hill obsequiously apologized in 1720 for an earlier satiric attack by lavishly praising Pope in *The Creation.*[8] Aware of Pope's hostility to Addison and Blackmore, Hill astutely critizes both men's treatment of his theme. After ridicule of several passages from Addison but before treating Sir Richard, Hill apologizes for his prolixity. "I am sliding insensibly," he says, "into a Theme, that requires rather a Volume, than a Page or two. . . ." Hill especially objects to Blackmore's unorthodox conceits. "He is," Hill insists, "too unmindful of the Dignity of his Subject, and diminishes it by mean, and contemptible Metaphors. Speaking of the Skies, he says they were 'Spun thin, and wove, on Nature's finest Loom.' What," Hill continues , "wou'd he [Longinus] have said of Sir Richard's Metaphorical Comparison of the CREATOR Himself to a Spinster, and a Weaver?"

Pope utilized Hill's hints to compile a larger "volume." Among the more obvious specific indebtednesses may be numbered Pope's "diminishing Figures" in Chapter XI and the overall conception of the superlative fifth chapter, wherein one who delves to achieve the true nadir of the bathetic must "be able, on the appearance of any Object, to furnish his Imagination with Ideas infinitely below it. . . . For example," Pope writes, "when a true Genius looks upon the *Sky*, he immediately catches the Idea of a Piece of *Blue Lutestring*, or a *Child's Mantle.*

Pr. Arthur p. 41-42.

The Skies, whose spreading Volumes scarce have room,
Spun thin, and wove in Nature's finest Loom,
The *new-born* World in *their soft Lap* embrac'd,
And all around their starry *Mantle* cast.[9]

Pope concludes the chapter by expanding Hill's original objection to inappropriate metaphorical representations of God's creative power. Eleven quotes from Blackmore's *Job* are wrenched from an already wretched context to show the deity now as a wrestler, now as an attorney, now as a baker.[10] In one sense, Pope's Scriblerus is more literal minded even than Hill, for at least Hill admitted that in a less religious context Blackmore's description of the sky "had been so far from Impropriety, as to have been pleasing, and praise-worthy."

Hill resumed his attack on Blackmore in the fifty-fourth number of the *Plain Dealer* for September 25, 1724. Used as an example of a poet who neglected the useful advice of literary criticism, Blackmore is described as "one of our most rapid, and voluminous Compilers of Poetry; who, though one wou'd imagine him too *heavy* to *ride Post;* yet, trusting wholly to Inspiration, breaks over Hedges and Ditches, and never checks his Horse's *Speed,* whether *out* of the Road, or *in* it." Blackmore's impetuous Pegasus is at its most unruly in the hymn which concludes *Creation.* Finding Sir Richard "no Niggard of his Fancy," Aaron Hill most vigorously objects to a passage which includes Blackmore's variation of Milton's creation metaphor:

Thro' the black Bosom of the empty Space,
The Gulphs confess th' Omnipotent Embrace:
And, pregnant grown, with Elemental Seed,
Unfinish'd Orbs, and Worlds in Embryo, breed.

"These fine Ideas, of His Creator," Hill criticizes, "at one, and the same Time, measuring the World with a Pair of Compasses—Omnipotently Embracing it—Impregnating it with Seed—

Breeding Orbs in Embryo—Picking Materials from the Crude Mass—Erecting it, with a Master-Hand—Labouring it—Cementing it—Nodding at it—and Setting it a rolling" involve such a profusion of metaphor as to finally produce only a "Shameful Heap of Inconsistencies." The metaphor of impregnation Hill, unaware of Blackmore's debt to Milton, finds "so indecent, so improper, so ill-express'd" as to be "almost blasphemous," a characterization certain to please Pope.

With whatever reluctance, however, Hill admits that Blackmore's verses are sometimes exceptional. He cites the opening of the hymn:

> Hail, King Supreme!—of Power, immense Abyss:
> Father of Light! Exhaustless Source of Bliss!
> Thou Uncreated, Self-existent Cause,
> Controul'd by no Superior Being's Laws.

"Since the first three Lines are so truly fine and poetical," Hill remarks, "what Pity, that the Author's Pride[11] depriv'd him of the Use of Criticism. Had he *buoy'd* himself, by the Help of *That*, He could never (though he had Sir *John Falstaff's Alacrity in Sinking*) have sunk, so soon, and so shamefully, as to tell us, in the 4th Verse—That *He, who is Supreme in Power, is controul'd by no Superior*." When Pope refers to the "*English* Author" who characterized the instinctive penchant for the bathous as "an *Alacrity of sinking*," he probably refers to Hill's criticism of Blackmore rather than Shakespeare's characterization of Falstaff.[12] The diving match in the *Dunciad* may also derive from Hill's ridicule of Sir Richard.

Pope finally gave this growing deprecation definitive form by publication of *Peri Bathous: Of the Art of Sinking in Poetry*. Thanklessly (and appropriately) lumping Aaron Hill with the flying fishes who struggle against nature when they seek to rise "out of the Profund," Pope borrows from Hill's critiques of Blackmore in the *Plain Dealer* to demolish whatever of Sir Richard's poetic reputation remained.[13] Unlike Aaron Hill's journalism, *Peri Bathous* itself is too well known to require even a cursory examination here. It should be adequate to reemphasize that Blackmore is indeed the chief dunce in that ambitious joke. The "Father of the *Bathous*, and indeed the *Homer* of it" receives citation forty-three separate times, far more than any other offender. Ambrose Philips, runner-up in this roll of infamy, is quoted a comparatively paltry eleven times. And despite the obvious unfairness of Pope's selective citation,[14] the modern reader can hardly wish that *Peri Bathous* were different than it is. Nor is our amusement abated to learn that the great scheme of Chapter XIII, "A Project for the Advancement of the Bathous," is simply Pope's elaboration of Blackmore's proposal in *Advice to the Poets* that his contemporaries, in default of adequate individual genius, combine to produce a poem worthy of Marlborough's campaigns.[15]

II *Eternity in Duncedom*

Peri Bathous was the prelude to the *Dunciad.* Pope intended to stir his antagonists into print with the *Bathous* and then squelch them once and for all with his modern epic. Blackmore, however, chose not to retaliate. His wife was dead not three months when *Peri Bathous* appeared and, in any case, Blackmore had not replied to any of his attackers since leaving London. Pope must have been disappointed because some of the wit of the overall design of *The Dunciad* depended on the juxtaposition of Pope's poem with Blackmore's *Kit-Cats* which it imitates at several points.[16] The "earliest" 1728 edition of *The Dunciad* which John Nichols examined had a frontispiece which shows an owl standing on a heavy pedestal on the ledge of which is written "P. and K. Arthur."[17] When Blackmore failed to reply, Pope altered *The Dunciad Variorium* the following year by placing the owl on top of a heap of volumes borne by a thistle-eating ass. Blackmore's works no longer appear on the frontispiece although Dennis's still remain. The conception of the frontispiece clearly comes, as was indicated earlier, from Blackmore's *The Kit-Cats.*

In one of the high heroic games in Book II of *The Dunciad,* Blackmore distinguishes himself as chief brayer. In a note, Pope indicates that he follows Sir Richard's lead by introducing the word "bray" into epic verse.[18] But the game ties in perfectly with the image of the frontispiece borrowed from the very author Pope indicts:

> So swells each Windpipe; Ass intones to Ass,
> Harmonic twang! of leather, horn, and brass. . . .
> But far o'er all, sonorous Blackmore's strain,

Walls, steeples, skies, bray back to him again:
In Tot'nam fields, the brethren with amaze
Prick all their ears up, and forget to graze;
Long Chanc'ry-lane retentive rolls the sound,
And courts to courts return it round and round:
Thames wafts it thence to Rufus' roaring hall,
And Hungerford re-ecchoes, bawl for bawl.
All hail him victor in both gifts of Song,
Who sings so loudly, and who sings so long. (II, 243-56)

Pope's note at this point disclaims responsibility for the burlesque Psalm and emphasizes Dryden's antagonism to the City Bard. It should also remind the reader that Pope's clever lines are merely a new turn to the old jests, for in a 1700 epistle of "Friendly Advice to Dr. B[ackmore]" the reader is informed that whereas Blackmore's stupidity had been previously disguised his poems now accuse him openly:

I'th Mountebank the Ass had lain conceal'd,
But his loud Braying has the Brute reveal'd.[19]

Pope's recurrent sneers in *The Dunciad* at the "pond'rous" pace of "everlasting" Blackmore's "endless line" are as predictable as they are amusing.

Immediately after the appearance of the 1728 *Dunciad*, Pope was criticized for including Blackmore as one of his dunces, not because Sir Richard deserved better but because the jokes seemed stale. "Sir *Richard*," according to one journalist, "has not for many Years been so much as nam'd, or even thought of among Writers as such; and whom no one except *P—pe*, would have had Ill-nature enough to revive."[20] *Mist's Journal* for June 8, 1728, flatly contended that "the sublime Poet *Maurus* [Blackmore], and his Arthurs, were introduced, to adorn the Work and save the expence of invention." Pope reacted to the first criticism by misquoting it to his own purpose in *The Dunciad Variorum*[21] and added *Mist's Journal* to the infamous catalogue of the frontispiece in place of "P. and K. Arthur."

As a further justification for his untimely attack on the retired physician-poet, Pope placed Blackmore's *Essays* last in "A List of Books, Papers, and Verses, in which our Author was abused, printed before the Publication of the *Dunciad*." "It is for a passage in pag.——of this book," Pope writes, "that Sir *Richard* was *put into the Dunciad.*"[22] Partially, at least, this is Pope's response to yet another of Curll's clever plays. As soon as *The Dunciad* first appeared Curll rushed into print with *A Complete Key To The Dunciad* in which, without Blackmore's approval, he quoted the relevant criticism of the Psalm burlesque from the *Essays.*[23] Apparently the inclusion of Blackmore's criticism aided sales, for Curll played it to the hilt. In the second edition of *A Complete Key,* issued barely a week after the first, Curll altered the title misleadingly to reflect his reprint of Blackmore's brief sentences. Curll now advertised the volume as *A Complete Key To The Dunciad. With a Character of Mr. Pope's Profane Writings. By Sir Richard Blackmore Kt. M.D. The Second Edition.* A third edition, similarly titled, appeared less than a month later. Thus, though the real Sir Richard was laboring inoffensively on a posthumously published *Essay upon Divine Eloquence*[24] during the summer following his wife's death, Curll resourcefully kept his war with Pope alive even in his absence.

Soon after the publication of *The Dunciad,* the anonymous author of *The Female Dunciad* defended Blackmore, arguing that Pope had ruined his reputation by indiscriminately lampooning men whose only offense to letters was a dislike of Pope's most dissolute and blasphemous productions.[25] While others waged war in Sir Richard's name, Pope was not content to forget Blackmore. Recently a 1732 lampoon entitled "Verses to be placed under the Picture of England's *Arch-Poet*" has been placed at Pope's doorstep, where it undoubtedly belongs.[26] This "ill-mannered and badly written squib"[27] appeared three years to the week after Blackmore's death, execrable poets being exempt from the universal injunction against speaking ill of the departed:

> See who ne'er was or will be half read!
> Who first sung *Arthur,* then sung *Alfred,*
> Prais'd great *Eliza* in God's anger,
> Till all true *Englishmen* cry'd, hang her!
> Made *William's* Virtues wipe the Bare A— —
> And hang'd up *Marlborough* in Arras: . . . [28]

One taste of this rotten apple suggests the tone of Pope's repeated references to Blackmore in his later Horatian poems.[29] It was, Theophilus Cibber opined in 1753, "as if to be at enmity with Blackmore had been hereditary to our greatest poets; we find Mr. Pope taking up the quarrel where Dryden left it, and persecuting this worthy man with yet a severer degree of satire."[30] His increasing infamy led poet after poet to hitch Sir Richard into rhyme whenever a dunce was called for. James Bramston is typical of the multitude of minor versifiers who modeled their opinions on Pope's. In *The Man of Taste* Bramston ridicules the pretender to taste who exclaims,

> Tho' *Blackmore's* works my soul with raptures fill,
> With notes by Bently they'd be better still.[31]

Defense of Blackmore was impossible, since even to be mentioned in the same couplet was a sort of infamy by association.

III *The Argument from Influence*

If neither his own works nor the merriment they occasioned in others seems sufficient apology for Sir Richard Blackmore's long career, it may be useful to consider that Pope's enmity did not completely suppress his influence on subsequent poets. If he had become a name in England, he was still respected in the more pious, or less fashionable, American colonies. There men as unlike as Mather Byles, Ben Franklin, and John Blair Linn seem to have been affected.[32] To Cotton Mather, whose works are filled with citations from Sir Richard, he is the "incomparable" Blackmore.[33] New England minister Benjamin Colman taught his daughter Jane to regard Blackmore as, after Watts, the true "laureate of the Church of Christ."[34] Ironically, Blackmore shares with Pope the distinction of having had the greatest influence on early 18th century American poetry.[35]

The same mixture of militant Christianity and melancholy reflection on death which enraptured the Americans in Blackmore's poetry probably influenced Edward Young to some extent, as verbal resemblances suggest.[36] In England, however, Blackmore's greatest contribution was the cultivation of the religious sublime in nature which led to the incredible popularity of James Thomson's *Seasons.*[37] Perhaps partially through David Mallet's *Excursion, Creation* became an "important example" for Thomson[38]; and the preface to the second edition of *Winter* (June 1726) defends poetry as a divine art in terms which clearly recall the preface to *Prince Arthur*.[39] The extent of Thomson's largely uninvestigated thematic and stylistic debt to Blackmore is best suggested by a few comparative quotations:

> And then advanc'd to wonders yet behind,
> Survey'd, and sung the vegetable kind.
>
> *Creation*, VII, 613-14
>
> A various sweetness swells the gentle race [of pears]
> In species different, but in kind the same.
>
> *Autumn*, 633-34
>
> Ferment the glebe, and genial spirits loose,
> Which lay imprison'd in the stiffen'd ground,
> Congeal'd with cold, in frosty fetters bound.
>
> *Creation*, II, 193-95
>
> Thick clouds ascend, in whose capacious womb
> A Vapoury deluge lies, to snow congealed.
>
> *Winter*, 225-26

The womb-cloud image which Thomson uses is one of Blackmore's favorites and occurs in the heroic poems as well as in *Creation*. "Glebe," of course, is one of Thomson's favorite words. The second quotation occurs in Blackmore's survey of the wonders of the changing seasons in Book II of *Creation* and suggests, what no critic has noted, that Thomson may be indebted to Blackmore for the overall design of his greatest work.[40]

Pervasive as Blackmore's influence on the *Seasons* was, *Creation* was even more of a catalyst to the Everest of eighteenth-century philosophic poetry, Pope's *Essay on Man*. Curious as this seems in light of Pope's contempt for Blackmore, the debt has not gone entirely unobserved. Johnson, noting that Blackmore excels at "ratiocination and description" in *Creation*, suggests that reasoning in verse "is a skill which Pope might have condescended to learn from him, when he needed it so much in his *Moral Essays*." Johnson does not suggest that Pope's *Essay on Man* does indeed borrow from Blackmore; but his editor, George Birkbeck Hill, feels so certain of Pope's indebtedness that he provides evidence of resemblances in a footnote.[41] Southey, similarly convinced that Pope "did not disdain to study and profit by *The Creation*," thought that Pope "should in gratitude, as well as in justice, have bestowed on [Blackmore] a redeeming verse in *The Dunciad*."[42]

An adequate documentation of Blackmore's influence on *An Essay on Man* would properly belong in a study of Pope. However, since the infrequent prior allegations have all rested solely on subjective response or on very scattered verbal resemblances,[43] some documentation seems necessary. Many resemblances, such as Blackmore's "wide inextricable maze" of the universe (p. 348) and Pope's "mighty maze" (I, 6), could indicate literal or figurative usages common at the time. The coincidence seems less likely to be accidental, however, when the resemblance is both thematic and rhetorical, as in the following:

> All these illustrious worlds, and many more,
> Which by the tube astronomers explore;
> And millions which the glass can ne'er descry,
> Lost in the wilds of vast immensity;
> Are suns, are centers, whose superior sway
> Planets of various magnitude obey.
> If we, with one clear comprehensive sight,
> Saw all these systems. . . . *Creation*, p. 349

> Thro' worlds unnumber'd tho' the God be known,
> 'Tis ours to trace him only in our own.
> He, who thro' vast immensity can pierce,
> See worlds on worlds compose one universe,
> Observe how system into system runs,
> What other planets circle other suns,
> What vary'd being peoples ev'ry star,
> May tell. . . . *An Essay on Man*, I 21-28

The history of society and government in Epistle III of *An Essay on Man* seems indisputably related to Blackmore's "Essay upon the Origin of Civil Power" in the 1716 volume of *Essays*.[44] But the linguistic debt is clearest when Pope adapts Blackmore's metaphor for the mutual dependence of all natural phenomena:

> The creeping ivy to prevent its fall,
> Clings with its fibrous grapples to the wall.
> Thus are the trees of every kind secure,
> Or by their own, or by a borrow'd power.
> *Creation*, p. 351

Man, like the gen'rous vine, supported lives;
The strength he gains is from th' embrace he gives.
An Essay on Man, III, 311-12

Enthusiasts of Pope recognize in Blackmore's last line one of Pope's favorite syntactic structures in *An Essay on Man.*

Blackmore's arguments from order and plentitude in Book III of *Creation* so closely anticipate Pope's first epistle that verse paragraphs might almost be exchanged. Perhaps as Blackmore had with Sandys, Pope is inviting a comparison between his and Blackmore's treatments of the same themes. The following juxtapositions are a suggestive few taken from many similarities in idea and metaphor:

(1) Now to the universal whole advert;
The Earth regard as of that whole a part.
Creation, p. 353

'Tis but a part we see, and not a whole.
An Essay on Man, I, 60

(2) Were all the stars, whose beauteous realms of light,
At distance only hung to shine by night,
And with their twinkling beams to please our sight?
Creation, p. 354

Ask for what end the heav'nly bodies shine,
Earth for whose use? Pride answers, "'Tis for mine."
An Essay on Man. I, 131-2

(3) Has all perfection which the place demands. . . .
Creation, p. 354

Say rather, Man's as perfect as he ought;
His knowledge measur'd to his state and place. . . .
An Essay on Man, I, 70-1

(4) Ye vain philosophers! presumptuous race!
Who would the Great Eternal Mind displace;
Take from the world its maker, and advance
To his high throne. . . .
Creation, p. 259

Presumptuous Man! . . .
Snatch from his hand the balance and the rod,
Re-judge his justice, be the GOD of GOD!
An Essay on Man, I, 35, 121-22

Examples might be multiplied but perhaps these are adequate to support Southey's contention that common gratitude as well as the charity so earnestly recommended in *An Essay on Man* should have inclined Pope to bestow upon Blackmore a few redeeming verses.

IV "*An Impartial Estimate*"

Nothing, however, was to redeem Blackmore's reputation. By mid-century he was remembered, when at all, as an illustration that it is genius and not rules that distinguished a poet from a poetaster, a Milton from a Blackmore.[45] James Beattie assumed that most reader's knowledge of Blackmore, in his day as in ours, would come from "the treatise on the Bathous," which abounds in examples of Sir Richard's propensity for degrading "into burlesque what he meant to raise to sublimity."[46] Before the end of the century, Blackmore ceased to be a distinguishable poetic entity; he merged into that troop of poetasters whose only excuse for immortality is to bear abuse. Even his defender, Samuel Johnson, justified as Blackmore's a couplet actually penned by Edward Howard in his epically atrocious *British Princes.*[47]

All this seemed unfair to a few. Blackmore was, above all, Theophilus Cibber insisted twenty-four years after the physician's death, "a chaste writer; he struggled in the cause of virtue, even in those times, when vice had the countenance of the great, and when an almost universal degeneracy prevailed. He was not afraid to appear the advocate of virtue, in opposition to the highest authority, and no lustre of abilities in his opponents could deter him from stripping vice of those gaudy colours, with which poets of the first eminence had cloathed her."[48] For all his lapses, Blackmore was not universally thought a fool. It was the opinion of Alexander Chalmers early in the nineteenth century that perhaps the time had come to judge Blackmore more even-handedly. "The fashion of the times," he explained, "or the mutual jealousies and animosities of contemporary wits and authors, often occasion great injustice to be done to worthy men and useful writers. But time will, generally, in a great degree, remove such prejudices; and those who form an impartial estimate of the character and various productions of Blackmore, will acknowledge, that as a writer, with all his faults, he had considerable merit; that as a man he was justly entitled to great applause."[49] Despite Chalmers' injunction, the injustice, if it is that, still stands.

Notes and References

Chapter One

1. Daniel Defoe, *A Tour through the Whole Island of Great Britain*, introductions by G. D. H. Cole and D. C. Browning (London, 1962), I, 280–85.

2. Albert Rosenberg, *Sir Richard Blackmore: A Poet and Physician of the Augustan Age* (Lincoln, Nebraska, 1953), p. 3. I am heavily indebted to Professor Rosenberg's fine and meticulous biography, having, with only minor exceptions, found his datings to be definitive.

3. Giles Jacob, *An Historical Account of the Lives and Writings of our most Considerable English Poets* (London, 1720), p. 9. Because Blackmore's name appears on no school documents there is some question whether he ever attended Westminster, despite his inclusion in *The Record of Old Westminsters*, 2 vols. (London, 1928), I, 133. However, since Blackmore was in London when Jacob's *Lives* was published and since Jacob's account (pp. 10–11) contains information concerning revisions and works not yet published which he probably received from Sir Richard or one of his close acquaintances, it seems likely that Blackmore sanctioned the details of his early liie.

4. William Turner, *A Compleat History of the Most Remarkable Providences* (London, 1697), p. 29. Blackmore is included as an example of "remarkable studiousness."

5. John Kettlewell, *A Compleat Collection of the Works of . . . John Kettlewell* (London, 1719), I, 11. All of Kettlewell's works are devotional.

6. Thomas Hearne, *Remarks and Collections of Thomas Hearne* (Oxford, 1885–1921), VIII, 101. Hearne matriculated into St. Edmund Hall some years after Blackmore left.

7. Public Records Office, S.P. 29/303/232–33. The full text of Pierce's letter is cited in Rosenberg, pp. 8–9.

8. Sir Richard Blackmore, *A Treatise of Consumptions and other Distempers Belonging to the Breast and Lungs* (London, 1724), pp. 92–93.

9. See William Tang, *Some Memoirs of the Life and Death of the Reverend Mr. John Shower. . . . Wherein is inserted. An Account of his Travels through France, Italy, Germany and Holland* (London, 1716), pp. 22–23; William Munk, *The Roll of the Royal College of*

Physicians (London, 1861), I, 305; and *Alumni Oxonieses*, IV, 1371. Rosenberg resists the temptation to construct a coherent interpretation out of the various bits of information available.

10. *Fifth Report of the Royal Commission of Historical Manuscripts* (London, 1876), I, 338.

11. Will and Ariel Durant, *The Age of Louis XIV* (New York, 1963), p. 71.

12. *The Diary of John Evelyn*, ed. E. S. De Beer (London, 1959), pp. 262-67.

13. Anthony A. Wood, *Fasti Oxonienses* (London, 1691), p. 888.

14. John Herman Randall, Jr., *The Career of Philosophy: From the Middle Ages to the Enlightenment* (New York, 1962), pp. 53-54, 65. See the same author's *The School of Padua and the Emergence of Modern Science* (Padua, 1961).

15. Evelyn, pp. 234-35, 241-42.

16. University of Padua, Archivic Antico Universitario, no. 284 c. 49v-50r. Cited in Rosenberg, p. 14. How long Blackmore lived in Padua is unknown. E. Hudson Long, citing the *Dictionary of National Biography*, contends he was a student for two years ("Notes on Sir Richard Blackmore," *MLN*, 58 (1943), 587). Rosenberg accurately notes that "the exact dates of his attendance are not recorded," p. 14.

17. Durant, p. 525.

18. C. D. O'Malley, "The English Physician in the Earlier Eighteenth Century," *England in the Restoration and Early Eighteenth Century: Essays in Culture and Society*, ed. H. T. Swedenberg, Jr. (Berkeley, California, 1972), pp. 151, 145-47.

19. Ibid., pp. 148, 154-55.

20. Ibid., pp. 153-54.

21. Sir Richard Blackmore, *A Treatise upon the Small-Pox* (London, 1723), pp. 47, 11.

22. *Poems on Affairs of State: Augustan Satirical Verse, 1660-1714. Volume 6: 1697-1704*, ed. Frank H. Ellis (New Haven, 1970), pp. 132-33. See also Ludwig Edelstein, "Sydenham and Cervantes," *Essays in the History of Medicine presented to Professor Arturo Castiglioni* (Baltimore, 1944), p. 61.

23. Sir Richard Blackmore, *King Arthur* (London, 1697), p. ix.

24. Rosenberg, pp. 17-18.

25. Sir George Clark, *A History of the Royal College of Physicians of London* (Oxford, 1966), II, 427-47, 480-84.

26. Blackmore's account, *A True and Impartial History of the Conspiracy against the Person and Government of King William III. Of Glorious Memory, in the Year 1695*, was not published until 1723, probably because the facts were embarrassing to politicians in William's government.

27. G. N. Clark, *The Later Stuarts: 1660-1714* (Oxford, 1940), p. 177.

28. Recorded in the Public Record Office, T 53/13/425 and T 52/19/275. On p. 35 Rosenberg incorrectly indicates that Blackmore received £2000 yearly.

29. *The Correspondence of John Locke and Edward Clark*, ed. Benjamin Rand (London, 1927), p. 567.

30. *The Report of the Physicians and Surgeons, Commanded to assist at the Dissecting the Body of His Late Majesty at Kensington* (London, 1702).

31. Rosenberg, p. 75–76.

32. William Pittis, *Some Memoirs of the Life of John Radcliffe, M.D.* 2nd ed. (London, 1715), p. 42.

33. See Albert Rosenberg's review of Campbell R. Hone, *The Life of Dr. John Radcliffe* (London, 1950) in *Isis* (October 1951), pp. 250–51.

34. Sir Richard Blackmore, *Discourses on the Gout, A Rheumatism, and the King's Evil* (London, 1726), p. li.

35. John Oldmixon, *The Life and Posthumous Works of Arthur Maynwaring, Esq.* (London, 1715), pp. 342–43.

36. Munk, I, 432; *Memoirs of the Life of the Most Noble Thomas Late Marquess of Wharton* (London, 1715), p. 106; *The Works and Life of the Right Honourable Charles, Late Earl of Halifax* (London, 1715), pp. 260–61.

37. *Verney Letters of the Eighteenth Century from the Manuscripts at Claydon House* (London, 1930), II, 81. Cited by Rosenberg, p. 132.

38. Blackmore, *A Treatise of Consumptions*, pp. v–vi.

39. Sir Richard Blackmore, *A Discourse upon the Plague* (London, 1721), preface.

40. Ibid., p. 87. Thomas N. Toomey thinks that Blackmore's account of typhus has permanent value, "Sir Richard Blackmore, M.D.," *Annals of Medical History*, 4 (1922), 180–88. Toomey is also impressed by the fact that Blackmore offers no commentaries on ancient authors, the common method of medical treatises at this time.

41. Sir Richard Blackmore, *A Treatise of the Spleen and Vapours: Or, Hypocondriacal and Hysterical Affections* (London, 1725) and *A Critical Dissertation upon the Spleen* (London, 1725).

42. Blackmore, *Discourses on the Gout*.

43. Sir Richard Blackmore, *Dissertations on a Dropsy, A Tympany, the Jaundice, the Stone, and a Diabetes* (London, 1727), p. xix.

44. See *Tatler* No. 3. Steele apologizes to Blackmore in *Tatler* No. 14.

45. *The Letters of Joseph Addison*, ed. Walter Graham (Oxford, 1941), pp. 1–2.

46. William Molyneux to John Locke in *Some Familiar Letters between Mr. Locke, and Several of his Friends* (London, 1708), p. 219. This volume certainly must have confirmed many readers in the high opinion they had of Blackmore's epics.

47. Sir Richard Blackmore, *Just Prejudices Against the Arian Hypothesis* and *Modern Arians Unmask'd*, both (London, 1721).

48. In volume 38 of *The Political State of Great Britain* (London, 1729), p. 392.

49. Rosenberg, p. 159. In the preface to Blackmore's posthumously published religious work, *The Accomplished Preacher* (London, 1731), the Reverend John White assures the reader that Sir Richard died as piously as he had lived. Perhaps Sir Richard had been reading Kettlewell's *Death Made Comfortable, or the Way to Die Well* (London, 1695).

Chapter Two

1. John Sheffield, "An Essay upon Poetry," *Criticism and Aesthetics: 1660–1800,* ed. Oliver F. Sigworth (San Francisco, 1971), p. 21.

2. John Dryden, "The Author's Apology for Heroic Poetry," *Of Dramatic Poesy and Other Critical Essays,* ed. George Watson (London, 1962), I, 198. Hereafter cited as "John Dryden, *Critical Essays.*"

3. Ibid., II, 96.

4. Ibid., II, 223.

5. Northrop Frye, "The Story of All Things," *The Return of Eden: Five Essays on Milton's Epics* (Toronto, 1965), p. 5.

6. "An Essay upon Poetry," p. 22.

7. W. Macneile Dixon, *English Epic and Heroic Poetry* (New York, 1964), pp. 224–52; E. M. W. Tillyard, *The English Epic and Its Background* (London, 1954), pp. 452–509.

8. P. K. Elkin, *The Augustan Defence of Satire* (Oxford, 1973), p. 3.

9. H. T. Swedenberg, Jr., *The Theory of the Epic in England: 1650–1800,* University of California Publications in English, Volume XV (Berkeley, 1944), pp. 27, 43.

10. *Poems on Affairs of State: Augustan Satirical Verse, 1660–1714. Volume I: 1660–1678,* ed. George de F. Lord (New Haven, 1963), p. 339.

11. Brendan O Hehir, *Harmony from Discords: A Life of Sir John Denham* (Berkeley, 1968), p. 249.

12. Richard Blackmore, *Prince Arthur. An Heroick Poem. In Ten Books* (London, 1695), preface. In *Boileau and the French Classical Critics in England: 1660–1830* (New York, 1965), p. 244, A. F. B. Clark believes Blackmore's preface to be the first practical application of Le Bossu.

13. For Boileau's view see *L'Art poëtique,* III, 193ff. On this point, Blackmore is less cautious than Le Bossu.

14. In his condemnation of the stage Blackmore mentions no names; however for an example perfectly fitting his description see the first act of Thomas Shadwell's *The Virtuoso* (1676).

15. *The Stage Acquitted* (London, 1698), p. 136.

16. George Saintsbury, *A History of English Criticism* (London, 1912), p. 137.
17. *Poems on Affairs of State,* VI, 130.
18. Thomas Rymer, *Monsieur Rapin's Reflections on Aristotle's Treatise of Poesie* (London, 1694). "The Preface of the Translator" is reprinted in *The Critical Works of Thomas Rymer,* ed. Curt A. Zimansky (New Haven, 1956), pp. 1–16.
19. Roberta Florence Brinkley, *Arthurian Legend in the Seventeenth Century.* Johns Hopkins Monographs in Literary History III (Baltimore, 1932), p. 123. James Douglas Merriman finds *Prince Arthur* a product of "grotesque egotism" whose "sources are in fact anything but Arthurian" in *The Flower of Kings: A Study of The Arthurian Legend in England between 1485 and 1835* (Lawrence, Kansas, 1973), pp. 64, 66.
20. Brinkley, p. 169.
21. Leah Rachel Clara Yoffie, *Creation, the Angels, and the Fall of Man in Milton's Paradise Lost and Paradise Regained and in the Work of Sir Richard Blackmore.* Unpublished dissertation (University of North Carolina at Chapel Hill, 1942), p. 2. Merriman admits that Blackmore's eclecticism is "remarkably ingenious," p. 67.
22. Brinkley, pp. 177, 108–13.
23. Sir Richard Blackmore, *Essays upon Several Subjects* (London, 1716), p. 43.
24. Samuel Johnson, *Lives of the English Poets,* ed. George Birkbeck Hill (Oxford, 1905), II, 237.
25. "The Story of All Things," p. 5.
26. *The Correspondence of Alexander Pope,* ed. George Sherburn (Oxford, 1956), III, 164.
27. John Hawkesworth, *Life of Swift* (Dublin, 1755), p. 20.
28. *Lives of the English Poets,* II, 238.
29. John Phillips, *A Reflection on our Modern Poesy* (London, 1695), preface.
30. *Monsieur Bossu's Treatise of the Epick Poem* (London, 1695), preface.
31. Ibid.
32. Edward Howard, *An Essay upon Pastoral* (London, 1695), The Proem. This twelve page pamphlet is not by the epic poet Edward Howard mentioned earlier.
33. *The Second, Fourth, and Seventh Satyrs of Monsieur Boileau Imitated* (London, 1696), p. 90.
34. John Oldmixon, *Poems on Several Occasions* (London, 1696), pp. 103-104, 72–73.
35. John Dennis wrote the prologue for Oldmixon's *Amyntas* in 1698. See H. G. Paul, *John Dennis: His Life and Criticism* (New York, 1911), p. 37.
36. *Lives of the English Poets,* II, 238.

37. Edmund Gosse, *History of Eighteenth Century Literature* (London, 1889), p. 394.

38. George Saintsbury cited in *The Critical Works of John Dennis*, ed. Edward Niles Hooker (Baltimore, 1939), I, 449.

39. Yoffie, pp. 50–51.

40. *The Critical Works of John Dennis*, I, 449.

41. Ibid., I, 49, 51.

42. Later, recognizing Milton's accomplishment, Dennis changed his mind and used Christian machinery in his pretentious *A Poem on the Battle of Ramillies. In Five Books* (London, 1707). The resemblance of that poem to *Prince Arthur* is striking. Satan and Discord aid the French against the Duke of Marlborough while God sends the Angel of Concord to protect him.

43. *The Critical Works of John Dennis*, I, 52–53, 55.

44. Ibid., pp. 60, 66.

45. Ibid., p. 83.

46. Ibid., pp. 104, 127.

47. Ibid., p. 138.

48. Ibid., pp. 70–71.

49. Charles Gildon in *The Lives and Characters of the English Dramatic Poets* (London, 1698), p. 38. For the same judgment by another writer see Giles Jacob's *The Poetical Register* (London, 1723), I, 68.

50. Sir Richard Blackmore, *Alfred, An Epick Poem* (London, 1723), p. ii.

51. In "Remarks upon Pope's Homer" in *The Critical Works of John Dennis*, II, 120.

52. Ibid., II, 402–403, 109–14.

53. No. 54, 25 September 1724.

54. *Lives of the English Poets*, II, 239.

55. William Pittis, *An Epistolary Poem to N. Tate, Esquire, And Poet Laureate to his Majesty: Occasioned by the taking of Namur* (London, 1696), preface.

56. *Miscellany Poems* (London, 1697), p. 35.

57. Colley Cibber, *Love's Last Shift* in *Plays of the Restoration and Eighteenth Century*, ed. Dougald MacMillan and Howard Mumford Jones (New York, 1931), p. 317. The play was first performed in January 1696.

58. Judith Drake, *An Essay in Defence of the Female Sex* (London, 1696), p. 50.

59. Edward Bysshe, *The Art of English Poetry* (London, 1702). Bysshe's book was reprinted seven times during Blackmore's lifetime. Only Milton and Dryden's translations are more frequently cited for admiration than Blackmore. The 1702 edition quotes seventy passages from *Prince Arthur* and *King Arthur*.

60. William Coward, *Licentia Poetica Discuss'd, or the True Test of Poetry* (London, 1709), p. 23.
61. Transcribed by Howard Maynadier, *The Arthur of the English Poets* (New York, 1907), p. 302.
62. *Lives of the English Poets,* II, 238 n.
63. Rosenberg, p. 30.
64. *Poems on Affairs of State,* V, 483.
65. When Newton wrote the *Principia,* as he told Richard Bentley, he "had an eye upon such principles as might work with considering men for the belief of a Deity." In another letter to Bentley he argued that "gravity may put the planets into motion, but without the divine power it could never put them into such a circulating motion as they have about the sun." See *Newton's Philosophy of Nature: Selections from His Writings,* ed. H. S. Thayer (New York, 1953), pp. 46, 53.
66. Blackmore, *King Arthur,* p. xiii.
67. *The Critical Works of John Dennis,* I, 334.
68. This is also Professor Yoffie's opinion
69. Yoffie, p. 2, disagrees with Raymond Dexter Havens' contention that Blackmore was a mere plagiarist. Cf. *The Influence of Milton on English Poetry* (Cambridge, Mass., 1922), p. 91.
70. Yoffie, p. 415.
71. Sir Walter Scott's *Life of John Dryden* has the fullest treatment.
72. *The Works of John Dryden,* ed. A. B. Chambers and William Frost (Berkeley, 1974), IV, 22.
73. Ibid., IV, 23.
74. A commonplace, see Charles E. Ward, *The Life of John Dryden* (Chapel Hill, N.C., 1961), p. 293.
75. See *Essays upon Several Subjects,* p. v and *Alfred,* p. xliv.
76. Dryden does seem to have encouraged William Walsh to attack Rymer in a similar manner. See *The Letters of John Dryden,* ed. Charles E. Ward (Durham, N.C., 1942), No. 24. Blackmore, of course, allied himself with Rymer in the preface to *Prince Arthur.*
77. *Essays of John Dryden,* ed. W. P. Ker (Oxford, 1900), II, 164. Watson reprints only a portion of the *Aeneis* dedication.
78. Because Dryden does not mention Blackmore by name any more than Blackmore does Dryden, no previous critic has noticed these passages as an attack on Sir Richard.
79. Ibid., II, 224–25.
80. Ibid., II, 244.
81. *The Critical Works of John Dennis,* II, 387.
82. *The Poems of John Dryden,* ed. James Kinsley (Oxford, 1958), III, 1435.
83. *Licentia Poetica Discuss'd,* pp. 23–24.
84. Dated 1699 but published anonymously in December 1698 as *A Short History of the Last Parliament.*

85. John Hughes, *The Triumph of Peace* (London, 1698), preface.

86. Molyneux quotes the lines on the constellations cited above in a subsequent letter to Locke.

87. *The Works of John Locke* (London, 1823), IX, 423, 426, 429–30.

Chapter Three

1. *A Short History of the Last Parliament* (London, 1699).

2. The phrase is Evelyn's.

3. *Miscellanies over Claret*, III, 61–62. The shortlived periodical was begun by Brown in late March or early April of 1697, just after the publication of *King Arthur.* See Benjamin Boyce, *Tom Brown of Facetious Memory* (Cambridge, Mass., 1939), pp. 57, 193.

4. *Liber Annalium Collegii Medicarum Lond.*, 6. 194. Cited in *Poems on Affairs of State*, VI, 60.

5. Clark, *A History of the Royal College of Physicians*, II, 443.

6. The best discussions of the controversy are found in Clark's *History of The Royal College*, II, 427–99, and in Frank H. Ellis's "The Background of the London Dispensary," *Journal of the History of Medicine*, 20 (1965), 197–212.

7. "Life of Garth," *Lives of the English Poets*, II, 63.

8. *The Present State of Physick* (London, 1701), preface. Cited in *Poems on Affairs of State*, VI, 62.

9. See *Poems on Affairs of State*, VI, 138 n. 87. For an argument that Blackmore intended Tom Brown see Benjamin Boyce, "The Dispensary, Sir Richard Blackmore, and the Captain of the Wits," *Review of English Studies*, 14 (1938), 453–58.

10. *Essays upon Several Subjects*, I, 190.

11. Ibid., I, 201, 192–93.

12. Ibid., I, 199, 207.

13. *Poems on Affairs of State*, VI, 131.

14. *Essays upon Several Subjects*, I, 214.

15. *A Satyr against Wit* (London, 1700), pp. 9–10. An excellently annotated and slightly modernized text of this poem is included in *Poems on Affairs of State*, VI, 135–54.

16. Cited from verses "To Mr. Charles Hopkins upon my Lending Him Mr. Wallers Poems" in *Poems on Affairs of State*, VI, 145.

17. Dryden, *Critical Essays*, I, 259–60.

18. In using Judith Drake's description of the fop poet who "is a Smuggler of Wit, and Steals *French* Fancies" in *An Essay in Defense of the Female Sex* (London, 1696), p. 79, Blackmore uses the ammunition provided by one enemy to attack another.

19. "Come on, ye Critics! Fine one fault who dare,/For, read it backward like a witch's prayer,/'T will do as well. . . ." Charles Sackville in *Poems on Affairs of State*, I, 338.

20. Ellis's characterization in *Poems on Affairs of State,* VI, 133.

21. *Letters of Wit, Politicks, and Morality,* ed. Abel Boyer (London, 1701), pp. 250–51.

22. In "To Sir W. S—," in *The Works of Monseiur Voiture* (London, 1705), pp. 128–30. Cited by Richard C. Boys in *Sir Richard Blackmore and the Wits.* University of Michigan Contributions in Modern Philology, No. 13 (Ann Arbor, 1949), pp. 10–11.

23. British Museum MS. Sloane 1731 A, F. 111.

24. *A Satyr Upon a late Pamphlet, Entituled, A Satyr against Wit* (London, 1700), pp. 4–5.

25. Samuel Cobb, *Poems on Several Occasions* (London, 1707), pp. 213–15. *Poetae Britannici* was revized to reflect Dryden's death and reprinted in Cobb's *Poems* as "Of Poetry."

26. In the letter "To Sir W. S—" dated 8 January [1700]. *Poetae Britannici* was advertised in the *Post Boy* for January 11.

27. Daniel Defoe, *The Pacificator* (London, 1700). Excellently edited in *Poems on Affairs of State,* VI, 160–80.

28. *A Satyr against Satyrs* (London, 1700).

29. Boys, *Sir Richard Blackmore and the Wits,* p. 60. He also feels that the war of the wits against Blackmore "has received far less attention than its importance warrants" (p. 2).

30. The title plays upon the notoriety of Henry and John Arthur, two robbers. John had been hanged and brother Henry killed in a tavern brawl the previous year.

31. Boys, *Sir Richard Blackmore and the Wits,* p. 49. Ellis entertains a similarly low opinion, *Poems on Affairs of State,* VI, 181.

32. This fact greatly complicates attribution. Boys remains the authority on the authorship of *Commendatory Verses.* See also his "The Authorship of Poems in *Commendatory Verses* (1700)," *Philological Quarterly,* 30 (1951), 221–22 and W. J. Cameron's useful suggestions in *Notes and Queries,* 208 (1963), 62–66.

33. Blackmore's *Paraphrase on the Book of Job* was advertised in the *London Gazette* two days after *Commendatory Verses* went on sale.

34. *Commendatory Verses, on the Author of the Two Arthurs and the Satyr against Wit; By Some of His Particular Friends* (London, 1700), p. i. Usefully reprinted with *Discommendatory Verses* in Boys's *Sir Richard Blackmore and the Wits,* pp. 61–130. For a full text of Sir Charles Sedley's undistinguished contribution see *Poems on Affairs of State,* VI, 187–88.

35. Richmond Bond damns Brown's work with the faintest of praise, finding his transversions "not without ingenuity" (p. 237).

36. *Discommendatory Verses, on Those Which are Truly Commendatory, on the Author of the Two Arthurs, and the Satyr against Wit* (London, 1700), p. ii.

37. Boys, *Sir Richard Blackmore and the Wits,* p. 37.

38. *The Works of Mr. Thomas Brown, Serious and Comical, In Prose and Verse. In Four Volumes. The Fifth Edition* (London, 1720), I, 232.

39. *The Critical Works of John Dennis,* II, 397.

40. *Letters of Wit, Politicks, and Morality,* pp. 217–19.

41. W. J. Cameron, p. 66, disputes Boys's contention that Garth contributed one poem to *Commendatory Verses.*

42. One possible objection to the very tentative suggestion of Dennis as editor of *Discommendatory Verses* is the attribution of the eighth poem in *Commendatory Verses.* Tom Brown's *Works* attributes the poem to William Burnaby who subsequently attacked Blackmore in the character of the physician Bloodem in *The Reformed Wife* (see F. E. Budd, *Dramatic Works of William Burnaby* [London, 1931], pp. 51–52). The rejoinder in *Discommendatory Verses,* however, attributes it to *"D[enn]is."* This may be a smoke-screen, a deliberate attempt to disassociate Dennis from *Discommendatory Verses.* It may also be the case that, having contributed a poem to *Commendatory Verses* (assuming the attribution in Brown's Works to be incorrect), Dennis would have tipped his hand had he not included a rebuttal to his own contribution along with the others. Further, if Burnaby was the author, Dennis may have wished to avoid squibbing him, since Burnaby's epilogue to Dennis's *The Comical Gallant* in 1702 suggests that the men remained on good terms.

43. Boys, *Sir Richard Blackmore and the Wits,* p. 43.

44. Yoffie, p. 32; Rosenberg, p. 52.

45. Nahum Tate, *Panacea: A Poem Upon Tea* (London, 1700), postscript. Nicholas Brady defended Tate in *Commendatory Verses.* Thus we have the unique situation of the King's Chaplain (Brady) defending the Poet Laureate (Tate) against the King's Physician (Blackmore). Tate doubtless viewed this play on the lower slopes of Parnassus as all in the order of things and took no offense. He later praised Blackmore as "the British Elijah."

46. *The Poetical Works of the Honourable Sir Charles Sedley* (London, 1707), p. ii.

47. Tom Brown, *Works,* I, 77.

48. Although Boys mentions a thirty-page issue of *Commendatory Verses* (1700), Ellis finds no copy extant (VI, 189, 755).

49. *Commendatory Verses,* p. 28.

50. In the *London Gazette,* February 29–March 4.

51. Tom Brown, *Works,* I, 235. From "To Madam —upon sending her Sir *Richard Blackmore's Job* and *Habakkuk."*

52. *Miscellanea Sacra: Or, Poems on Divine and Moral Subjects,* ed. Nahum Tate (London, 1696), dedication.

53. Ibid., pp. 98, 102–106, 110, 100, 101.

54. Swedenberg, *The Theory of the Epic in England: 1650–1800,* p. 73–74.

55. Richard F. Jones, "Science and Criticism in the Neo-Classical Age of English Literature," *Journal of the History of Ideas,* I (1940), pp. 395–97.

56. *L'Art poëtique,* III, 193 ff.

57. Blackmore does seem to have been the first English epic poet to employ Nordic Mythology—i.e., Thor in *Prince Arthur.*

58. See Swedenberg, *The Theory of the Epic in England: 1650–1800,* pp. 306–34.

59. *Essays upon Several Subjects,* I, 49–51.

60. See Dennis's objection to Blackmore's contention that an epic may end unfortunately (*Essays upon Several Subjects,* I, 79) in "To Sir Richard Blackmore on the Moral and Conclusion of an Epick Poem, 1716," *Critical Works of John Dennis,* II, 109–14.

61. Dryden, *Critical Essays,* II, 84.

62. The "Commendatory Verses" prefixed to Sandys's *Paraphrase upon Job* may have been an additional stimulant to the wits' imaginations when burlesquing Blackmore with *Commendatory Verses.*

63. George Sandys, *A Paraphrase Upon the Divine Poems* (London, 1648), p. 20 of the subsection "A Paraphrase upon the Songs Collected out of the Old and New Testament."

64. Sir Richard Blackmore, *A Paraphrase on the Book of Job* (London, 1700), p. 285.

65. In *The Theory of the Epic in England: 1650–1800,* Swedenberg notes that those favoring rhyme were in the minority and were usually apologetic concerning their preference, p. 341.

66. *Essays upon Several Subjects,* I, 111–12.

67. Havens, p. 62.

68. Richard Gwinnett, *Pylades and Corinna: Or, Memoirs of R. G. . . . and Mrs. E. Thomas* (London, 1731), II, 178–79.

69. "The Devil, A Wife, and a Poet" included in *The Grove* (London, 1721), p. 42.

70. Tom Brown, "A Lent-Entertainment: Or, A Merry Interview by Moon-light, betwixt a Ghost and the City-Bard" in *Poems on Affairs of State,* VI, 193.

71. Brown, *Works,* III, 22.

72. Krapp, p. 81.

73. Samuel Wesley, *An Epistle To A Friend Concerning Poetry* (London, 1700), pp. 18, 20.

74. *Poems of John Dryden,* IV, 2059.

75. *Letters of John Dryden,* p. 130.

76. Dryden, *Critical Essays,* I, 86.

77. Ibid., II, 164. In the preface to *Examen Poeticum* (London, 1693).

78. Ibid., II, 270.

79. Ibid., II, 291–94. Dryden's words proved prophetic. See Pope's

An Essay on Criticism, 11. 462–63: "Might he [Dryden] return, and bless once more our Eyes,/New *Blackmores* and new *Milbourns* must arise." If Blackmore's audacity in urging his comparison to Dryden seems inconceivable, consider Luke Milbourne's renditions of Virgil which he appended to his criticism of Dryden's *Aeneis* as examples of the way Maro should be translated. To call them excrable is a kindness.

80. *Poems of John Dryden*, IV, 1531–32.

81. The smell and appearance of excrement were considered vital to a proper diagnosis.

82. *Poems of John Dryden*, IV, 1758–59.

83. Colley Cibber, *An Apology for the Life of Colley Cibber*, ed. B. R. S. Fone (Ann Arbor, 1968), p. 149.

84. Tom Brown, *Works*, II, 148–49.

85. *Homer and Virgil Not to Be Compar'd with the TWO ARTHURS* (London, 1700), pp. 78, 64.

86. Ibid., pp. 93–97, 87, 106–107, 116, 117–19.

87. Ibid., pp. 69, 143, 138–39, 74–75.

88. Suckling introduced the genre from Italy with *A Session of the Poets* (1637, published 1646). Forty years later the mode was popularly revived by Buckingham or Rochester.

89. Daniel Kenrick, *A New Session of the Poets, Occasion'd by the Death of Mr. Dryden* (London, 1700), p. 2.

90. For Pope's improvement of these lines see *An Essay on Criticism*, 11. 241–42.

91. Kenrick, pp. 5–6.

92. The Yale copy, from which I worked, has "Tho: Phillips" in an eighteenth-century hand on the title page:

AN
EPISTLE
Tho: TO *Phillips*
Sr. Richard Blackmore,
Occasion'd by
The New Session of the POETS.

93. *An Epistle to Sr. Richard Blackmore* (London, 1700), pp. 5–6, 9. The author mistakes Dryden's epilogue for his prologue.

94. Although the poem speaks of the tomb as already completed, Montagu never built the memorial.

95. *A Satyr against Wit*, pp. 10–11.

96. *An Epistle to Sr. Richard Blackmore*, p. 12.

97. In Charles Gildon's *Examen Miscellaneum* (London, 1702), p. 84.

98. By Thomas Cheek in Boyer's *Letters of Wit, Politicks, and Morality*, p. 285.

99. *Religio Poetae: Or A Satyr on the Poets* (London, 1703), p. 6.

100. *The Town Display'd, In A Letter to Amintor in the Country* (London, 1701), p. 15.
101. So characterized in *Spite and Spleen; Or the Doctor Run Mad* (London, n.d. [1703]).
102. Abel Boyer, *The English Theophrastus: Or, The Manners of the Age* (London, 1702), p. 2.
103. "The Court," *Poems on Affairs of State,* VI, 252.
104. Bysshe's *Art of English Poetry* (1702 edition) has seventy citations from Blackmore. Mopas's song is found on pp. 276–77.
105. Tom Brown, "A Lent-Entertainment," *Poems on Affairs of State,* VI, 193–94.
106. Brown, *Works,* III, 21–22.
107. Boyce, *Tom Brown of Facetious Memory,* pp. 120–21.
108. Ellis thinks that internal evidence suggests Brown's authorship but doubts that his name would have been withheld from the posthumous poem. See *Poems on Affairs of State,* VI, 680.
109. Ibid., VI, 701–702.
110. Boys, *Sir Richard Blackmore and the Wits,* p. 17.
111. *Lives of the English Poets,* II, 252.

Chapter Four

1. Blackmore has been most seriously discussed as an influence on religious poetry. See Hoxie Neale Fairchild, *Religious Trends in English Poetry, Volume I: 1700–1740* (New York, 1939), pp. 189–201, and David B. Morris, *The Religious Sublime: Christian Poetry and Critical Tradition in 18th-Century England* (Lexington, Kentucky, 1972), pp. 83–84.
2. Bysshe, pp. 14, 16.
3. *A Hymn to the Light of the World* is dated 1703. However, since it takes Christ's nativity as its subject and since it is listed in *The History of the Works of the Learned* for December of 1702, I assume it was actually on sale at Tonson's "within *Grays-Inn Gate*" during Christmas.
4. Fairchild, p. 193.
5. Rosenberg, pp. 71–72.
6. Public Records Office, T 29/13/247. Cited in Rosenberg, p. 74. The Lord Treasurer awarded him £200, a sum equal to his yearly retainer.
7. Sir Richard Blackmore, *The Lay-Monastery* (London, 1714), pp. 181–83.
8. Ibid., pp. 183–85.
9. Ibid., pp. 186, 188.
10. Ibid., pp. 189–90.
11. *A Collection of Divine Hymns and Poems Upon Several*

Occasions (London, 1704), dedication. Blackmore contributed two Psalm paraphrases to the collection.

12. Reprinted in *Eighteenth-Century Critical Essays*, ed. Scott Elledge (Ithaca, N.Y., 1961), I, 155, 157. In later years Blackmore dissuaded Watts from praising him again in the preface to Watts's *Imitation of the Psalms of David;* see Rosenberg, pp. 125–26.

13. *An Entire Set of the Monitors* (London, 1715), p. 10. Nahum Tate's poem, "An Essay in Praise of Divine Poesie," appeared in the *Monitor* of March 2, 1713.

14. Theodore F. M. Newton, "Blackmore's Eliza," *Harvard Studies and Notes in Philology and Literature*, 18 (1935), 113.

15. *Lives of the English Poets*, II, 242.

16. Newton, p. 121.

17. Pittis, *Some Memoirs of the Life of John Radcliffe*, p. 51.

18. Newton, p. 117, n. 10.

19. Pittis, *Some Memoirs of the Life of John Radcliffe*, p. 46. Pittis has been described as "a first-rate drunkard and a second-rate journalist."

20. See Rosenberg's review of Campbell R. Hone's *The Life of Dr. John Radcliffe* in *Isis* (October 1951), 250-51.

21. Cited in Newton, p. 117.

22. Ibid., pp. 117–18.

23. See issues of Defoe's *Review* for August 2, 7, and 14 of 1705.

24. Newton, pp. 122–23.

25. G. N. Clark, p. 201.

26. *An Epistle To Sir Richard Blackmore, Kt. On occasion of the Late Great Victory in Brabant* (London, 1706), p. 1. Whether one should read the *Epistle* as a straightforward panagyric for Blackmore and Marlborough (as Blackmore's biographer, Rosenberg, p. 88) or as entirely ironical (as F. H. Ellis, *Poems on Affairs of State: Augustan Satrical Verse, 1660–1714: Volume 7: 1704–1714* (New Haven, 1975), VII, 196) is debatable. The Narcissus Luttrell copy has the inscription "A Banter on Sr. Richard." However, even Ellis admits that the appeal to Blackmore seems "freighted with credibility" (VII, 195). Whichever interpretation one elects, it was certainly not accidental that the *Epistle* appeared on July 20, just prior to Blackmore's *Advice to the Poets.* If straightforward, the poem stimulated interest for the forthcoming praise by the Whig poet; if hostile, it would have been intended to undercut Blackmore's poem in much the same way the wits had maligned *Job* in *Discommendatory Verses.*

27. Sir Richard Blackmore, *Advice to the Poets. A Poem. Occasion'd by the Wonderful Success of her Majesty's Arms, under the Conduct of the Duke of Marlborough, in Flanders* (London, 1706). The copy in William Andrews Clark Memorial Library has the date "23 July" written in a contemporary hand.

28. Pope's *Guardian* No. 78 and the fifteenth chapter of *Peri Bathos* draw their inspiration from Blackmore's conception.

29. *Advice to the Poets,* p. 11. This last couplet together with the last line on p. 27—"Arms, Anna, Malbro', Dyle, Ramillia's Plain"—served as the catalysts for one of Pope's wittiest couplets against Sir Richard.

30. *A Panegyric Epistle (Wherein is given An Impartial Character of the present English Poets)* (London, 1706), p. 7. Philips himself has been suggested, probably incorrectly, as the author of his own defense.

31. Leonard Welsted, *A Poem to the Memory of the Incomparable Mr. Philips* (London, 1710).

32. Edumnd Smith, *A Poem on the Death of Mr. John Philips* (London, n.d. [probably 1709]). Smith ridicules Blackmore's Bunyanesque style which prolongs "lean Homilies" to ten pages, a complaint justified by passages of *Eliza* and a practice totally unorthodox in traditional epic theory.

33. *The British Warriour, A Poem. In a Letter to His Excellency The Lord Cutts: Occasion'd by the late Glorious Success of Her Majesty's Arms* (London, 1706). The clanking occurs on p. 10.

34. This precedes Addison's rehabilitation of that ballad in the *Spectator.*

35. *The Flight of the Pretender, With Advice to the Poets. A Poem, In the Arthurical,—Jobical,—Elizabethecal Style and Phrase of the sublime Poet Maurus* (London, 1708).

36. The great tapestries Marlborough had made of his victories may still (1980) be seen at Blenheim.

37. See No. 14.

38. The publisher was socially subordinate to most of the Kit-Cat's membership. See Robert J. Allen, *The Clubs of Augustan London* (Cambridge, Mass., 1933), pp. 41–42. Allen mistakenly characterizes Blackmore's poem as an "elaborate attack" on the club, p. 45.

39. British Museum, 816 M. 19(34). Reprinted entire in Rosenberg, p. 93.

40. Richmond P. Bond, *English Burlesque Poetry: 1700–1750* (Cambridge, Mass., 1932), p. 157.

41. Sir Richard Blackmore, *The Kit-Cats. A Poem* (London, 1708), p. 4. The Clark Library copy is dated 22 May.

42. Yoffie (p. 45) notes Pope's indebtedness to this passage of *The Kit-Cats* for the frontispiece to *The Dunciad.* Unaware of Yoffie's dissertation, James Means elaborates James Sutherland's suggestion of the same possibility in "Sir Richard Blackmore and the Frontispiece to *The Dunciad Variorum* (1729)," *Scriblerian,* 6:2 (1974), 101–102.

43. P. 13. Tom Brown was still alive when the poem was written but died before it was published.

44. See John C. Hodges, "Pope's Debt to One of his Dunces," *Modern Language Notes,* 51 (1936), 154–58. Hodges sees *The Kit-Cats*

as a much stronger influence on *The Dunciad* than Dryden's "Mac Flecknoe," p. 158.

Chapter Five

1. Locke, *Works,* IX, 423.
2. See Z. S. Fink, "Milton and the Theory of Climatic Influence," *Modern Language Quarterly* (March 1941), 67–80.
3. Edward Tyson, *Orang-Outang, sive Homo Sylvestris: Or the Anatomy of A Pygmie Compared with that of a Monkey, an Ape, and a Man* (London, 1699).
4. Sir Richard Blackmore, *The Nature of Man* (London, 1711), p. 4.
5. *Lives of the English Poets,* II, 242–43.
6. *The Works of William Cowper,* ed. Robert Southey (London, 1835–37), II, 139.
7. Brinkley, p. 218.
8. Fairchild, I, 195.
9. William Powell Jones, *The Rhetoric of Science: A Study of Scientific Ideas and Imagery in Eighteenth-Century English Poetry* (Berkeley, 1966), pp. 86–87.
10. Maren-Sofie Røstvig, *The Happy Man: Studies in the Metamorphosis of a Classical Ideal. Volume II: 1700–1760* (Oslo, 1958), p. 450.
11. Fairchild, I, 189.
12. Arthur O. Lovejoy, *The Great Chain of Being* (Cambridge, Mass., 1936), p. 135.
13. The phrase is Alfred North Whitehead's.
14. See Charles T. Harrison, "The Ancient Atomists and English Literature of the Seventeenth Century," *Harvard Studies in Classical Philology,* XLV (1934), 1–80. Blackmore's *Creation* is discussed on pp. 54–56. In "Cremes" Blackmore identifies Epicurean chance creation with Hobbes's natural state of war. See Johannes Hendrik Harder, *Observations on Some Tendencies of Sentiment and Ethics Chiefly in Minor Poetry and Essay in the Eighteenth Century until the Execution of Dr. W. Dodd in 1777* (Amsterdam, 1933), p. 34.
15. Thomas Shadwell, *The Virtuoso,* ed. Marjorie Hope Nicolson and David Stuart Rodes (London, 1966), p. 9.
16. *Titus Lucretius Carus. The Epicurean Philosopher, His Six Books, De Natura Rerum Done into English Verse with Notes* (Oxford, 1682). Issued in 1700 "by the Booksellers of London and Westminster" together with Dryden's translations from Lucretius.
17. Wolfgang Bernard Fleischmann, *Lucretius and English Literature: 1680–1740* (Paris, 1964), p. 266.
18. See Richard S. Westfall, *Science and Religion in Seventeenth-Century England* (New Haven, 1958).
19. *The Works of Richard Bentley, D.D.,* ed. Alexander Dyce

(London, 1838), III, 52. Bentley's influential Boyle lectures were delivered in 1692.

20. See Newton's letters to Bentley on this subject, Ibid., III, 203–15.

21. William Molyneux, *Dioptrica Nova* (London, 1692), pp. 279–80.

22. See W. P. Jones, p. 2.

23. Basil Willey, *The Eighteenth Century Background: Studies on the Idea of Nature in the Thought of the Period* (Boston, 1961), p. 35.

24. John Ray, *The Wisdom of God Manifested in the Works of Creation,* 3rd ed. (London, 1701), p. 304.

25. London, 1696.

26. Edwards believes the heavens roll around the earth, see Book I, Chapter II.

27. Ibid., I, xv, xi, 74–75, 200.

28. Ibid., II, 151. Book II, Chapter VII is "An Apology for Physicians."

29. Willey, p. 39.

30. William Derham, *Physico-Theology* (London, 1713), p. 38. Cited in Willey, p. 40.

31. By W. P. Jones, p. 84.

32. Ibid., p. 47.

33. Majorie Hope Nicolson, *Newton Demands the Muse: Newton's "Opticks" and the Eighteenth Century Poets* (Princeton, 1946), pp. 57–58.

34. Harrison, p. 55. These resemblances are more carefully documented in Fleischmann's *Lucretius and English Literature,* pp. 228–34.

35. Sir Richard Blackmore, *Creation: A Philosophical Poem. In Seven Books* reprinted in *Works of the English Poets,* ed. Alexander Chalmers (London, 1810), X, 325. I have elected to cite Chalmers' edition because of its general availability.

36. Fairchild, I, 200.

37. This phrase, which occurs prominently in the last paragraph of the preface (p. 335), suggests Blackmore's debt to Locke's own deistic *Reasonableness of Christianity* (London, 1695).

38. As Newton writes to Bentley: "You sometimes speak of gravity as essential and inherent to matter. Pray, do not ascribe that notion to me; for the cause of gravity is what I do not pretend to know. . . ." *Works of Richard Bentley,* III, 210.

39. See *De Rerum Natura,* I, 80–102.

40. Compare to *An Essay on Man,* I, 267–80. Pope's pervasive and almost wholly ignored debt to *Creation* is discussed in Chapter 7.

41. W. P. Jones, p. 89.

42. Nicolson, *Newton Demands the Muse,* pp. 114, 66–67.

43. Ibid., p. 103.

44. Majorie Hope Nicolson, *Science and Imagination* (Ithaca, N.Y., 1956), p. 180.

45. *The Critical Works of John Dennis,* I, 350.

46. See *Bibliotheca: A Poem Occasioned by the Sight of a Modern Library* (London, 1712) and "A Letter from Mr. *Thomas D'Urfey,* to a Friend," *Whig and Tory: Or, Wit on both Sides* (London, 1712).

47. *Spectator,* ed. Bond, III, 261.

48. Ibid., IV, 444.

49. Enquiring why Blackmore "surpasses" himself in *Creation,* Johnson records an account which a bookseller received from Addison's intimate, Ambrose Philips: "That Blackmore as he proceeded in this poem laid his manuscript from time to time before a club of wits with whom he associated, and that every man contributed as he could either improvement or correction; so that . . . there are perhaps no where in the book thirty lines together that now stand as they were originally written," *Lives of the English Poets,* II, 243. George Birkbeck Hill finds "somewhat similar lines" in *Creation* and Addison's brief "Hymn" which concludes *Spectator* No. 465.

50. Stephen Switzer, *The Nobleman, Gentleman, and Gardener's Recreation* (London, 1715), p. 106. Blackmore is in the vanguard of the "natural sublime" with its progression from great objects (nature) to great thoughts (order and magnificence of God's creation) to feeling (awe) and finally to poetry. See the introduction to Oliver F. Sigworth's *Criticism and Aesthetics: 1660–1800,* esp. xix.

51. Thomas Foxton, *The Character of a Fine Gentleman* (London, 1721), p. 59.

52. *The Works of Henry Needler,* 2nd ed. (London, 1728), p. 34. This poem was published first in Thomas Hollier Ridout's *Poems and Translations* (London, 1717), pp. 6–8. William Duncombe included it in *The Works of Mr. Henry Needler* in 1724. The admiration for Blackmore's use of medical knowledge suggests that Ridout, a surgeon, may have been the author after all.

53. For Blackmore's influence on Needler see Fairchild, I, 254–58; W. P. Jones, pp. 94-96; and Herbert Drennon, "Henry Needler and Shaftesbury," *PMLA,* 46 (1931), 1095–1106.

54. In his *Life of Erasmus Darwin* (London, 1887), p. 138, Ernest Krause attempts to refute the German critics who see Blackmore's *Creation* as Darwin's model.

55. *The Critical Works of John Dennis,* II, 120.

56. Charles Gildon, "The Complete Art of Poetry," *Critical Essays of the Eighteenth Century: 1700–1725,* ed. Willard Higley Durham (New Haven, 1915), pp. 35, 37.

57. Theophilus Cibber [and Robert Shiels], *The Lives of the Poets* (London, 1753), v, 180.

58. *Lives of the English Poets,* II, 246, 253.

59. Ibid., II, 244. Ironically, had Blackmore in fact written nothing else, he almost certainly would have enjoyed a more felicitous reputation.

60. Ibid., II, 254.
61. Sir John Hawkins, *Life of Johnson* (London, 1787), p. 348.
62. *William Cowper, Works,* ed. Robert Southey, XV, 93.
63. Ibid., II, 140.
64. John Robert Moore, "Gay's Burlesque of Sir Richard Blackmore's Poetry," *Journal of English and Germanic Philology,* 50 (1951), 83–89.
65. Aaron Hill, *The Creation. A Pindarick Illustration of a Poem, Originally Written by Moses, On That Subject* (London, 1720), p. 12. Interestingly, a recent critic finds the fullest use of "poetic diction" in didactic poems of natural description such as *Creation* and Henry Brooke's *Universal Beauty.* See John Arthos, *The Language of Natural Description in Eighteenth-Century Poetry* (Ann Arbor, 1949), p. 16.
66. Leslie Stephen, *History of English Thought in the Eighteenth Century,* 3rd ed. (London, 1927), II, 259–60.
67. *The Letters of Joseph Addison,* pp. 1–2.
68. Ibid., pp. 30, 47.
69. Ibid., p. 280.
70. From the Yale manuscript. "Sweat" is printed "tremble" in the version included in *Letters, by Several Eminent Persons Deceased,* 2nd. ed. (London, 1773), I, 122–23, the version cited by Rosenberg, p. 106. The Yale manuscript has a notation identifying Blackmore and recording that his *Creation* "is deserving of great praise."
71. *The Letters of Joseph Addison,* pp. 488–89. Only Blackmore's contributions are discussed below.
72. *Letters, by Several Eminent Persons Deceased,* I, 144.
73. Charles Gildon, *The Post-Man Robb'd of his Mail* (London, 1719), p. xiv.
74. Allen, *The Clubs of Augustan London,* p. 211.
75. Walter Graham, *English Literary Periodicals* (New York, 1930), pp. 94–95.

Chapter Six

1. *The Journal of James Yonge: 1647–1721: Plymouth Surgeon,* ed. F. N. L. Poynter (Hamden, Conn., 1963), p. 215. In 1716 Blackmore served as a Censor of the Royal College and in August of the same year was named an Elect. See Rosenberg, p. 114.
2. See Maren-Sofie Røstvig, *The Happy Man,* II, 100.
3. Joseph Spence, *Observations, Anecdotes, and Characters of Books and Men,* ed. James M. Osborn (Oxford, 1966), I, 17.
4. See *The Correspondence of Alexander Pope,* I, 373.
5. All citations from Pope's poetry are from the Twickenham Edition, 11 vols (London, 1939–69).
6. See I, 134 and *Creation,* VII, 36 or II, 56–57 and *King Arthur,* p. 4.

7. *Correspondence of Alexander Pope,* I, 218 (19 April 1714).

8. *The Correspondence of Jonathan Swift,* ed. Harold Williams (Oxford, 1963-65), II, 43. George Sherburn agrees that these are the seeds of *Peri Bathous.* See *The Early Career of Alexander Pope* (New York, reissued 1963), p. 81.

9. Loyd Douglas, "A Severe Animadversion on Bossu," *PMLA,* 62 (1947), 690-706.

10. *The Prose Works of Alexander Pope,* ed. Norman Ault (Oxford, 1936), I, 115.

11. Ibid., p. 116.

12. Ibid., pp. 117-20.

13. Blackmore's praise is in the "preface" to "An Essay upon Epick Poetry," *Essays upon Several Subjects,* I, vi.

14. Ibid., I, 12-16, 45, 49, 51, 79, 89, 111-12, 119, 121.

15. *The Diary of Dudley Ryder: 1715-1716,* ed. William Matthews (London, 1939), pp. 194-95. Quoted in Rosenberg, p. 116.

16. *Essays upon Several Subjects,* I, 217.

17. Ibid., I, xlviii.

18. Ibid., I, xxxi, xxxiv.

19. Ibid., I, xlvii-xlviii.

20. Ibid., I, 305-306, 310, 347, 358, 374.

21. Ibid., I, xxxi.

22. Thomas Hearne, *Reliquiae Hearnianae,* ed. P. Bliss (London, 1869), II, 44.

23. Jonathan Swift, *A Tale of a Tub,* ed. A. C. Guthkelch and D. Nichol Smith, 2nd ed. (Oxford, 1958), p. 182.

24. Ibid., p. 183.

25. See Irvin Ehrenpreis, "Four of Swift's Sources," *Modern Language Notes,* 70 (1955), 95-100.

26. *A Tale of a Tub,* p. 248.

27. *Correspondence of Alexander Pope,* I, 359.

28. See Sherburn, pp. 149-85, for the full context of Pope's abhorrence of Curll.

29. *The Prose Works of Alexander Pope,* I, 262-63, 266.

30. Reprinted by Norman Ault in *New Light on Pope* (London, 1949), p. 156.

31. Sherburn's characterization, see *The Correspondence of Alexander Pope,* I, 342, n. 2. Also see Pope to Swift (20 June 1716) and Pope to Teresa Blount (7 August 1716).

32. For example, see J. V. Guerinot, *Pamphlet Attacks on Alexander Pope: 1711-1744* (New York, 1969), pp. 113-14.

33. Sir Richard Blackmore, *Essays upon Several Subjects* (London, 1717), II, 169-70.

34. *Correspondence of Jonathan Swift,* II, 214 (30 August 1716).

35. *Correspondence of Alexander Pope,* I, 371 (14 November 1716).

36. *John Gay: Poetry and Prose,* ed. Vinton A. Dearing (Oxford, 1974), I, 205.
37. Advertised in the *Evening-Post,* June 26–28, 1716.
38. *The Critical Works of John Dennis,* II, 107.
39. For the date of *A Farther Account* see Ault's *Prose Works of Alexander Pope,* I, c–ci.
40. Ibid., I, 275, 383.
41. Ibid., I, 276.
42. Ibid., I, 284. See also a letter of Pope's referring to Blackmore about this time, *Correspondence,* I, 373.
43. Jonathan Swift, *Miscellaneous and Autobiographical Pieces, Fragments and Marginalia,* ed. Herbert Davis (Oxford, 1962), p. 254. Swift is not alone in misreading the tone of *Freeholder* No. 45; see Rosenberg, p. 116. No one, besides Blackmore himself, has taken notice of Addison's attack in *Freeholder* No. 40.
44. *The Critical Works of John Dennis,* II, 457.
45. Peter Smithers, *The Life of Joseph Addison,* 2nd ed. (Oxford, 1968), p. 287.
46. *Essays upon Several Subjects,* I, xlv, 221.
47. *The Critical Works of John Dennis,* II, 109.
48. *Essays upon Several Subjects,* II, 277.
49. Ibid., II, 279–87.
50. Guerinot, pp. 47–68.
51. *Essays upon Several Subjects,* II, xlvii–xlviii.
52. Reprinted entire in *Popeiana IV: On Literary Farces: 1715–1733* (New York, 1974). Interestingly, Curll is still fomenting trouble between Blackmore and the Buttonians on the one hand and Pope on the other. In Breval's farce Pope proclaims to Arbuthnot:

> Not BUTTON'S Wits from my Lampoons are free,
> And Thou, and BLACKMORE are but *Worms* to me. (p. 5)

53. *Essays upon Several Subjects,* II, lix.
54. Ibid., II, 246.
55. Sir Richard Blackmore, *A Collection of Poems on Various Subjects* (London, 1718), p. v.
56. Ibid., p. xii.
57. Ibid., pp. 129–30.
58. Ibid., p. 307.
59. Ibid., p. 434.
60. Rosenberg, p. 115.
61. *A Collection of Divine Hymns and Poems Upon Several Occasions,* 3rd ed. (London, 1719), preface.
62. For the full text of the inscription see Rosenberg, p. 126.
63. *The Correspondence of Jonathan Swift,* II, 303–4.

64. Sir Richard Blackmore, *A New Version of the Psalms of David, Fitted to the Tunes Used in Churches* (London, 1721), preface.

65. Bodleian Library, Rawl. MSS. D. 389 (137). Cited in Rosenberg, p. 130.

66. Rosenberg, pp. 137–41.

67. Sir Richard Blackmore, *Just Prejudices Against the Arian Hypothesis* (London, 1721), p. 18.

68. Joseph Pyke, *An Impartial View of the Principal Difficulties that Affect the Trinitarian, or Clog the Arian, Scheme* (London, 1721).

69. Thomas Morgan, *A Refutation of the False Principles Assumed and Apply'd by the Reverend Joseph Pyke in his Book, Intitled, An Impartial View* (London, 1722).

70. Sir Richard Blackmore, *Modern Arians Unmask'd* (London, 1722).

71. Thomas Morgan, *A Letter to Sir Richard Blackmore; Occasioned by his Book, intituled, Modern Arians Unmask'd* (London, 1721), p. 81.

72. Sir Richard Blackmore, *Redemption: A Divine Poem. In Six Books. The three first demonstrate the Truth of the Christian Religion, The three last the Deity of Christ. To which is added, A Hymn to Christ the Redeemer* (London, 1722).

73. Fairchild, I, 194.

74. Fairchild's remark, see I, 200.

75. Giles Jacob, *Lives and Characters of the English Poets,* p. 11.

76. A claim Blackmore's biographers can make nothing of; see Rosenberg, p. 134.

77. *Lives of the English Poets,* II, 249–50.

78. *Letters, by Several Eminent Persons Deceased,* III, 83–84.

79. Sir Richard Blackmore, *Alfred. An Epick Poem. In Twelve Books* (London, 1723), pp. iii–x.

80. Ibid., p. xxviii.

81. Ibid., p. xxx.

82. Ibid., p. xl.

83. *The Remains of Thomas Hearne: Reliquiae Hearnianae,* ed. John Buchanan Brown (Carbondale, Ill., 1966), p. 258.

84. Ibid.

85. *Lives of the English Poets,* II, 250.

86. Blackmore, *A Treatise of Consumptions,* p. xviii.

87. The work of morality published the year before his death is *Natural Theology: Or, Moral Duties Consider'd apart from Positive* (London, 1728). It seeks to prove, by arguments abstracted from his earlier work, that natural law teaches the same morality as revealed religion.

88. *Lives of the English Poets,* II, 253.

89. *Lives and Characters of the English Poets,* p. 10.

90. *The Political State of Great Britain* (London, 1729), p. 392.

Blackmore's old enemy, Abel Boyer, may not have written this obituary since he died the same year.

Chapter Seven

1. *Lives of the English Poets,* II, 252.
2. For an elaboration of this significant parallel see J. V. Guerinot, pp. lviii–lix.
3. *Correspondence of Alexander Pope,* I, 373.
4. *Essays upon Several Subjects,* I, 207.
5. See *Homer and Virgil Not to be Compar'd with the Two ARTHURS,* p. 64 for a passage which Pope includes in *Peri Bathous* [*The Art of Sinking in Poetry: A Critical Edition,* ed. Edna Leake Steeves (New York, reprint 1968), p. 35] and again ridicules in *The Dunciad Variorum* [II, 380 n.].
6. *Peri Bathous,* p. 99 of the commentary.
7. With ironic effect, Pope, in *The Dunciad Variorum,* adopts the device of quoting Dennis's criticism of *Prince Arthur* from its effective use in *Homer and Virgil* (p. 87).
8. Aaron Hill, *The Creation,* preface. Partially reprinted in *The Correspondence of Alexander Pope,* II, 35.
9. *Peri Bathous,* pp. 20–21.
10. Ibid., pp. 22–24.
11. Criticism seized early on Blackmore's reputed pride. "He was said," Dudley Ryder wrote of a coffeehouse conversation in March of 1716, "to be a man very much conceited of him self." See *The Diary of Dudley Ryder: 1715–1716,* pp. 194–95. Cited in Rosenberg, p. 116.
12. The sinking metaphor was, as mentioned previously, popular during the *Commendatory Verses* quarrel. The Earl of Dorset had earlier characterized Blackmore's progenitor in heroics, Edward Howard, as possessed of a "way of writing without thinking," a "strange alacrity in Sinking." See *Poems on Affairs of State,* I, 339.
13. The fascinating story of Pope's attack on Aaron Hill in the *Bathous* and his subsequent hypocritical evasion of responsibility for the hit possesses all the drama of literary blackmail but is no part of the present study.
14. For example, see Professor Steeves' note to *Peri Bathous,* p. 173. Interestingly, Pope used Bysshe's *Art of English Poetry* to supplement the absurdities he found in his 1714, 4th edition of *Prince Arthur* and the 1716, 2nd edition of *Job;* see *Peri Bathous,* p. 154 (52:6).
15. See Loyd Douglas, pp. 704–705. The idea is implicit earlier in the bank of wit in Blackmore's *Satyr against Wit.* See *"On Sir R—— Bl——re's Noble Project to Erect a Bank of Wit," Commendatory Verses,* pp. 21–22.

16. John C. Hodges, "Pope's Debt to One of His Dunces," pp. 154-58.

17. John Nichols, *Illustrations of the Literary History of the 18th Century* (London, 1817), II, 752.

18. Alexander Pope, *The Dunciad,* ed. James Sutherland, 3rd ed. (London, 1963), p. 130. In this, Blackmore follows Milton, *Paradise Lost,* vi, 209.

19. *Commendatory Verses,* pp. 16-17.

20. *Characters of the Times* (London, 1728), p. 25.

21. See note to II, 256 (p. 131).

22. *The Dunciad,* p. 210.

23. Edmund Curll, *A Complete Key To The Dunciad* (London, 1728), p. 19.

24. *The Accomplished Preacher; Or, an Essay upon Divine Eloquence* (London, 1731).

25. *The Female Dunciad* (London, 1728), p. 46.

26. Ault, *New Light on Pope,* pp. 248-58.

27. W. H. Irving, *John Gay: Favorite of the Wits* (Durham, N.C., 1940), p. 141.

28. Alexander Pope, *Minor Poems,* ed. Norman Ault and John Butt (London, 1964), p. 290.

29. See under "Blackmore" in *The Poems of Alexander Pope: Volume XI: Index,* ed. Maynard Mack (London, 1969), p. 14.

30. *Lives of the Poets of Great Britain and Ireland,* V, 179. In this regard, see "A Parallel of the Characters of Mr. Dryden and Mr. Pope," Appendix VI of *The Dunciad Variorum.*

31. James Bramston, *The Man of Taste. Occasion'd by an Epistle of Mr. Pope's On that Subject* (London, 1733), p. 7.

32. See Mather Byles' poem "Golieth" which quotes a passage from *Prince Arthur.* For Franklin see *Benjamin Franklin, Representative Selections,* ed. F. L. Mott and C. E. Jorgenson (New York, 1936), p. cxxxii. Blackmore and Pope are mentioned with equal respect in Linn's "The Poet."

33. Cotton Mather, *The Christian Philosopher* (London, 1721), p. 211. Mather's book is "a Collection of the Best Discoveries in Nature, with Religious Improvements." The title page describes it as written by "Cotton Mather and Fellows of the Royal Society," additional evidence that Blackmore was respected in the London scientific community.

34. Ebenezer Turell, *Memoirs of Mrs. Jane Turell* (Boston, 1741), pp. 29-30.

35. The opinion of William P. Trent, *History of American Literature, 1607-1865* (New York, 1920), p. 82.

36. Compare *Creation,* II, 473-76, with *Night Thoughts,* I, 285-86. Besides *Night Thoughts* see Young's *Paraphrase on Part of the Book of Job.*

37. Alan Dugald McKillop, *The Background of Thomson's Seasons* (Minneapolis, 1942), p. 129.

38. The phrase is McKillop's, p. 11. Dwight L. Durling says the same in *Georgic Tradition in English Poetry* (New York, 1935), p. 45.

39. Røstvig (*Happy Man*, I, 254) notes the general resemblance between Thomson's preface and Blackmore's arguments.

40. Blackmore's tarnished reputation probably made Thomson reluctant to acknowledge his debts to Blackmore, an influence which to judge from the early "Paraphrase of Psalm CIV" began in his youth.

41. *Lives of the English Poets,* II, 254, n. 3.

42. *Cowper's Works,* II, 139.

43. See Alexander Pope, *An Essay on Man,* ed. Maynard Mack (London, 1950), notes at lines III, 105; III, 173–74; IV, 156.

44. See especially pp. 425, 429–32.

45. See Thomas Leland, *Dissertation on the Principles of Human Eloquence* (London, 1764).

46. James Beattie, *Essays* (Edinburgh, 1776), p. 357.

47. For the relevant quote see *Spectator,* I, 184–85.

48. *Lives of the Poets of Great Britain and Ireland,* V, 178.

49. *The General Biographical Dictionary,* revised and enlarged by Alexander Chalmers (London, 1812), V, 338–39.

Selected Bibliography

PRIMARY SOURCES

Only Blackmore's major English literary works are included.

Prince Arthur. An Heroick Poem. London, 1695. Issued in facsimile. Menston, Yorkshire, England: The Scolar Press, 1971.

King Arthur. An Heroick Poem. London, 1697.

A Satyr against Wit. London, 1700. Reprinted as pp. 129–54 of *Poems on Affairs of State: Augustan Satirical Verse: Volume 6: 1697–1704,* ed. Frank H. Ellis. New Haven: Yale University Press, 1970.

A Paraphrase on the Book of Job. London, 1700.

A Hymn to the Light of the World. London, 1703.

Eliza. An Epick Poem. London, 1705.

Advice to the Poets. London, 1706.

The Kit-Cats. London, 1708.

Instructions to Vander Bank, A Sequel to the Advice to the Poets. London, 1709.

The Nature of Man. London, 1711.

Creation. A Philosophical Poem. London, 1712. The most popular of Blackmore's poems, *Creation* exists in sixteen separate editions and was reprinted in Samuel Johnson's and in Alexander Chalmers' collections of the English poets.

The Lay-Monastery. London, 1714. Collected essays originally issued as *The Lay-Monk.*

Essays upon Several Subjects. 2 volumes. London, 1716–1717. The first volume was published in 1716, the second in 1717. The first volume has been issued in facsimile. New York: Garland, 1971.

A Collection of Poems on Various Subjects. London, 1718.

A New Version of the Psalms of David. London, 1721.

Redemption: A Divine Poem. London, 1722.

Alfred. An Epick Poem. London, 1723.

SECONDARY SOURCES

AULT, NORMAN. *New Light on Pope.* London: Methuen, 1949. Chapter VIII deals with Pope's burlesque version of the First Psalm.

Chapter XV attributes "Verses on England's Arch-Poet," an anti-Blackmore squib, to Pope.

BOYCE, BENJAMIN. "The Dispensary, Sir Richard Blackmore, and the Captain of the Wits," *Review of English Studies,* 14 (1938), 453-58. Identifies Tom Brown as the leader of the attack on Blackmore in *Commendatory Verses.*

BOYS, RICHARD C. "The Authorship of Poems in *Commendatory Verses* (1700)," *Philological Quarterly,* 30 (1951), 221-22.

——. *Sir Richard Blackmore and the Wits.* University of Michigan Contributions in Modern Philology, No. 13. Ann Arbor: University of Michigan Press, 1949. A valuable reprint of *Commendatory* and *Discommendatory Verses.* Although unsympathic to Blackmore as a serious poet, Boys provides an informative and entertaining introduction. See the review by V. DeSola Pinto in *Philological Quarterly,* 29 (1950), 261-62.

BRINKLEY, ROBERTA F. *Arthurian Legend in the Seventeenth Century.* John Hopkins Monographs in Literary History III. Baltimore: The Johns Hopkins Press, 1932. Frequently inaccurate, this remains the fullest treatment of Blackmore's Arthurian epics.

CAMERON, W. J. "The Authorship of *Commendatory Verses,* 1700," *Notes and Queries,* 208 (1963), 62-66.

DOUGLAS, LOYD. "A Severe Animadversion on Bossu," *Publications of the Modern Language Association,* 62 (1947), 690-706. Argues persuasively that Pope in his "Receit to make an Epick Poem" (*Guardian,* No. 78) ridicules Blackmore rather than Le Bossu.

FAIRCHILD, HOXIE N. *Religious Trends in English Poetry: Volume I: 1700-1740.* New York: Columbia University Press, 1939. Pages 189-201 give the fullest treatment of Blackmore as a religious poet. Fairchild finds Blackmore "a satisfyingly representative figure," especially valuable to "the student of the history of thought" (p. 201).

FLEISCHMANN, WOLFGANG B. *Lucretius and English Literture: 1680-1740.* Paris: A. G. Nizet, 1964. Deals with Blackmore's debt to Lucretius in *Creation.*

HODGES, JOHN C. "Pope's Debt to One of His Dunces," *Modern Language Notes,* 51 (1936), 154-58. Documents Pope's debt in the *Dunciad* to Blackmore's *The Kit-Cats.*

JONES, WILLIAM P. *The Rhetoric of Science.* Berkeley: University of California Press, 1966. Best treatment of *Creation* in terms of eighteenth-century physicotheology.

KELLEY, MICHAEL. "Sir Richard Blackmore in the Judgment of His Fellow-Writers," *Journal of the History of Medicine,* 16 (1961), 186-89.

LIIS, OSKAR. *Die Arthurepen des Sir Richard Blackmore.* Strasbourg, 1911. Documents Blackmore's debt to Virgil and Milton.

LONG, E. HUDSON. "Notes on Sir Richard Blackmore," *Modern Language Notes,* 58 (1943), 585-89. Biographical.

MEANS, JAMES. "Sir Richard Blackmore and the Frontispiece to *The Dunciad Variorium* (1729)," *Scriblerian*, 6:2 (1974), 101-102.

MOORE, JOHN R. "Gay's Burlesque of Sir Richard Blackmore's Poetry," *Journal of English and Germanic Philology*, 50 (1951), 83-89. In *The Shepherd's Week*.

NEWTON, THEODORE F. M. "Blackmore's Eliza," *Harvard Studies and Notes in Philology and Literature*, 18 (1935), 113-23. The Blackmore-Radcliffe quarrel.

ROSENBERG, ALBERT. *Sir Richard Blackmore: A Poet and Physician of the Augustan Age*. Lincoln: The University of Nebraska Press, 1953. The only modern study of Blackmore. Almost entirely biographical.

SWEDENBERG, H. T. *The Theory of the Epic in England: 1650-1800*. University of California Publications in English, Volume XV. Berkeley: University of California Press, 1944. Cites Blackmore repeatedly.

TOOMEY, THOMAS N. "Sir Richard Blackmore, M.D.," *Annals of Medical History*, 4, (1922), 180-188. As medical writer.

Index

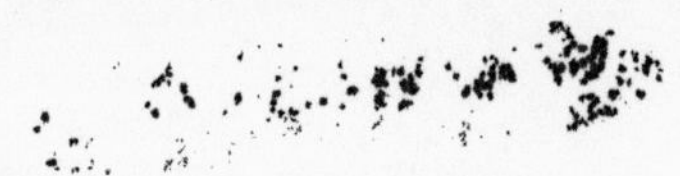